Culture and Contra-Culture

James Biser Whisker
John R. Coe

K D P Amazon 2021

Printed in the United States of America
and distributed by
K D P Amazon

John R Coe was born and raised in Parkersburg, WV. He was the youngest child of the late Dr. Donald E. Coe and Jacqueline Ann Galka. He received his B.S. degree in biology from Glenville State College, his MS from WVU, and his Ed. D. from Liberty University. He is also a retired central office administrator from the Wood County schools. John is currently an independent businessman . The businesses include an analytical chemistry lab as well as a restaurant. He is an avid firearm collector of both pistols rifles and muzzle loaders. He can be found almost any day on the rifle range. He has been married for over 31 years to his college sweetheart Rosemary.

James B Whisker is professor emeritus from West Virginia University where he taught for over 37 years. He was adviser to the WVU College Republicans during most of his tenure. He received his Ph. D. in 1969 from the University of Maryland. He is author or co-author of books on gunsmiths and arms makers of eighteen states. He co-authored books on clockmakers and silversmiths of Pennsylvania and also Maryland. Among his other books are *The Alien Tort Claims Act, The Militia, The Right to Hunt; The Citizen-Soldier and U.S. Military Policy, Our Vanishing Freedom: The Right to Keep and Bear Arms,* and the *Rise and Decline of the American Militia System.* He currently resides in Everett. In August 2020 he and, the former Sheila Elaine Bailey celebrated their Golden Wedding anniversary.

Contents

Introduction

A yearbook for a middle school in Lewisville, Texas, has sparked controversy on account of its back cover which was designed with Black Lives Matter art. The yearbook was published under the theme, "We Stick Together." Downing Middle School art teacher Kayla Mick is on leave after she approved the cover art designed by her eighth grade students for their yearbook. The cover had phrases including "I can't breathe" and "Black Lives Matter" designed on it.[1]

Both proponents and opponents of the juvenile yearbook agreed on one thing: it is the result on emphasis on Critical Race Theory (CRT). The great question is: is that a good thing or a bad thing? Has it, will it, make us stick together? To proponents, it is so important to teach CRT that it matters not whether parents, or, for that matter, students like it. In a sense, its overpowering import is so great that it is legitimate to force feed its contents. The fact that it has annoyed white parents is merely proof that virulent racism exists and must be eradicated.

To opponents, schools should be a place of leaning academic subjects and not a nursery for advancement of socially and politically correct agendas. It is simply one more nail in the educational coffin, one more diversion from instruction in language, science, history, mathematics, and other academic subjects. It is no wonder, than, that scores on standardized tests plummet. Moreover, it is propelled by black racism that teaches that whiteness is an illness that must be cured. So moved are CRT advocates that they are willing to tear at the very fabric of education. Testing is racist, designed to perpetuate white supremacy. Tests are biased against black culture and skewed toward traditional Western civilization. When there are insufficient persons of color scoring well, it is the tests that are at fault and so must be discounted.

Affirmative Action for blacks is only a beginning. It must be extended to all people of color, all excluded races, including groups with no history of oppression in the United States such as Ethiopians, South Asia (Indians) and, for awhile in the 1970s, East Asians. No matter what the nature of the group, so long as it is not Caucasian, action must be taken on it behalf, whether it asks for assistance and recognition or not.

---

1 *Dallas Morning News,* 24 May 2021.

Anti-racist thought in the United States in recent years has been dominated by issues, related to what has become known, as wokeness, or woke culture. The word "woke" was added to dictionaries in 2017, a now-legitimatized slang term for awake. In its contemporary use, "woke" means social awareness, being alert to social issues, racism, discrimination and injustice. Some of the goals of the woke culture are: dissolution of the nuclear family, abolition of capitalist economic system, elimination of traditional religion, re-writing of the constitution so its is politically and socially acceptable, and raising children in a gender neutral climate. Certainly not each and every woke activist accepts most or all these stances.

Other actions by the woke culture include canceling socially objectionable movies, removing certain cartoon characters, banning politically incorrect books, and boycotting environmentally irresponsible organizations and corporations. Many woke protesters are active in the defunding law enforcement movement, banning and confiscating privately owned handguns and so-called assault rifles, while refusing to prosecute crimes committed with firearms. The leftist ideology of the woke culture is so pervasive in our lives today that we find it in virtually every field of human activity: in education, in the media, in entertainment and even in sports.

Attacks upon the nuclear family are hard to comprehend when we consider that seven out of ten black children grow up in single parent households. 80% of youth in prison grew up in fatherless homes. Those deprived of maturation in the nuclear family are far more likely to drop out of school, commit crimes, experience depression and being suicidal. One might conclude that it is not the dissolution, but the restoration of families, that will help people of color.

The woke culture has chosen to ignore the moist obvious economic fact: people who flee the Third World have found that their socialist systems do not work. Economic opportunities can be found in the world that capitalism has provided, where prosperity was the direct result of a free market economy. Capitalism, as an economic system, gives rise to competition, which leads to economic growth, market share and opportunities, that benefit everyone. Capitalism is not the problem, but rather corruption and undue corporate influence in politics are responsible for the ever growing income inequalities and other ills of society.

CRT enthusiasts condemn capitalism because, they assert, it

was founded upon, and made prosperous by, slave labor. They offer reams of economic and social history to back that claim. While rejecting that claim, let us, just for the sake of argument, allow that conclusion. First, we might ask, what system, since the beginning of history, has not had slavery, until that last two hundred or so years in the capitalist West? Second, has socialism, by one name or another, produced a New World of economic equality? One might view the slave labor camps in any communist nation. Perhaps one might read Friedrich Hayek's well-reasoned classic, *The Road to Serfdom,* which has often been denied but never successfully refuted. Will translation from capitalism to whatever woke ideology is successful somehow undo the evils of slavery past?

Successful societies are those which have created a sense of individual responsibility in which inhabitants do not dwell on blaming society, rather than themselves, responsible for their crimes. Perhaps we should blame a killing on a gun rather than the shooter, saying were there no gun there would have been no killing. Ultimately, that murder was the fault of the maker of the ammunition and the gun's manufacturer. If one fails an examination, should one blame the examination or one's self? If one scores low on an entrance examination, clearly it is the fault of the examiners for having produced a racially insensitive and politically exclusive examination that is designed to uphold and maintain white racial dominance.

In addition to promoting its agendas through the media and academia, the woke culture's other chief strategy to further its cultural influence is political correctness. A standard definition of political correctness is the "avoidance of action, that is perceived to insult, or marginalize certain groups of people." Were it true that really all there is to political correctness, no reasonable person would oppose it. But, as is the case with many other dissident ideologies, there is far more hidden deep inside that can be discerned only by careful analysis. While waving the banners of "tolerance" and "social justice", the woke culture denounces as racist anyone or anything that holds differing views. The protesters view life through the lens of racism, sexism, homophobia, trans-phobia, and xenophobia.

They claim they believe in free speech, but will only allow speech that fits their ideological perspective, suppressing free thought and heterodox intellectual inquiry. They have no tolerance for a diversity of opinions, done in the name of tolerance. This is censorship, designed to intimidate and "cancel" those with dissenting views and reach a uniformity of thought.

Which brings us to counter culture, which may be defined as a way of life and set of attitudes opposed to or at variance with the prevailing social norm. Counter-culture is a mind set whose values and norms of behavior differ substantially from those of mainstream society, sometimes diametrically opposed to mainstream cultural mores. A counter-cultural movement expresses the ethos and aspirations of a specific population during a well-defined era. When oppositional forces reach critical mass, counter-cultures can trigger dramatic cultural changes. Such has become the objective of the present ideology of the anti-racist counter-culture.

The origins of the present counter-culture movement are a bit vague. John Milton Yinger has been said to have coined the term "contra-culture" in an academic journal article.[2] Dr. Yinger suggested the use of the term contra-culture "wherever the normative system of a group contains, as a primary element, a theme of conflict with the values of the total society, where personality variables are directly involved in the development and maintenance of the group's values, and wherever its norms can be understood only by reference to the relationships of the group to a surrounding dominant culture."

Another important early contributor to the making of contra-culture was Professor Theodore Roszak.[3] Rejection of mainstream culture was quickly embodied in the new genres of psychedelic rock music, pop-art and explorations in new quasi-religious movements.

A small but highly vocal minority of the anti-racist movement have found it expedient to reject, then attack, traditional Christianity. The Black Islam movement ante-dates the present CRRT era, but has had significant influence upon it. Christianity is not the religion for blacks, while Islam is the proper choice for persons of color. Some protesters are willing to accept Christianity, provided Jesus and Mary are depicted as blacks while others see them purely as Caucasians who are symbols of white supremacy. The most radical wish to destroy images of all Christian figures since the Hebrew Bible clearly accepted slavery and St. Paul wrote a book specifically telling a slave

2 Yinger, J. M., "Contraculture and Subculture," *American Sociological Review,* 25: 5 (1960), pp. 625-35.

3 Roszak, Theodore. *The Making of a Counter Culture: Reflections on the Technocratic Society and Its Youthful Opposition.* University of California Press, 1995.

to accept his lot in life while instructing the slave's owner to treat his slaves like brothers.

But Christian monuments are only a tiny fraction of the offensive monuments that the contra-culture seeks to obliterate. In the name of anti-racism, they seek to remove images of all slave holders. Monuments to various figures associated in any way with the Confederate States of America make the easiest, but certainly not the only, targets. Founding Fathers like Thomas Jefferson, George Washington, James Madison, and George Mason must go for their held slaves. Perhaps, if one truly believed that the true and only reason to remove such monuments were glorification of slave holding, one might be persuaded. But the monuments were erected in tribute to their statesmanship and democratic vision, not to their roles as slavers. One soon begins to suspect that these are assaults on their vision and greatness, not on their pro-slave lifestyles, perpetrated by hoodlums who have never contributed to the quality of American life.

Insurrection

In 1968 while a student at University of Maryland I met Ted, a chap who owned a modest size grocery store in one of the poorest sections of Washington, largely, but not exclusively a black neighborhood. His prices were competitive with the large chains and he was well known for his charity. He gave away foods reaching their expiration dates rather than discarding and he was recognized as a soft touch if one was really desperate.

Then came the riots following the King assassination. Young hoodlums hit the liquor stores first and, fully inebriated, looted and burned down businesses, including Ted's market. He lost everything, no insurance compensated his loss, no one rebuilt his shop, and locals had to go elsewhere to shop. We climbed atop an eight story high building and watched the red glow as the nation's capital burned, thinking that London must have looked like this during the Nazi blitz.. One Washington newscaster Tony Sylvester late that first night of the right noted that as firemen attempted to extinguish blazes, sharpshooters were firing at them. He also saw a middle-age woman pushing a baby carriage over the fire hoses and in it were two television sets. Tony asked the reporter on the spot what was happening and he responded "unless she's moving at three A.M., she looted those TVs." No one challenged such looters. Perhaps they were just "undocumented shoppers."

We drove downtown and the mass destruction looked exactly like the bombed out European and Japanese cities. We saw our capitol surrounded by barbed wire and Congressmen being carted to work in jeeps by soldiers with .50 caliber machine guns as protection. A few weeks later, Ted received a summons for his burned out automobile that the city had removed from the parking lot of his fire-gutted shop.

From the top floor of a high-rise University of Maryland dormitory we watched Washington burn during those 1968 riots. A huge red glow lit up the sky to our south-south-east. We thought, "this is what London must have looked like during the blitz" or "Japan must have been so after General Curtis LeMay fire-bombed it." A few days later we drove down U.S. One and took a short tour of Washington. Indeed, it was like one of the bombed-out cities, with piles of rubble all along the streets, trash that last week took the form of buildings. Washington burned while President Lyndon Johnson dallied. Few were arrested, the news media never used words like insurrection or revolution. I wondered if this was black privilege since no Caucasians were involved in that riot.

Ever after, no one hated blacks as much as did Ted. He often quoted the Preamble to the US Constitution, wherein the Founding Fathers pledged to "establish justice, insure domestic tranquility, provide for the common defense, promote the general welfare, and secure the blessings of liberty" for all Americans. Why had his dream, his whole life, been destroyed by people to whom he had treated fairly and charitably. At the end of that year I left West Virginia where I had taken a teaching position to defend my doctoral dissertation back at the University of Maryland. I decided to visit my friend Ted. Stopped at a red light two blocks from where Ted's store once was located, a middle age black woman walked up to my car and spit on the windshield.

That was more than 50 years ago and most of us hoped we had moved beyond that level of protest. But in 2020 the news media has castigated our President for calling for full legal restraint of lawbreakers, and for suppression of domestic rebellion. The media refers to insurrectionists, rioters, looters, incendiaries, and revolutionaries as "protesters" and "demonstrators" and actually treats them as though they have something legitimate to convey. A public low cost housing unit in Minneapolis of 168 apartments was torched, just as was Ted's market. Why is it, if righteous anger and frustration are the prime movers of riots, that the very first places the rioters hit are the liquor stores and beer distributors? Must the insurrectionists be drunk before they can vent their anger?

Like Ted, I wonder why the government puts no emphasis on maintenance of "domestic tranquility" and denies justice to shop owners, and why it is "inflammatory" for our President to suggest suppression of lawlessness by force. Democratic candidate Biden, along with other prominent Democratic leaders, charge the President with inciting racial hatred while doing nothing to calm the lawless mob behavior. In the end it is all us tax-paying citizens who will pay for the millions upon millions of dollars in destruction that the insurrectionists have caused.

I have watched in absolute amazement as the news media has pandered to the insurrectionist terrorist "Black Lives Matter" irrespective of its violent teachings and actions. Even more amazing is the apparent agreement with a black insurrectionary who counseled "attack the cops, leave the National Guard alone." The left-wing news media, which would have you believe it is mainstream American, has supported disciplining of police who push back against rioters. One would think that responsible citizens would back fully our President who demanded protection for the lives and property of all citizens.

One recent (June 2020) Congresswoman asked "What's the big deal about looting" as though this act of stealing is somehow acceptable reaction to some injustice. It is not surprising that many Christian fundamentalists, and perhaps others, see some fulfillment of the predictions in the Book of Revelation. I also shudder to think how our Founding Fathers, who gave us a Constitution dedicated to securing domestic tranquility, along with justice, would deal with wholesale defiance of the laws of our republic. Is it not amazing that these patriots could forge a nation without looting one British shop or burning one English owned building?

Many years ago I visited briefly a protest camp set up on the national mall in Washington, D.C. Its adherents called it Resurrection City while others of us referred to it as Insurrection City. One vivid scene etched in mind's eye was human feces many places, presumably caused by defecation wherever the inhabitants wished. I though then, and still believe, we needed men of dedication, as were George S. Patton, Jr. and Douglas A. MacArthur when they moved out the so-called

Bonus Expeditionary Force on 28 July 1932.

The news in May and June 2020 was filled with images of shattered storefronts and small businesses on fire as protests over the death of George Floyd more than occasionally devolved into looting. But as many restaurant owners see it, the attention on looting ignores much bigger threats to their businesses, One of the most preposterous assertions found on the mainstream media involves the coverage of small businesses damaged by looters during protests. It alleges that focusing on rioting and theft ignores even bigger threats that these businesses face. The news story chose to comment on what it called even "greater threats" that restaurants, including reduced capacity dining rooms, increased operational costs, and unforgiving rent payments, in the months to come. It even asserted that some restaurant owners, despite being victims of looting, say that their problems are secondary to the social issues that protesters are fighting for.

Those who have studied revolutions – and make no mistake in seeing the insurrections of spring 2020 as orchestrated revolutionary activities-- have discovered that such violent social and political upheavals occur when oppressive conditions are being positively addressed and elimination of evils has begun. As with so many things, Karl Marx was positively wrong when he claimed that his beloved revolution that would end capitalism must occur when conditions are at their absolute worst. Studies of real events show that at rock bottom either revolutions do not occur or, if they should take place, they are immediately and harshly repressed.

The fact that revolutions have occurred, not in the 1870 to 1960 eras when matters were indeed intolerable for blacks, but after 1960, and continuing well into the twentieth century, shows that society and its weak political leaders would prefer to accept the consequences of riots and revolution due to assumed guilt of past errors. These ineffective leaders refuse to see that positive changes come best through legal and Constitutional means and that looting and consequent property destruction hurts all. Moreover, unlawful behavior is the single greatest factor in perpetuating class and racial hatred, and even setting matters back by reintroducing hatreds from the past.

I should like to share another true story from my early teaching days at West Virginia University. So-called protesters, in reality dedicated nihilistic anarchists, had occupied the park area near Washington Monument and called it Resurrection City, although to many it was Insurrection City. It was filthy and unkept with essentially no police. As one walked its pathways, one had to avoid human feces. The late 1960s had brought unrestrained riots in our cities so intense that members of Congress were escorted to the nation's capitol in jeeps replete with live machine guns.

Some of my militant students, as well as many of my esteemed colleagues, were celebrating those defiant acts as a statements of people's power and freedom. A middle-age student sought to speak. She identified herself as a refugee from Uganda. She spoke of the former dictator, Idi Amin Dada (1925-2003), who practiced ritual cannibalism, who was affectionately known as "the Butcher of Uganda, who ruled in large by practicing voodoo, and who was among the most brutal despots even known, fully as horrid as Hitler, Mao, Stalin, or Kim. His regime was exposed in "The Last King of Scotland" and psychotic Amin was brilliantly portrayed by Forest Whitaker.

She related how Ugandans prayed for relief which came when the Tanzanian Army in 1979 ousted Amin. But the anarchy which followed Tanzania's withdrawal was even worse. Widespread rape, rapine, slaughter of wildlife, butchery, robbery, and general mayhem followed almost immediately. Amin's former soldiers used civilian homes for target price and slaughtered elephants for their ivory. Life was indeed brutal, short, and terribly unpleasant. There was no answer at 9-1-1.

I pray to God daily that the anarchy so valued by the Left is restrained by responsible men, such as those who framed our Republic. With anarchy there is no compromise possible or desirable and no responsible leader should seek to negotiate with pure evil by lowering basic values.

Rhetoric and Revolution

One of the most important descriptive terms I have seen, if not a basic definition, of a republic is a political arena in which rhetoric and debate have superseded violence. When humans have chosen to live in proximity of one another they must choose law and order over destructive behavior. They must denounce the law of self-preservation with collective security of a state that exists under the rule of law. Law must apply equally to all.

In Seattle, Washington, in June 2020, a group of protesters have cornered off several city blocks and established the Capitol Hill

Autonomous Zone as the center for its protest haven. There were virtually no police are in sight. President Donald Trump correctly branded the protest society as a group of "ugly Anarchists" and "Domestic Terrorists." Naturally, the city's mayor, Jenny Durkan, claimed that the President "just doesn't get it." She claimed that "It's a group of people gathering lawfully and exercising their First Amendment right of free speech. . . . It is patriotism." Washington Governor Jay Inslee chimed in saying, "A man who is totally incapable of governing should stay out of Washington state's business." Instead of supporting their police, city council members and other officials criticized police and labeled their actions criminal and irresponsible.

How did that anarchist enclave come about? The mob gathered after forcing Seattle police to abandon its precinct in the Capitol Hill neighborhood on Monday. The mayor and other officials ordered police to abstain from violence and forcible defense of the facility, effectively handing the area over to the insurrectionists with whom police had clashed for days. The "Capitol Hill Autonomous Zone" stretches over a couple city blocks and sprung up after police on Monday removed barricades near the East Precinct and basically abandoned the structure after officers used tear gas, pepper spray and flash bangs over the weekend to disperse demonstrators they said were assaulting them with projectiles.

The ultra-left took control of this six block area, declared it separate from the rest of Washington, created specific borders, and immediately ordered out a specific group of people who were forbidden to return. Compare this to the actions against Waco when the far right set up a separatist community. Try also to imagine the coverage of such a far right enclave by CNN, CBS, ABC, and MSNBC.

Television programs showing heroic deeds performed by police are either canceled, rewritten, or modified. Parmount took the first bold steps by removing police shows from its left-wing network. Perhaps the cop shows can be replaced by ":Looters" or "Insurrectionists" or even "Revolutionaries" with the lawless breeds as heroes.

Eighteen days after the death of George Floyd, Minneapolis City Council unanimously passed a resolution to replace the police department with a community-led public safety system. A veto-proof totality of the council announced plans to disband its police department and invest in community-based public safety programs. Mayor Jacob Frey, announced a plan to "end our city's toxic relationship with the Minneapolis Police Department." The city council will begin a year-long process of engaging "with every willing community member in Minneapolis" to develop a new public safety model, having acknowledged that the present police system is so corrupt that it cannot be reformed or purged. City Council president Lisa Bender declared the entire Minneapolis police department to be guilty of institutional racism and thus guilty of Floyd's death.

Let's take a close look at the cast of characters. Derek Chauvuin was a 19 year veteran of the police department, having also served as a military policeman. During his tenure he was subject of 18 complaints and twice was cited for valor. Interestingly, one case in which Chauvin was reviewed was overseen by current Democratic vice-presidential aspirant Amy Klobuchar, who was then serving as chief prosecutor for the county. After full review Klobuchar declined to bring charges. The same was true for Klobuchar in more than two dozen cases of police killing civilians in Minneapolis while she was in office.

George Floyd had moved to Minneapolis after being released from Texas prison for aggravated robbery. He was under the influence of fentanyl and methamphetamine at the time of arrest. He went to jail for at least 5 times and a look at George Floyd’s profile as per court documents reads like a career criminal involved in drug abuse, theft, criminal trespassing, aggravated robbery as well as entering a woman’s home and pointing a gun at her stomach while looking for drugs and money.

Although Joe Biden has declared that he does not support the call for defunding the police, an investigation has found that 99.64% of the Black Lives Matter’s ‘Defund the Police’ donations go to Joe Biden via ActBlue, a Democrat fundraising platform that is the top donor to Biden for President campaign.

Meanwhile, an effort to defund the police department is gaining momentum. Los Angeles Mayor Eric Garcetti said the city would look to cut $100 million to $150 million from its nearly $2 billion annual police budget and redirect that money to assist black communities. Mayor Bill de Blasio pledged for the first time to cut New York City’s police funding following ten nights of mass protests against police violence and mounting demands that he overhaul a department whose tactics have caused widespread consternation. DeBlasio declined to say precisely how much funding he planned to divert to social services from the New York Police Department, which has an annual budget of $6 billion, representing more than 6% of de Blasio's proposed $90 billion budget.

One of the very few religious organizations which had the backbone to take offense at the governmental interference with its religious services was the Mormons, also known as the Church of Jesus Christ of Latter-day Saints. Speaking at the Religious Freedom Annual Review at Brigham Young University, Elder David A. Bednar of the Quorum of the Twelve Apostles of The Church of Jesus Christ of Latter-day Saints went on record opposing such governmental interference as occurred in spring 2020, saying that government power must have limits and shared examples that he said illustrated "a profound devaluing of religion." The pandemic provided evidence that balancing public health needs and religious exercise during a crisis can be a major challenge. When governments around the world swiftly banned religious gatherings as COVID-19 advanced, they dangerously breached boundaries protecting the free exercise of religious freedom and proved just how tenuous it is. The pandemic was a wake-up call about the fragility of religious freedom. He said government power must have limits and shared examples that he said illustrated "a profound devaluing of religion." The pandemic provided evidence that balancing public health needs and religious exercise during a crisis can be a major challenge. Elder Bednar did not claim that religious freedom is unlimited during a pandemic or that all government officials disregarded religious rights. What he said was that while strong measures to address COVID-19 were justified, "extraordinary assertions of governmental power" can dramatically constrain basic freedoms. He continued: "We cannot deny and we should not forget the speed and intensity with which government power was used to shut down fundamental aspects of religious exercise. . . . "These decisions and regulations were unprecedented. For nearly two months, Americans and many others throughout the free world learned firsthand what it means for government to directly prohibit the free exercise of religion."

Barbarians at the Gate

The barbarians are at the gate in the form of mobs tearing down statues and memorials representing our history and our heritage. They started with Confederate political leaders and generals, but many of us understood from the very outset that the Confederate leaders were clearly a Trojan horse.

In a true civilization, rhetoric and debate take the place of violence. To have mobs take the law into their own hands is not only unacceptable in a civilized society, but it is downright dangerous. Such actions erode the rule of law, which is precious, valuable, and very fragile. It is far easier to destroy the rule of law than it is to build it up in the first place.

Typical of the ill-learned self-appointed leaders is Shaun King, probably the most visible of the Black Lives Matter gang. He has proclaimed, "I think the statues of the white European they claim is Jesus should also come down. Yes. All murals and stained glass windows of white Jesus, and his European mother, and their white friends should also come down. They are a gross form of white supremacy. Created as tools of oppression. Racist propaganda. They should all come down." King's anti-Christian rantings follow well former president Obama's belittling of rural Americans who cling to God and their guns.

The new racist barbarians have made war not only upon the statues of slave holders, they have attacked the leaders of the very foundation of the Republic: George Washington, Thomas Jefferson, Abraham Lincoln, and James Madison. They have vandalized the likenesses of the military heroes who sustained the Republic, such as U. S. Grant and Douglas A. MacArthur. The criminals who destroy public property themselves have contributed nothing of positive value to either the nation or the debate over police powers.

Their cowardly political allies have joined in. Maryland removed the statue of Roger Taney, our second most significant Chief Justice of SCOTUS, following John Marshall. As it was, his decision in *Scott v Sanford* was very good law under the Constitution as then written. His many other decisions, buttressing Justice Marshall, helped form the Republic. Justice Taney, like Justice Marshall, avoided the sociological jurisprudence that has more recently undermined the rule of law. One of the great ironies here is that the opinions of Justices Marshall and Taney regarding the definition of, and control over, interstate commerce allowed the ultra-left wing Earl Warren Court to rule in favor of sustaining the Civil Rights Act of 1964 in Heart of Atlanta Motel vs *Katzenbach*.

It should be obvious that the barbarians are fully capable of shouting down the truth. It is not facts they seek but organized nihilism, anarchist attacks upon civilization. They do not care to really examine the facts, and judge the totality of human contributions. Having decided that an historical figure does not meet their litmus test, there is no question as to his removal (Have the barbarians yet attacked any women as unworthy in their petty insights?) In the overall schema of things, it is incredible that barbarians who have accomplished nothing positive on their own, and who never will add to the nation's accomplishments, can arrogate to themselves the power to censor history and dismiss the giants of the past.

While I would not force people to act as I would recommend, it would behoove revolutionaries to read one or more of the better dystopian novels such as *1984*. Specifically in that work it is the job of protagonist Winston Smith to rewrite history, even in newspaper articles, removing or reinterpreting those individuals who have fallen out of favor with the current government. By removing and rewriting it is as though the real past never occurred. History becomes retroactive fiction.

Can one truly envision American history with no mention of George Washington, Thomas Jefferson, Abraham Lincoln, Robert E. Lee, James Madison, James Monroe, and Andrew Jackson? Can one understand and fully appreciate world history if one removes mention of all slave-owning figures? Was Columbus really such a bad guy as to merit his disappearance? When we decide which slave-holders to cause to disappear will it be only those who owned black slaves? Or will we go back and include all slave-owners from all epochs of history? My own guess is that, should we discard all slave owners, we would have very short histories. While I would never list Diane Feinstein among the great figures of American history, and thus worthy of recognition by having a building named after her, the reason for my exclusion of Ms Feinstein would not be because she replaced a desecrated Confederate flag from an historical exhibit.

As the barbarians reinterpret history for their own purposes, how will we view organizations that are in opposition to their transcended values? Should the United Confederate Veterans (UCV), one depicted on U.S. stamps, now be called a hate organization? Should the Southern Poverty Law Center add the Daughters of the Confederacy to its allegedly definitive list of professional racists? Must we disband the various genealogical societies who trace their ancestors back to slave-holders? Perhaps the Bible, at least in the Book of Philemon, be revised to remove any pro-slavery thoughts. The latter deed could be done while looking for the presumed Biblical condemnation of the institution of slavery.

It is most disturbing to see the mainstream news media refer to criminals, insurrectionists, arsonists, vandals, incendiaries, and looters merely as demonstrators. It is even worse when political leaders respond to them by giving in to their every demand and granting their every pipe-dream. All human lives matter precisely because each life is an act of God Almighty. We don't protect those lives though violent acts. In an open society such as our own rhe toric replace s violence, at least among civilized people.

Required Right Thinking

Americans in their righteous wrath should stand up against the Democratic Majority in the House of Representatives action in denying Marjorie Greene (R-GA) her committee assignments in January 2021 because of her free speech associations. As one who, over 40 years, witnessed frontal assaults on free speech in an academic environment, it comes as absolutely no surprise. Undoubtedly, they claim she is a racist and thus unworthy to appear among them in that august body.

When I was growing up there was the strong undercurrent that FDR had "set up" Pearl Harbor on 7 December 1941 in order to get United States involved in the World War in order to rescue Churchill and England, a view held by several members of Congress and popularized by several credible historians. Even today there are members of Congress who would posthumously exonerate murderers Sacco and Vanzetti, insurrectionist John Brown, and treasonous spies Julius and Ethel Rosenberg. Should such persons be subject of Congressional discipline?

Should black members of Congress be removed from committees if they adhere to teachings of John Lewis or Malcolm X? The sheer nonsense preached by candidate for socialist sainthood, deceased US Representative John Lewis (D-GA) claimed that not only were 100 million slaves were thrown overboard from slave ships, but that the migratory pattern of sharks were changed because of their feeding off these dead bodies. That untenable myth originated with Rep. John M. Payne (D-NJ).

How about the fictional origins of the black race? In his book

"*Message to the Blackman in America,*" Black Islam Prophet Elijah Muhammad wrote that "Negroes are descended from an ancient tribe named Shabazz. Allah has declared that we the so-called Negroes are descendants of the Asian Black Nation and the tribe of Shabazz." Malcolm X picked this up and embellished it, as related by convicted plagiarizer Alex Haley in his "Autobiography of Malcolm X."

Many Christians assert that the Book of Mormon was really a purloined fictional manuscript written by Solomon Spaulding on Westmoreland County. One Congressman, a Bedford resident long ago, Honorable John Cessna, so charged . Should Mormon Mit Romney be disciplined for holding that belief to be true?

To many, the longest fictional work in any language is the Warren Commission report on Kennedy Assassination. How should we judge? Was it or was it not a true and honest inquiry? Then there was the TV program "Men Who Killed Kennedy" broadcast by History Channel, one segment of which accused Lyndon Johnson! Many viewers bought one or another accusation. Which way to demand "the truth" on this issue?

Another group, largely from the West Coast, has demanded that any positive memory of various notable Americans be discarded because they fail their litmus tests of political correctness. Must all admirers of Jefferson, Washington, Lincoln, Lee, and Jackson do penance in sackcloth in order to serve on Congressional committees?

Is this merely the first broadside, in a war which will soon reject all traditional Christian moral stances and whose adherents will be denied committee assignment for holding their Biblical beliefs? Such socialistically rejected beliefs would most likely include traditional marriage, sanctity of human life, freedom of religion, and family lifestyle.

Kwanza: Counter-Christmas

For reasons that doubtless are racist, and doubtless anti-Christian, it has become necessary to invent, resurrect, discover, or uncover days of special concern, as the politically correct term is, to rival and someday take the place of Christmas. Go back fifty years and try to find references to Diwali or Kwanza! One could not possibly find anything about Kwanza because its founders had not yet created it.

Not especially surprising, to join others at the cutting edge of political correctness, the local scandal sheet ran complimentary articles on Kwanza wholly ignores its racist nature and violent origins. Kwanza was designed to the first specifically African-American holiday, celebrated over the Christmas/New Year period. The reported goal was to "give Blacks an alternative to the existing holiday and give Blacks an opportunity to celebrate themselves and history, rather than simply imitate the practice of the dominant society."

Kwanza was the handiwork of a black hate group, US, founded in 1965 by Hakim Jamal and Ron "Dr. Maulana" Karenga as a more militant [in politically incorrect language-- revolutionary] organization than the Black Panthers. One of the early slogans was, "Wherever US is, We are." US stands for us Black people vs 'them' the oppressors." The Black Panthers referred to the US organization as the "United Slaves", a name never actually used by members of US but which is often mistaken for the group's official name.

The US Organization, spreaded its hate through a magazine, *Message to the Grassroot* in which Karenga was listed as chairman and Jamal as founder of the new group. US promotes seven collectivist [essentially Marxist] principles: Black Unity (Umoja), Black Self-Determination (Kujichagulia), Collective Work and Responsibility (Ujima), Cooperative Socialist Economics (Ujamaa), Racial Purpose (Nia), Creativity (Kuumba), and Faith (Imani).

Although some of their most high-profile leaders were drug dealers and murderers, and some members harbored great ethnic hatred, generally the Black Panthers did not seek armed revolution.

On January 17, 1969, there was an epic gun battle on the UCLA campus between US and Black Panthers which ended in the deaths of Panthers. This led to a series of retaliatory shootings that lasted for months. Later in 1969, two other Black Panther members were killed and one other was wounded by US members. In 1971, Karenga, together with his fellow travelers Louis Smith, and Luz Maria Tamayo, was convicted of felony assault. After his release in 1975 Karenga re-emerged as US leader as it operates it today. The phony holiday of Kwanza is his principal legacy.

Karenga gained new following when in a widely quoted 1995 interview he claimed that "O. J. Simpson had been framed murder by the FBI, the CIA, the State Department, Interpol, the Chicago Police Department." As columnist Ann Coulter recently pointed out, "Karenga's invented holiday is a nutty blend of schmaltzy 1960s rhetoric, black racism and Marxism. The seven principles of Kwanzaa are the very same seven principles of the Symbionese Liberation Army."

In a world which recently has come down hard on white supremicist organizations and leders it is odd that white liberals have so strongly supported a militant separatist black organization. Suppose US's rhetoric were translated to white militancy by neo-nazis, the Klan, etc.

This batch of sheer nonsense mixed in heavily with Marxism has survived only beacuse it originated witgh the black community. Even more significantly, it grew out of the far left of the black community. The so-called mainstream media has long since decided that anything truly "black" must be from the ultra-left. Anything conservative is a remnant of slavery and thus insulting to blacks. Were Caucasians to invent such nonsense the media would immediately jump on it and it would soon be consigned to the purifying flames. But Kwanza is one of the end results of black expressionism and thus legitimate and desirable. Happy Kwanza!

The laudatory and highly complimentary articles on Kwanza wholly ignore its racist nature and violent origins. Kwanza was designed to the first specifically African-American holiday, celebrated over the Christmas/New Year period. The reported goal was to "give Blacks an alternative to the existing holiday and give Blacks an opportunity to celebrate themselves and history, rather than simply imitate the practice of the dominant society."

Black Lives Matter 2

It has become one of the imbecilities of our age that to be remembered one must have a background as pure as Ivory Soap. Pete Rose, for example, has been denied admission to Baseball Hall of Fame because he once bet on sports. Ignore his accomplishments, condemn his sins. Today, the ill-informed nihilists have chosen to ignore Justice Taney's brilliant and nation-forming decisions because of one perfectly good decision in terms of the Constitution as it existed in 1856. It is one of the imbecilities of our times that those who would consign Justice Taney to oblivion do not understand that his decision in *Charles River Bridge v Warren Bridge* formed an important precedent when Chief Justice Earl Warren's court upheld the 1964 Civil Rights Act in the *Heart of Atlanta Motel v Katzenbach.*

Self-appointed leaders who have contributed nothing to the commonweal dare to condemn Washington, Monroe, Madison, Jefferson, Jackson and others who forged a Republic Some even condemn the God-Man who came into this world to save mankind because he was incarnate as a Caucasian. Were that a legitimate position, to wholly condemn a single sin, I, as an academician dedicated to to maintaining the highest standards of integrity, should demand the destruction of Martin Luther King memorials since, according to the *New York Times*, he plagiarized his doctoral dissertation. In any ordinary situation, proof of a plagiarized thesis would be more than sufficient reason to rescind the culprit's degree.

I do not understand why black lives matter more than blue lives. It make great sense that if a criminal would attack an armed policeman he would an even greater danger to civilians. That thin blue line is out only defense against all lawless activities. I don't understand why blacks don't protest more against the racist Margaret Sanger's advocacy of abortions for unborn blacks.

I do not understand why black leaders don't try to disperse mobs bent on looting and arson, or why they bristle at white leaders like Spiro Agnew who chide them for failing to do so. I do not understand why criminal acts directed against police or property owners are not listed as hate crimes but painting over a BLM drawing on a street is hateful. Why should lawless crowds assume a right to interrupt my free passage on roads my taxes helped pay for by marching, laying down on the roadway, or otherwise preventing travel?

As Thomas More taught, we must seek the protection of law for our own safety for, when we strike down law to get after whatever present devil, the devil will turn round on us and we will have nowhere to hide, the law having been flattened.

The two greatest dangers to this great Republic are: [1] destroying its history so that we'll make same errors again; [2] allowing any group, no matter how noble its cause, to win its objective by lawless behavior. Our history is not without blemishes of many kinds, but if we look at the history of human kind, we one of very few nations which constantly seek to rectify evils and advance good. Whites did not invent slavery, but whites ended it, at least in the West.

James Biser Whisker

Marxism and the Black Experience

What must be understood before embarking on an exploration of Marxism is that it exists fundamentally as an attack on, and critique of, capitalism. As an ideology, it will disappear immediately after the fall of capitalism for it has no substance of its own, no program to offer, no better world to live in. Marx never completed his ideology, perhaps because it could not be brought to some conclusion. The best he could offer for the communist Utopia was slogans, such as "from each according to his ability, to each according to his needs" without ever explaining how to get there, let alone how it would operate. It should be obvious that, when so-called Marxist regimes have come to power, they have been only brutal dictatorships, with the promised dictatorship *of* the proletariat being a dictatorship *over* the people. Celebrations are held all across the American fruited plain, with radicals worshiping the ideals of communism which, simply stated, is an ideology calling for government control over our lives.

Marx admitted that he had not explained sufficiently the dialectic, his motor power of history. Before dying, Marx admitted that he had never written a full explanation of the dialectic. For Marx's intellectual mentor G. W. F. Hegel, the dialectic was a tool used in the philosophical field of logic. It was a mode of explanation that sought to increase understanding by contrasting opposed ideas. Traditional logic had sought to increase understanding by seeking likeness, not diversity, as when Jesus taught "the Kingdom of Heaven is like unto . . . ." Hegel did conceive of the dialectic as an entity which could propel history, or, for that matter, do anything. The dialectic was a mental construct with no life or being of its own.

Having taken Hegel's ideas, Marx eviscerated them, removing the deity which as the *Weltgeist* [World Spirit] propelled history. Marx's materialism had no place for God, but drew upon the dialectic, an immaterial mental construct, to motivate history. Somehow that blind force slowly, but inexorably, moves humankind to increasingly higher planes until it brought about communism.

For some unexplained reason, the dialectic, having brought about communism, grinds to a halt, creating no new hybrid. Marx never conceived that the dialectic would move on after communism, creating a new class of exploiters who controlled the exploited class below. That was left to Jugoslav theorist Milovan Djilas, who showed that the communist masters, the commissars, the new exploiting class, were now the power devastating the poor, now known as the comrades. Indeed, the dialectic continued its march toward newer, and presumed higher, standards of human existence.[4]

Marx's theory of history, known as dialectical and historical materialism, centered around the idea that forms of society rise and fall as they further and then impede the development of human productive power. Marx asserted that the historical process proceeds through a necessary series of modes of production, culminating in communism. Marx's economic analysis of capitalism is based on his version of the labor theory of value, and includes the analysis of capitalist profit as the extraction of surplus value from the exploited proletariat. The analysis of history and economics come together in Marx's prediction of the inevitable economic breakdown of capitalism, to be replaced by communism. However Marx refused to speculate in detail about the nature of communism, arguing that it would arise through historical processes, and was not the realization of a predetermined moral ideal. One appeal of Marxism to American black writers is to be found in its method of analysis and theoretical critique of capitalism which views it as a system which fosters social divisions which Marxist revolution alone can correct.

Having no clear vision of a future Utopia, Marx never articulated either a new way of arranging the basic building blocks of the state and society or created new entities to replace the corrupted capitalistic building blocks. All previous systems had arranged essentially the same building blocks, such as sovereignty; legislative, judicial and executive powers; money and banking; and the like. What previous generations had discovered was that there were only a few ways to join those blocks and have a functioning system. Marx rode roughshod over these concepts, expending his energy on on damning the present arrangement. When asking, the, how different his brave new world would be, Marx would be unable to answer. When Lenin, who adopted Marxism, wanted to decide how to deal with money, banking, and commerce, he had to admit that neither he nor Marx had even the most remote idea of how to deal with such matters without full reference and application to the traditional way these matters were handled under the hated capitalist system.

---

4 Djilas, Milovan. T*he New Class*. Praeger, 1958.

Marx the Bigot

It is incredibly odd that so many black American writers and protesters have become enamored of Marxism and its chief exponents when it is fundamentally racist. As radicals demand that political entities tear down statues of everyone deemed racist, those dedicated to communism's principal spokesbeing, Karl Marx have thus far evaded the woke mob's wrath. Yet his comments and observations were critical of virtually every race and nationality except Gentiles in Western Europe. One cannot find in any other well-known writer any more virulent racism than one finds in the essays and letters of Karl Marx.[5]

On the Jewish Question, also known as *A World Without Jews*, is a work by Karl Marx, written in 1843, and first published in Paris in 1844 under the German title *Zur Judenfrage* as an article in the *Deutsch–Französische Jahrbücher* [German-French Yearbook]. It was one of Marx's first attempts to develop what would later be called the materialist conception of history. Marx's father was a practicing Jew who joined the Lutheran Church for economic and political, if not religious, reasons.[6] Marx wrote of the Jewish people:

> Money is the zealous one God of Israel, beside which no other God may stand. Money degrades all the gods of mankind and turns them into commodities. Money is the universal and self-constituted value set upon all things. It has therefore robbed the whole world, of both nature and man, of its original value. Money is the essence of man's life and work, which have become alienated from him: this alien monster rules him and he worships it. . . . .The God of the Jews has become secularized and is now a worldly God. The bill of exchange is the Jew's real God. His God is the illusory bill of exchange. "What is the foundation of the Jew in our world? Practical necessity, private advantage. "What is the object of the Jew's worship in this world? Usury. What is his worldly God? Money. . . . Very well then: emancipation from usury and money, that is, from practical, real Judaism.[7]

Marx did not hesitate to use the forbidden N-word in describing one of his intellectual rivals, Ferdinand Lassalle. Ferdinand Las-

---

5 Chris Talgo, Chris. "Karl Marx Was a Horrific Racist," St*opping Socialism,* 22 June 2020

6 Greenblatt, Stephen J., "Marlowe, Marx, and Anti-Semitism," *Critical Inquiry*, 5: 2 (1978), pp. 291–307; Wheen, Francis. *Karl Marx: A Life.* Norton, 2001. Wheen argued that this was actually a defense of Jews.

7 Marx, Karl. *A World Without Jews*. Dagobert Runes, ed., trans., intro. Philosophical Library, n.d.

salle was a Prussian-German jurist, philosopher, socialist and political activist best remembered as the one who introduced the social democratic movement in Germany and many considered a forerunner of Marxism in Germany. In 1862 Marx wrote the following to Friedrich Engels in Manchester:

> The Jewish nigger Lassalle who, I'm glad to say, is leaving at the end of this week, has happily lost another 5,000 talers in an ill-judged speculation. The chap would sooner throw money down the drain than lend it to a 'friend,' even though his interest and capital were guaranteed.... It is now quite plain to me—as the shape of his head and the way his hair grows also testify—that he is descended from the negroes who accompanied Moses' flight from Egypt (unless his mother or paternal grandmother interbred with a nigger). Now, this blend of Jewishness and Germanness, on the one hand, and basic negroid stock, on the other, must inevitably give rise to a peculiar product. The fellow's importunity is also nigger-like.[8]

Writing to his collaborator, Friedrich Engels, concerning Pierre Trémaux (1818--1895), a French architect, Orientalist photographer, and author of numerous scientific and ethnographic publications, Marx observed that Trémaux"proved that the common Negro type is the degenerate form of a much higher one ... a very significant advance over Darwin."[9] In a letter to Paul Lafargue's wife, who was Marx's daughter, Engels, who assumed that Lafargue had partially black heritage, wrote, "Being in his quality as a nigger, a degree nearer to the rest of the animal kingdom than the rest of us, he is undoubtedly the most appropriate representative of that district." Engels was of opinion that LaFargue, who lived near the city zoo, was an octoroon, one-eighth black.

When the United States annexed California after the Mexican War, Marx sarcastically asked, "Is it a misfortune that magnificent California was seized from the lazy Mexicans who did not know what to do with it?" Engels shared Marx's contempt for Mexicans, explaining: "In America we have witnessed the conquest of Mexico and have rejoiced at it. It is to the interest of its own development that Mexico will be placed under the tutelage of the United States."[10]

---

8 Karl Marx Was a Horrific Racist. Here Are the Quotes to Prove It | INDIAN LIBERTY REPORT

9 Marx, Karl, letter to Friedrich Engels, dated 7 August 1866.

10 Quoted in Williams, Walter E., "The Ugly Racism of Karl Marx," *The Daily Signal,* 10 May 2017.

Given Marx's absolute insistence that capitalism would fail, beginning with its most advanced application, probably in Germany or Great Britain, and then into the other Western European nations, and the United States, it is not at all surprising that he denounced Russian exiles who sought to bring communism to Russia. Marx viewed Russia as just emerging from feudalism, in which the aristocrats were the oppressors and the serfs the exploited ones. It was the fact that part of the United States was just emerging from servile feudalism that prompted Marx to postpone the communist revolution there. But the rejection of Russia's suitability for a communist revolution should not have sparked a racist outburst against Slavic peoples. Nonetheless, Marx wrote,

> This splendid territory [the Balkans] has the misfortune to be inhabited by a conglomerate of different races and nationalities, of which it is hard to say which is the least fit for progress and civilization. Slavonians, Greeks, Wallachians, Arnauts, twelve millions of men, are all held in submission by one million of Turks, and up to a recent period, it appeared doubtful whether, of all these different races, the Turks were not the most competent to hold the supremacy which, in such a mixed population, could not but accrue to one of these nationalities.[11]

Marx's comments on slavery, taken from an early work, justified its use in the United States. He wrote, "Without slavery, North America, the most progressive of countries, would be transformed into a patriarchal country. Wipe out North America from the map of the world and you will have anarchy— the complete decay of modern commerce and civilization. Abolish slavery and you will have wiped America off the map of nations."[12] This fits well with his comments made some twenty years later, regarding the American Civil War. For the slaves, according to Marx, life was much better because of cradle to the grave care the slave masters provided. Northern wage slaves enjoyed no such paternalistic care. It was imperative that Marx conclude in this way since he had insisted that the exploitation of the poor increased with each advance of the dialectic. Capitalism was a higher form of economic life and so its mistreatment was necessarily greater than slavery which was a form of feudalism.[13]

---

11 Marx, Karl, *The Russian Menace to Europe,* (1853).

12 Marx, Karl, *The Poverty of Philosophy,* 1847. This work was a biting attack on Pierre Joseph Proudhon's *Philosophy of Poverty* (1846).

13 Marx, Karl and Friedrich Engels, *The Civil War in the United States*. Interna-

Marx was pitted inexorably against the Third World. Advances of historical and dialectical materialism occurred only in the West. No similar progressive stages are to be found in Asia or Africa. It was logical, then, that Marx castigated the peoples of the Indian sub-continent in his correspondence with a New York newspaper. Marx wrote, "Indian society has no history at all, at least no known history. What we shall call its history is but the history of the successive invaders who founded their empires on the passive basis of that unresisting and unchanging society."[14]

Despite its many failures, Marxism has successfully attracted support from the Third World, who have accepted the absurd bit of illogic that concludes that socialism, not capitalism, is the economic way of the future. They believe its rhetoric that capitalism exploits the poor far worse than any other economic system and that capitalism was built on the backs of slaves. Marxism has been able to successfully camouflage the many "ethnic cleansings" and starvation practices used by Marxists in Russia, China, and elsewhere. It has effectively covered up the horrid mass murders, such as the red terror in Ethiopia and the killing fields of Pot Pol's khmer rouge. Hiding its own blood--red hands, Marxism has accused capitalism of being the ideology of hate, prejudice, exploitation, and assassination. Black intellectuals, in part seduced by leftist ideologues, have embraced Marxism in significant numbers and around the world.[15]

Marxism Infiltrates Black Thinking

One of the early and highly influential communist black advocates was Festus Claudius McKay (1889—1948). He was a Jamaican-born writer and poet, and a central figure in the Harlem Renaissance. In 1919 McKay wrote *If We Must Die* his best known work. McKay was attracted to communism in his early life, although always claimed that he never became an official member of the Communist Party. There is no question of his close ties to active members, his attendance at communist-led events, and his months-long stay in the Soviet Union from 1922-23, which he wrote about very favorably. Claude McKay, co-executive editor of *The Liberator* alongside socialist Max

tional Publishers, 1937.

14 Marx, Karl Marx, in the *New York Daily Tribune,* 8 August 1853

15 Marable, Manning. "Rethinking Black Liberation: Towards a New Protest Paradigm." *Race and Class* 38: 4 (1997), pp. 1–13.

Eastman, traveled to the Soviet Union, attending the Fourth Congress of the Communist International in 1922. He declared in 1919: "Every Negro who lays claim to leadership should make a study of Bolshevism and explain its meaning to the coloured masses. It is the greatest and most scientific idea afloat in the world today." McKay joined the Industrial Workers of the World (IWW or Wobblies) in autumn 1919 while working in a factory following his time as a dining-car waiter on the railways .

According to his autobiographies *A Long Way From Home* and *My Green Hills of Jamaica*, he claimed he was drawn to the Communist party because it offered independence. McKay later denounced Stalin and his bloody version of Marxism which alienated him from most of the other black intellectuals of the Harlem school. He eventually converted to Roman Catholicism. Despite his changing ideas, his early espousal of the Marxist line left an indelible legacy followed by many black intellectuals.[16]

Antiracists oppose capitalism itself. Ibram X. Kendi, perhaps the nation's most prominent "antiracist," says that "to truly be antiracist, you also have to truly be anti-capitalist." Ibram Xolani Kendi was born Ibram Henry Rogers on 13 August 1982. He is an American anti-racist activist, and historian of race and discriminatory policy in America. In July 2020, he assumed the position of director of the Center for Antiracist Research at Boston University. A New York Times #1 Best Seller in 2020, *How to Be an Antiracis*t is Kendi's most popular work. One adherent called it the "most courageous book to date on the problem of race in the Western mind".Another praised the book's introspection and wrote that it was relatable in the context of ongoing political events. In it, Kendi advanced the idea of transferring government oversight to an unelected Department of Antiracism.

According to Kendi, in the United States the government defends the capitalist economic system and its class and race hierarchies. The ideological crisis of the state is brought on by a crisis of legitimacy, when significant parts of the population reject its authority and its rule. They can make nations ungovernable. The US is at such a moment of crisis. The US, however, remains the vanguard of the

---

16 Cooper, Wayne F. *Claude McKay: Rebel Sojourner in the Harlem Renaissance.* Baton Rouge: Louisiana State University Press, 1987. See also Tillery, Tyrone. *Claude McKay: A Black Poet's Struggle for Identity.* University of Massachusetts Press, 1992.

global movement to save western capitalism and white civilization. It is the military strike force of western hegemony. Its strength is weakened, and its hegemony challenged by the rise of an energized Chinese socialism and new global alliances of non-western nations and political forces.

Capitalist United States defends "the outmoded but exploitative capitalist economic system along with its class and race hierarchies." It is thus a necessary part of the ruling elite's ideological intervention to thwart the development of anti-racist consciousness, and prevent formation of united fronts against racism. One revealing part of Kendi's book is how it deals with the race/class dialectic and racial capitalism. "To love capitalism is to end up loving racism", Kendi insists. Kendi defined capitalism by its policies, but not as a system. It integral policies are "theft and racism and sexism and imperialism." Such are the evil policies from which capitalism must disentangle. Racist policies and capitalist policies are twins; therefore, anti-capitalist policies must be joined to antiracist ones. Thus, not a good a true Marxist, Kendi assumes that one can change capitalist policies, and, if it can be changed, it may not be necessary to replace the capitalist economic system

His view may stem in part from the upside-down, ahistorical narrative put forth in *The New York Times*' pernicious "1619 Project." Parts of that long supplement asserted that slavery was a capitalist institution and without slavery there would have been no capitalism. Setting aside that in practice, many of the world's socialist regimes have proven uniquely bigoted, capitalism tends to punish discrimination and reward people regardless of their skin color. Socialism tends to generate pervasive inequity—a cadre of ultra-rich elites, and a mass of impoverished humanity.

As the late Walter Williams wrote: "Before the rise of capitalism, the way people amassed great wealth was by looting, plundering and enslaving their fellow man," creating and perpetuating inequity. Conversely, "Capitalism made it possible to become wealthy by serving one's fellow man." Perhaps the antiracists believe that a return to "looting, plundering and enslaving," if done by and to the "right" people, is "equitable"—but in practice, regimes encouraging such behavior are always rife with inequity, if they are to even survive in the first instance.

Harry Haywood

The most radical early black American Marxist was Harry Haywood (1898—1985). He was a leading figure in the Communist Party of the United States (CPUSA) and was quickly accorded much attention by the Communist Party of the Soviet Union (CPSU). His stated goal was the connection of Communist ideology with the issues of race in the United States.

In 1926, he joined other black Communists and traveled to the Soviet Union to study the effect of Communism on racial issues found in the United States. Pleased with his work there, t he CPSU promoted him to be the head of the CPUSA's Negro Department. The CPUSA platform changed by the late 1930s and began to move away from advocating self-determination. Some Communists considered Haywood's narrow nationalism, along with Marcus Garvey's "back to Africa" movement, to be reactionary, and hence antithetical to orthodox Marxist thinking. However, others viewed Haywood's nationalism to be a very legitimate development within the overall Black Freedom Movement. Unwilling to compromise with the CPUSA's changing platform, Haywood began to lose his importance within the party.[17]

One of his successes was in the agitation designed to help rescue the "Scottsboro boys," which was one of the most unjust cases of prosecution based on race ever to disgrace the United States. While the defendants underwent several trials, none which met modern standards of justice and due process of law, their case drew much worldwide attention.

Haywood wrote his first book, *Negro Liberation,* published in 1948. Following his expulsion from the CPUSA, he wrote an autobiography entitled *Black Bolshevik*, which was also published in 1978.[18] He contributed major theory to Marxist thinking regarding the place of blacks in the United States. To draw attention to his thoughts, he associated with the Maoist New Communist movement.

He had come to believe that a distinct African-American nation within the territorial boundaries of the United States. That emergence satisfied the criteria laid out by Stalin in his *Marxism and the*

---

17 Perkins, William Eric, "Harry Haywood (1898-1985)," in Mari Jo Buhle et al., eds. *Encyclopedia of the American Left.* New York: Garland, 1990.

18 Haywood, Harry. *Black Bolshevik: Autobiography of an Afro-American Communist.* Chicago: Liberator Press, 1978.

National Question. American blacks now constituted an historically constituted, stable community of people, formed on the basis of a common language, territory, economic life, and psychological makeup manifested in a common culture. Blacks in the South constituted such a nation, and Haywood asserted that the correct response was a demand for self-determination, up to and including the right to separate from the United States. Their national territory was historically the South, and they deserved full equality everywhere else in the United States. Haywood believed that only with genuine political power, which from a Marxist point of view included control of the productive forces, such as land, could African Americans obtain genuine equality. Their gaining of equality was a prerequisite for broader working class unity.[19]

Collaboration between Marxists and black radicals in the United States originated in the 1920s and 1930s when the CPUSA began to recognize that American blacks constituted a fertile recruiting ground, one which no other ideology had yet exploited. Early black communists like Harry Haywood helped to elucidate what the CPUSA called the "Negro Question." Black leaders struggled against the assignment of a subsidiary position in the revolutionary movement to black writers. The Sixth World Congress of the CPUSA in 1928 passed resolutions regarding the American Negro Question. That Congress supported Haywood's contention that American blacks were an "oppressed nation which had the right to self-determination,"and that the Southern "Black Belt" was ready for revolutionary activity.[20]

Angela Davis

Many regard Angela Davis (1944--) as the founding philosopher of Critical Race Theory. She was born in Birmingham, Alabama, where both her parents were employed as school teachers. She is the best known black female nihilist-activist in America. Angela attended a small private school known as the 'Little Red School House' in Greenwich Village in New York City where she became enamored of

---

19 Harry Haywood, *For a Revolutionary Position on the Negro Question.* Chicago: Liberator Press, 1975; Robinson, Cedric J. *Black Marxism: The Making of the Black Radical Tradition*. University of North Carolina Press, 2000.

20 Robinson, Cedric J. 1983. *Black Marxism: The Making of the Black Radical Tradition.* London: Zed, 1983; James, C. L. R., "The Revolutionary Answer to the Negro Problem in the U.S.A." [1948] in Grimshaw, Anna, ed. *The C. L. R. James Reader.* Cambridge, MA: Blackwell, 1992, pp. 182-89.

socialism and communism.

She befriended the children of the leaders of the Communist Party, including her lifelong friend, Bettina Aptheker, daughter of longtime communist activist Herbert Aptheker. Herbert Aptheker (1915--2003) was an American Marxist historian and political activist. He wrote more than fifty books, mostly in the fields of black history, most notably *American Negro Slave Revolts* (1943), the standard reference in the field. He also compiled the seven volume *Documentary History of the Negro People* (1951–1994). In addition, he compiled a wide variety of primary documents supporting study of African-American history. He was the literary executor for the works of W. E. B. Du Bois. Beginning in the 1940s, Aptheker was a prominent figure in U.S. scholarly discourse on the place of communist theory in American life. Aptheker was blacklisted in academia during the 1950s because of his Communist Party membership. He succeeded V. J. Jerome in 1955 as editor of *Political Affairs*, an academic journal concerned with Marxist theory.

An accomplished scholar, Angela received a full scholarship to Brandeis University in Massachusetts, where she met German-Jewish philosopher Herbert Marcuse (1898-1979).

Marcuse was a philosopher, sociologist, and political theorist, the best known associate of the Frankfurt School of critical theory. He was a prominent figure in the Frankfurt-based Institute for Social Researc which developed into the Frankfurt School. His written works were highly critical of capitalism, modern technology, the Soviet Russian brand of Communism, and entertainment culture, arguing that they represent new forms of social control. Between 1943 and 1950, Marcuse worked in U.S. Office of Strategic Services (OSS) where he critiqued the official ideology, and e specially the practices, of the Communist Party of the Soviet Union in the book *Soviet Marxism: A Critical Analysis* (1958). In the 1960s and the 1970s he became known as the preeminent theorist of the New Left and the student protest movements of West Germany, France, and the United States; some consider him "the Father of the New Left." His best known works are *Eros and Civilization* (1955) and *One-Dimensional Man: Studies in the Ideology of Advanced Industrial Society* (1964). His Marxist-based scholarship inspired many radical intellectuals and political activists in the 1960s and 1970s, both in the United States and internationally.

Several of his critics have described Marcuse as essentially anti-Marxist, because he ignored Marx's critique of Hegel. Supposedly, Marcuse also discarded Marx's explanation of history as a story of inevitable class struggle, alleging that Marcuse taught in its stead an inverted Freudian reading of human history in which all social rules could and should be discarded to create a "New World of Happiness." Marcuse's ideal society was to be ruled despotically by an enlightened group [who] have realized in themselves the unity of Logos and Eros, and thrown off the vexatious authority of logic, mathematics, and the empirical sciences, a sort of advanced Platonic ruling elite.

Other critics have asserted that Marcuse falsely assumed consumers were completely passive, uncritically responding to corporate advertising. Some even charged that n early all of Marcuse's key positions are false. In any event, Marcuse was not an orthodox Marxist. Like many of the Frankfurt School, Marcuse wrote of "critical theory" not of "Marxism."[21]

Partially under Marcuse's tutelage she studied Marxian communism, and the existentialist-nihilists Albert Camus, and Jean-Paul Sartre. She spent a summer in Paris and Helsinki, where she met with the Cuban students and became a supporter of Fidel Castro and Cuba. Then she continued her studies at the University of Frankfurt, graduating in 1965. Davis eared a Ph. D. in philosophy from Humboldt University in East Germany. She returned to the United States and obtained a lectureship at UCLA during the 60s. By that time she was a radical feminist and a member of the Communist Party USA and soon associated with the Black Panther Party. She was fired from University of California in 1969 because of her membership in the Communist Party.

Soviet leader Leonid Brezhnev hosted her and the Soviets used her name and image in Soviet propaganda. The Soviets brought her to schools, factories, collective farms, displaying her as a victim of capitalism and American racism. Although many Russian dissidents demanded equality and the right to travel to U.S. prisons, Davis refused to meet with them. Angela Davis ran for Vice President of the United States as a candidate from the Communist Party USA in 1980

21 Bleich, Harold. *The Philosophy of Herbert Marcuse*, Washington: University Press of America, 1977; Kellner, Douglas, *Herbert Marcuse and the Crisis of Marxism*. London: Macmillan, 1984; and Macintyre, Alasdair. *Herbert Marcuse. An Exposition and a Polemic,* Viking, New York, 1970.

and 1984 in company with the Communist Party leader Gus Hall as the presidential candidate.

She has served as the Presidential Chair and Professor with the History of Consciousness Department at the University of California, Santa Cruz campus, and was also director of the Feminist Studies department. She retired in 2002. She has actively opposed the Death Penalty in California. In 2017, Davis was a featured speaker and made an honorary co-chair of the Women's March on Washington in protest of Donald Trump's election and inauguration. Strongly opposed to the American prison system, Davis was a co-founder of Critical Resistance, an organization that aims to end what they call "the prison industrial complex."

CRT fitted Davis's political thinking and teaching well. Black Americans have always organized, she noted. From Black women teaching children and adults to read at Sunday schools during the era of slavery, to the rise of the NAACP and the Urban League, to the work of activists such as sociologist W.E.B. Du Bois and journalist Ida B. Wells. "For hundreds of years, Black people have passed down this collective yearning for freedom from one generation to the next," she says. "We are doing now what should have been done in the aftermath of slavery."

Before eliminating racism, Davis believes we must eradicate racial capitalism, a term Davis designed to "encourage people to think about the ways in which capitalism and racism are interlinked." According to her way of thinking, "There is no capitalism without racism." Police departments and prison systems are "the most dramatic expression of structural racism," according to Davis. When people seek to defund the police, they are really trying to re-imagine the meaning and nature of public safety.

What has been forgotten—perhaps because it is often purposely hidden—is that Antif and BLM both were born from a peculiarly American form of radical and violent Marxism. The actual word used to describe this ideology is in one sense not important: understanding how those who lead and fund these groups think is what matters. In fact, as soon as one uses the word "Marxism" today, the activists and intellectuals begin scoffing in disdain.

Black Lives Matter Movement

The Black Lives Matter movement was created and is led by

radical Marxist racialists. Their heroes and teachers are the violent radicals of the 1960s and '70s. As Murray Bessette points out in "Listen When They Tell You Who They Are,"[22] we know this because they tell us so. They call themselves "trained Marxists." Their ultimate aim is to destroy the family and abolish private education and private property along with the police. Marxist political organizations —such as Antifa, BLM, and the Movement for Black Lives (M4BL) —operate alongside the movement for police reform and seek to create the appearance that the millions of peaceful protesters in the streets support their radical agenda to transform America into a socialist state. The Marxist roots of Antifa, short for *Antifaschisitsche Aktion*, have fully been documented

M4BL explicitly and openly admits "We are anti-capitalist." The socialistic view is shared by the three co-founders of BLM—Patrisse Khan-Cullors, Alicia Garza, and Opal Tometi. As reported by the *New York Post,* Cullors explicitly asserted in an interview with Jared Ball of the Real News Network that both she and Garza "are trained Marxists. We are super-versed on, sort of, ideological theories."

Opal Tometi, born in 1984, is the daughter of Nigerian immigrants, the oldest of three children, who grew up in Phoenix, Arizona, but now lives in Brooklyn, New York. She received a Bachelor of Arts degree in History from the University of Arizona; a Masters in Communication and Advocacy from Arizona State University; and an honorary doctor of science degree from Clarkson University. She was formerly a case manager for survivors of domestic violence. Ms Tometi was a co-founder of Black Lives Matter. Tometi has been credited with setting up the social media portions of the movement. She is the former Executive Director of the United States' first national immigrant rights organization for people of African descent, the Black Alliance for Just Immigration.[23] As a co-founder of the Black Lives Matter, she recently called for a boycott of the British royal family following Meghan Markle's claims of royal racism in her interview with Oprah Winfrey. Opal Tometi openly supports socialist Venezuelan dictator Nicholas Maduro, by writing a lengthy letter of

---

22 Bessette, Murray, "Listen When They Tell You Who They Are," *The American Mind,* 1 September 2020.

23 Dalton, Deron, "The Three Women Behind the Black Lives Matter Movement," *Madame Noire*, 4 May 2015. See also "Black Lives Matter Founders Chosen As Glamour's "Women Of The Year," *Essence*, 2 November 2016.

support for him and the socialist revolution he leads. She has also condemned the "defamation of late President Hugo Chavez [by] labeling him a dictator."

The Marxian call to abolish the family, as expounded in the in the *Communist Manifesto* is clearly an antecedent to BLM's commitment "to disrupting the Western-prescribed nuclear family structure requirement by supporting each other as extended families and 'villages' that collectively care for one another, and especially 'our' children to the degree that mothers, parents and children are comfortable." Communist antecedent is likewise seen in M4BL's demand for the "progressive restructuring of tax codes at the local, state, and federal levels to ensure a radical and sustainable redistribution of wealth," as well as its commitment to "an end to the privatization of education."

M4BL proposes the nationalization of land ownership and management. One of its basic objectives is the "right to restored land, clean air, clean water and housing and an end to the exploitative privatization of natural resources—including land and water. We seek democratic control over how resources are preserved, used and distributed and do so while honoring and respecting the rights of our Indigenous family."

One can find dozens of articles, books, web sites, and apologists ready to defend Marx and claim that his racist views are merely a matter of misunderstanding, advanced by enemies of the people who are also undoubtedly racists at heart. I recall specifically debating the issue many years ago when the moderator interrupted my time, asserting that Marx was simply a part of his time and had he taken an aggressive anti-racist stance he would have been ostracized. Really, if we only understood, Marx had great compassion for the poor and outcast, the academic insisted.

Many black intellectuals view Marxism as the only effective mode of analysis of the social divisions which they have assumed exist in Western society. They view Marxism as the most powerful tool explaining class-consciousness, specifically among the black working class. Having preconceived the idea that revolution is vital, perhaps indispensable, to achieving their goals, the see Marxism as the most viable path to successful social upheaval. Marxism alone contends development of class consciousness is essential to revolution. Many laud Marxism's dismissal of culture" and ignore its theoretical myopia on the issue of race. Many blacks view themselves as a class apart, an underclass, a sub-proleteriat. Thus, for many black intellectuals, race, rather than being an incidental dimension of class, provides a significant subtext for the theorizing of radical change.[24]

Richard Edgar Pipes (1923--2018) was a Polish-American academic who specialized in Russian history, and who espoused a strong anti-communist point of view throughout his career. Regarding the appeal of communism, Dr. Pipes wrote, "Intellectuals, by the very nature of their professions, grant enormous attention to words and ideas. And they are attracted by socialist ideas. They find that the ideas of communism are praiseworthy and attractive; that, to them, is more important than the practice of communism." So it would seem with black writers who are drawn to Marxism like the proverbial moth to its demise in the flames.

Vice-president Kamala Harris

Kamala Harris' father was an avowed Marxist professor in the Economics Department at Stanford University. Both of Harris' parents were active in the Berkeley based Afro-American Association; Fidel Castro and Che Guevara were among the heroes lauded in the Afro-American Association. The group's leader, Donald Warden who preferred to be known as Khalid al-Mansour, mentored two young Afro-American Association members, Huey Newton and Bobby Seale; they created the Maoist-inspired Black Panther Party which gained strong support from Communist China; the Black Panther Party served as the model for creation of the Black Lives Matter Marxist organization Khalid al-Mansour subsequently went on to arrange financing and facilitated for Barack Hussein Obama to be accepted as a student to matriculate at Harvard Law School.

Following her graduation from college, Harris returned to California and subsequently became the close associate of 60-year-old the married Speaker of the California Assembly, Willie Brown, Jr. Brown's political campaigns were supported and funded by Dr. Carlton Goodlett, the owner of *The Sun Reporter* and several other left--wing newspapers. Brown was elected as Mayor of San Francisco, and strongly endorsed Harris' Marxist political philosophy; he guided Harris' political rise in California politics, leading to her election as

24 Sivanandan, A. "The Liberation of the Black Intellectual," *Race and Class,* 18: 4 (1977), pp. 329–342.

California's Attorney General. Willie Brown, Jr. was a well-known long-time Communist sympathizer. Willie Brown, Jr. was initially elected to public office with the substantial help of the Communist Party USA. Today, Willie Brown is widely regarded as one of the Chinese Communist Party's close t supporters in the San Francisco Bay Area.

While serving as San Francisco District Attorney, Kamala Harris mentored a young San Francisco Radical Maoist activist, Lateefah Simon, who was a member of Standing Together to Organize a Revolutionary Movement (STORM), which was especially active from 1995 until 2002. One of the most formative "political education sessions" of this period was a group trip to Cuba in the summer of 1999. Several STORM members participated in the Venceremos Brigade to see and support one of the world's few surviving socialist states. Members came back with" a heightened understanding of both socialism and capitalism" and a stronger commitment to socialist politics. Simon currently chairs the Bay Area Rapid Transit (BART) Board. Simon has always been close friends with the founder of Black Lives Matter, Alicia Garza, as well as STORM member, Van Jones. Of course, Harris has been openly and aggressively supporting the Black Lives Matter movement.

Doug Emhoff, husband of Kamala Harris, works for the law firm DLA Piper, which "boasts nearly 30 years of experience in Communist China with over 140 lawyers dedicated to its 'Communist China investment Services' branch. Emhoff was recently appointed to a professorship at Yale.

When she was elected to the US Senate, Kamala Harris appointed as Chief of Staff, Karine Jean-Pierre, a gay activist. Jean-Pierre was active with the New York-based Haiti Support Network. The organization worked closely with the pro-Communist China/Communist North Korea Workers World Party and supported Jean-Bertrand Aristide, the far-left Communist former president of Haiti and the radical Lavalas movement. Since January 2021, she has been White House Principal Deputy Press Secretary in the Biden Administration. Jean-Pierre served as the chief of staff for Democratic vice presidential nominee Kamala Harris on the 2020 United States presidential campaign.

Negativism in Black Leadership

There is an increasingly popular notion that the United States of America has evolved into a post-racial society, which assertion is denied by militant nihilistic black American authors. These scholars argue that discussions on race tend to be non-comprehensive and oversimplified. When assessing the current socioeconomic dilemmas unique to blacks, scholars on both sides of the political spectrum often overlook a critical component of the African-American condition: the looming threat of black negativism.

One of the earliest black writers to describe strong negative thought within the African-American community was Cornel West (1953--), the grandson of a Baptist minister from Oklahoma who matured in Sacramento, California. West became a radical democrat and socialist who focused on studying and writing about race and gender. In his book *Race Matters* (1994), West discussed negative thought, which he entitled negativism, beginning with his own life experiences. He wrote,

> Nihilism is to be understood here not as a philosophic doctrine that there are no rational grounds for legitimate standards or authority; it is, far more, the lived experience of coping with a life of horrifying meaningless, hopelessness, and (most importantly), lovelessness. The frightening result is a numbing detachment from others, and a self-destructive disposition toward the world. Life without meaning, hope, and love breeds a coldhearted, mean-spirited outlook that destroys both the individual and others.[25]

West believed that nihilistic thought existed in epidemic proportions within the black community. He likened it effect to diseases like alcoholism and drug addiction. The causes of this alienation according to West are "market forces and market moralities" which accompany various black institutions, leaving the community naked against anti-black forces. It is the result of "devastating exposure" to overwhelming institutional, spiritual and psychic violence against African-Americans. On the ever-shifting grounds of the black environment black existence, which is already fragile, becomes fractured.

According to West, black life becomes meaningless since meaning is an aspect of whiteness which excludes blacks. Blacks then

25 West, Cornel. *Race Matters.* Vintage, 1994, p. 23

live in a world of absurdity and that absurdity is their world.[26]

Floyd Hayes responded to Cornel West's theory of black negativism, offering a counter-theory of his own making. Black negativism is a natural reaction to the negativism they observed in the dominant Caucasian culture combined with a reaction to the anti-black attitude which white negativism had produced. He argued that black resentment that began with the transportation of slaves across the Atlantic. Engendered by thoughts of revenge, anger, and rebellion, black negativism coalesced as the logical culmination of black alienation. Resentment came about as a response to white racial prejudices.[27]

The role of the *foco*, as taught by nihilist Regis Debray, is to mobilize the people, although that is not always possible. He predicted its applicability to the American scene, with emphasis on the South. In some respects it resembles the way the Students Non-violent Coordinating Committee (SNCC) functioned in the American South in its early years despite the apparent opposition between the military character of the guerrilla band and the formal nonviolence of SNCC. The point is that both forms exist in rural areas where a peasantry is relatively scattered and subject to a vicious military rule which seems invincible. The function of the *foco* as of the SNCC workers was to show that this power was not invincible, either by getting away with military opposition or by challenging its laws and customs openly and engaging the support of other sections of the country. The result, in each case, must be the transformation of the struggle, in the first case to a popular army based on the peasantry, in the second to an indigenous movement locally led.[28]

Negativism has become a major issue within the black culture. Negativism is a reaction to the hopelessness that African Americans face. Many African Americans have lost hope in their lives. Negativism does not invade every black person's life because not all black people are engaged in a racial struggle. Lawlessness and injustice are not always seen inside the black communities. Black America has become completely engrossed with the multi-media. Reliance upon the

---

26 See Mills, *Charles. Blackness Visible*. Cornell University Press, 1998.

27 Haynes, Floyd W., "Cornel West and Afro-Nihilism: A Reconsideration," in George Yancy, ed. *Cornel West: A Critical Reader*. Blackwell, 2001, pp. 245-60.

28 Moten, Fred, "Blackness and Nothingness," *South Atlantic Quarterly,* 112: 4 (2013), pp. 737-80.

media's mass marketed morality and negativism are both diseases that take a heavy toll in black America.

The black population can be divided into two main groups depending on their respective theories of how to rise and overcome their oppressed condition. On the one hand, structuralists believe that the ills of black society are the result of political and economic oppression. Thus, the disparity in the black community is society's fault. Countering that belief, on the other hand, behaviorists place the blame on a lack of the Protestant work ethic within black society. For this group, disparity within the black community is the result of a failure of blacks themselves to work hard.

Both of these camps have obvious merit, but for various reasons they both miss or ignore the pervasive and pathological mindset within the community which many contemporary black writers and journalists call "the nihilistic threat." From the context of African American history and culture, one must form one's own appropriate definition of negativism as a lifestyle, a very familiar consequence of the ideology.

Politics of Hope

One of the most controversial themes developed in the late twentieth century has been called the Politics of Hope. The concept embraces a combination of promises about the condition and position of African-Americans in the United States, and includes the concepts of equality, economic justice, justice under the law, guarantees of real freedoms, and a host of other matters that always seem to be just beyond the reach of blacks. The black nihilists[29] refer to it as cruel optimism, arguing that it is really detrimental because it actually strengthens the very anti-black system which it promises to end. The politics of hope essentially pursues an impossible outcome. In concentrating on obtaining the impossible, adherents of the politics of hope, in their optimistic enthusiasm, have ignored anti-black laws, policies, contracts, practices, and attitudes. Politics of hope then pretends to bring blacks closer to that which does not exist. Black nihilists seek to destroy what they judge to be the illusion, not substance, of the politics of hope.[30]

---

29 See Berlant, Lauren, *Cruel Optimism.* Duke University Press, 2011.

30 Warren, Calvin L., "Black Nihilism and the Politics of Hope," *New Continental Review,* 15: 1 (2015), pp. 215-48.

Since negativism is a spiritual-psychic disorder within the black community, its cure must be sought within the spiritual realm. Nihilistic blacks are sorely in need of deliverance from false hope. West argued that blacks, especially those who had fallen into nihilistic patterns, were nonetheless deeply spiritual persons. False politics had disrupted their lives so redemption can come about only after the removal of false political hopes and promises. Some have even come to regard anti-black sentiments and actions as a form spiritual idolatry. Destroying much black hope, while simultaneously adding to black negativism, is the racist Christianity taught be many, especially among Southern Protestants.[31] One author wrote, "The white western god-man is an idol that seeks to determine what is normal. It is a nor m by which society governs the body politic, or regulates, measures, evaluates, and, indeed, judges what is proper or improper. . . ."[32] The conclusion that many blacks draw is that the politics of hope preserve anti-black structures and prolong black suffering.[33]

The Soledad Brothers

George Lester Jackson (1941-1971) was an African-American ultra-left-wing activist, avowed Marxist, author, member of the Black Panther Party, and co-founder of the Black Guerrilla Family. Jackson achieved fame as one of the Soledad Brothers and was later shot to death by guards in San Quentin Prison. In George Jackson's book *Soledad Brother,*[34] one can discover the key characteristics of the detrimental phenomenon of black racist negativism.

Soledad Brother is the autobiographical story of George Jackson who was arrested at age nineteen for stealing $70 at gunpoint from a gas station and sentenced to a one year to life in prison. He was advised to plead guilty, on the understanding that the one year part of the deal would see him out of the clink in next to no time. He started his sentence in 1960 and spent the next decade in prison. At the time, conditions in the California penal system were intensely racist, pitting blacks, Aryan Brotherhood whites and Mexicans against

---

31 Carter, J. K. "Christian Atheism" in *Religious Dispatches*, 23 July 2013. See also Jones, William R. *Is God a White Racist?* Beacon, 1997.

32 Carter, *op. cit.*, p. p. 3. See also Wynter, Sylvia"Unsettling the Coloniality of Being," *New Centennial Review*, 3: 3 (2003), 257-337.

33 Warren, *op. cit,.*, at 242.

34 Jackson, George. *Soledad Brother: The Prison Letters Of George Jackson.* Lawrence Hill, 1994

one other deliberately according to Jackson's accounts. In prison, he became politically aware and read widely: Mao, Lenin, Marx and others of the far left. He joined the Black Panther party. His book talks about his self-education during years of solitary confinement and the injustice in the penal system heavily weighted against African-Americans.

The Soledad Brothers were three African-American inmates charged with the murder of a white prison guard, John Vincent Mills, at California's Soledad Prison on January 16, 1970. George Jackson, Fleeta Drumgo, and John Clutchette murdered Mills in retaliation for another guard, O. G. Miller, having shot to death three black prisoners who were engaged in a prison fight in the exercise yard three days prior. On January 13, 1970, fourteen black inmates and two white inmates from the maximum-security section of Soledad Prison were released into a recreation yard after having been confined for several months without release into the exercise yard. Reportedly, the black prisoners were ordered to the far end of the yard, while the white prisoners remained near the center of the yard. A fight ensued and Miller opened fire on the prisoners below and three black inmates were killed in the shooting. Two men, W. L. Nolen and Cleveland Edwards, died in the yard, while Alvin Miller died in the prison hospital a few hours later. A white inmate was wounded. Jackson claimed that his close friend Nolen and the others were "murdered by a pig." On January 16, 1970, a Monterey County grand jury convened, then exonerated Miller in the deaths of Nolen, Edwards, and Miller with a ruling of justifiable homicide.[35]

On 7 August 1970, George Jackson's seventeen-year-old brother Jonathan entered a courtroom during the trial of a different prisoner who had been charged with the attempted stabbing of a Soledad guard. Jonathan Jackson armed McClain and freed the three San Quentin prisoners. They took as their prisoners Superior Court Judge Harold Haley, Deputy District Attorney Gary Thomas, and three female jurors. Jonathan had intended to secure the freedom of the Soledad Brothers. As they attempted to leave the court house, police killed Jackson, McClain, and a prisoner named William Christmas. Judge Haley died as the result of the discharge of a sawed-off

---

35 Bernstein, Lee. "The Age of Jackson: George Jackson and the Radical Critique of Incarceration" in Bernstein, L., *America is the Prison: Arts and Politics in Prison in the 1970s*. University of North Carolina Press, 2010.

shotgun which the prisoners had been fastened to his neck. Thomas, another prisoner, and one of the jurors were wounded. Two days after his brother's death, in George Jackson's last letter in his collection of letters written while in prison, he wrote a letter to his deceased brother, signing it: Ultra-left-wing activist and supposed academic Angela Davis, had purchased the guns used in the escape attempt, but escaped justice.[36]

On 21 August 1971, just a few days before his trial in the guard's killing, the 29-year-old Jackson led a riot at San Quentin while armed with a handgun that someone had apparently smuggled into the prison. Gun in hand, Jackson first released an entire floor of prisoners from the maximum-security wing. During the incident three guards were killed, as were two prisoners suspected of being snitches. George Jackson rushed out into the yard where he was shot and killed by a guard.[37]

Various black performers, especially in the music world, have dedicated work to the story of George Jackson along with other violent prison riots, such as the Attica, New York, prison uprising that followed. Dedicated anti-Creationism author Stephen Jay Gould, in his 1981 book *The Mismeasure of Man,* wrote lovingly of George Jackson's death in context of his initial indeterminate one-year-to-life sentence for stealing seventy dollars from a gas station. Jackson's life, beliefs and ultimate fate were the topic of one of the many audio tapes recorded at the Jonestown commune in Guyana in 1978. Alleged preacher Jones asserted that it was his firm belief that Jackson's death was a racist assassination.[38] The 2007 film *Black August* starring Gary Dourdan as George Jackson is a nearly two hour-long retelling of the last fourteen months of Jackson's life.[39]

Amiri Baraka

Amiri Baraka was born Everett LeRoi Jones (1934 –2014), was variously known as LeRoi Jones and Imamu Amear Baraka He was an American author of poetry, drama, fiction, essays and music criticism and the author of numerous books of poetry. He taught at

---

36 Caldwell. Earl. "Angela Davis Acquitted on All Charges," *New York Times*, 5 June 1972

37 Streeter, Harold V., "'Soledad Brothers' Conflict Incites 11 Violent Deaths," *San Francisco Examiner,* 29 August 1971.

38 "George Jackson" in Wikipedia.

39 Information on Black August is found on IMDB.com.

several universities, including the State University of New York at Buffalo and the State University of New York at Stony Brook.[40] Under whatever name, his career spanned nearly 52 years, and his themes range from black liberation to white racism. He was known as the revolutionary poet of the Black Arts Movement.[41]

Baraka's poetry and writing have attracted both high praise and condemnation in the African-American community. Some blacks compared Baraka to James Baldwin and recognized him as one of the most respected and most widely published black writers of his generation. Others have pointed out that his writings are filled with gratuitous violence, misogyny, and homophobia. Recent authors have claimed that Baraka's homophobia and misogyny stemmed from his efforts to conceal his own history of same-sex encounters. Overall, his production constituted defining texts of the nihilistic African-American culture. His first wife was Jewish and they were parents of two children, but he apparently thought that he was betraying his own people if he remained in that marriage.[42]

In 1968, he was arrested in Newark for carrying an illegal weapon and also for resisting arrest during the 1967 Newark riots. Convicted, he was sentenced to three years in prison. His poem "Black People", published in the *Evergreen Review* in December 1967, was read by the judge in court, including the memorable phrase: "All the stores will open if you say the magic words. The magic words are: "Up against the wall motherfucker this is a stick up!" He borrowed that phrase from the *Up Against the Wall Motherfuckers* organization and it was used as a slogan by other radical groups.[43] Shortly afterward an appeals court reversed the sentence. Not long af-

40 After being promoted to full professor of African Studies at Stony Brook in 1985, Baraka took an indefinite visiting appointment in Rutgers University's English department in 1988. See Sollors, Werner. *Amiri Baraka / LeRoi Jones: The Quest for a "Populist Modernism.* Columbia University Press, 1978.

41 Jones, LeRoi, alaso known as Baraka, Imamu Amiri, "Blaxck Art Drama is the Same as Black Life," *Ebony,* 1971. See also his *Black magic: Sabotage, Target Study, Black Art;: Collected Poetry, 1961-1967*. Bobbs-Merrill, 1969.

42 Schudel, Matt, "Amiri Baraka, 79: Architect of Black Arts Movement," [obituary] *Washington Post*, 10 January 2014.

43 Up Against the Wall Motherfucker, often shortened as The Motherfuckers or UAW/MF, was a Dadaist and Situationist anarchist affinity group based in New York City. This "street gang with analysis" was famous for its Lower East Side direct action and is said to have inspired members of the Weather Underground and the Youth International Party or Yippies.

ter the 1967 riots, Baraka generated even more controversy when he went on the radio with a Newark police captain and Anthony Imperiale, a local politician. All three of them blamed the Newark riots on "white-led, so-called radical groups" and "Communists and the Trotskyites."

In the late 1960s and early 1970s, Baraka he wrote some strongly anti-Jewish poems and articles, adopting a stance similar to that of the Nation of Islam. In one well-known poem, "Black Arts,"[44] Baraka suggested that police officers should be killed and have their 'tongues pulled out and sent to Ireland." He later admitted his prejudices in, "I was an AntiSemite" in *The Village Voice.*[45] He held a particular loathing for Jews, as was apparent in the different intensity and viciousness of his call in the same poem for 'dagger poems' to stab the 'slimy bellies of the ownerjews' and for poems that crack 'steel knuckles in a jewlady's mouth. He was also an outspoken enemy of Israel, seeing its anti-Arab policies as a form of racism.[46]

His brief tenure as Poet Laureate of New Jersey during 2002 and 2003 produced substantial controversy when there was a public reading of his poem "Somebody Blew Up America?" Many accused that poem of blatant anti-Semitism, thus producing condemnation of most of his works by politicians and literary critics.[47] In July 2002, ten months after the September 11 attack on the World Trade Center in New York City, Baraka wrote a poem entitled "Somebody Blew Up America?" To say the least, it was highly controversial and was immediately met with harsh criticism. The poem was also highly critical of what he claimed was institutional racism in America. It contained. includes nasty depictions of Caucasian public figures such as Trent Lott, but was most bitter in its depictions of conservative blacks such as Clarence Thomas, and Condoleezza Rice. Baraka also charged that Israel had fore-knowledge of the World Trade Center destruction. According to Baraka, President George W. Bush also had advance

44 Originally published in *The Liberator* in January 1966

45 Baraka, A. "I Was an AntiSermite," *Village News*, 1 (20 December 1980).

46 Salaam, Kaluma. "Historical Overviews of the Black Arts Movement", in *Oxford Companion to African-American Literature.* Oxford University Press, 1997. See also Gafio, Jerry. *Amiri Baraka: The Politics and Art of a Black Intellectual.* New York University Press, 2001.

47 Quotes in McAlister, Melani, "One Black Allah: The Middle East in the Cultural Politics of African American Liberation, 1955-1970". *American Quarterly*, 51: 3 (1999). See also "Miri Baraka" in Wikipedia.

knowledge of the September 11 attacks, but for whatever reasons allowed the assault to take place. He claimed that this information had been reported both in the American and Israeli press and on Jordanian television. He denied that the poem is antisemitic and pointed to his accusations, which were directed against Israelis rather than Jews as a people.[48] Nonetheless, the Anti-Defamation League denounced the poem as antisemitic,although Baraka and his defenders continued to define his position as anti-Zionism.[49] Baraka died on January 9, 2014, at Beth Israel Medical Center, Newark, New Jersey, probably from complications of diabetes.

Angela Davis

Angela Davis (1944--) was born in Birmingham, Alabama, where both her parents were employed as school teachers. She is the best known black female nihilist-activist in America. Angela attended a small private school known as the 'Little Red School House' in Greenwich Village in New York City where she became enamored of socialism and communism. She befriended the children of the leaders of the Communist Party, including her lifelong friend, Bettina Aptheker, daughter of longtime communist activist Herbert Aptheker. An accomplished scholar, Angela received a full scholarship to Brandeis University in Massachusetts, where she met German-Jewish philosopher Herbert Marcuse. In the company of Marcuse, she participated in a political rally against President John Kennedy's handling of the Cuban Missile Crisis.

Partially under Marcuse's tutelage she studied Marxian communism, and the existentialist-nihilists Albert Camus, and Jean-Paul Sartre. She spent a summer in Paris and Helsinki, where she met with the Cuban students and became a supporter of Fidel Castro and Cuba. Then she continued her studies at the University of Frankfurt, graduating in 1965. Davis eared a Ph. D. in philosophy from Humboldt University in East Germany.

She returned to the United States and obtained a lectureship at UCLA during the 60s. By that time she was a radical feminist and a member of the Communist Party USA and soon associated with the

---

48 Sommers, Ephraim Scott, "The Poem of Anger: Amiri Baraka, Tory Dent, and Adrian C. Louis," *Cream City Review*. 20: 2(2016), pp. 40–63

49 Jacobs, Andrew. "Criticized Poet Is Named Laureate of Newark Schools," *New York Times*, 19 December 2002. See also "Amiri Baraka" in Wikipedia. See also Anti-defamation League website.

Black Panther Party. She was fired from University of California in 1969 because of her membership in the Communist Party. That move was backed by Governor Ronald Reagan although she was later re-hired.

In 1970, her name appeared on the FBI's Most Wanted List, although she was able to evade the police for two months. She spent eighteen months in the Women's Detention Center in New York awaiting the trial. Reportedly, she had purchase firearms used in a court room riot in California in which fleeing insurrectionists murdered the trial judge. In 1972, John Lennon and Yoko Ono supported her with their song "Angela" and Rolling Stones recorded their song "Sweet Black Angel" advocating her release. She was tried and acquitted of all charges.

Soviet leader Leonid Brezhnev hosted her and the Soviets used her name and image in Soviet propaganda. The Soviets brought her to schools, factories, collective farms, displaying her as a victim of capitalism and American racism. Although many Russian dissidents demanded equality and the right to travel to U.S. prisons, Davis refused to meet with them. Angela Davis ran for Vice President of the United States as a candidate from the Communist Party USA in 1980 and 1984 in company with the Communist Party leader Gus Hall as the presidential candidate.

Davis opposed the Million Men March in Washington in 1995 because, she alleged, it promoted male chauvinism. She has served as the Presidential Chair and Professor with the History of Consciousness Department at the University of California, Santa Cruz campus, and was also director of the Feminist Studies department. She retired in 2002. She has actively opposed the Death Penalty in California. In 2017, Davis was a featured speaker and made an honorary co-chair of the Women's March on Washington in protest of Donald Trump's election and inauguration. Strongly opposed to the American prison system, Davis was a co-founder of Critical Resistance, an organization that aims to end what they call "the prison industrial complex."

Paul Coates

Ta-Nehisi Paul Coates (1975--) is an American author and journalist who was born in Baltimore, Maryland. His father, William Paul Coates, was a Vietnam War veteran, former Black Panther, publisher, and librarian. His mother, Cheryl Lynn (Waters), was a teacher. Coates' father founded and ran Black Classic Press, a publisher specializing in African-American titles. The Press grew out the George Jackson Prison Movement. Black Classic Press was established with a table-top printing press in the basement of the Coates family home.

Nehisi gained a wide following during his time as national correspondent at *The Atlantic* magazine, in which he wrote about cultural, social, and political issues regarding African Americans included a discussion of the grassroots organization, the Contract Buyers League. The focus of Coates' article was not so much on reparations for slavery, but was instead a focus on the institutional racism as practiced in housing discrimination.[50]

His fame spread after the penned an article for *The Atlantic,* "The Case for Reparations." Coates claimed that he had worked on that story for almost two years, weighing various alternatives for compensation for blacks whose ancestors had been enslaved. Among other books, he had read and was greatly influenced by Rutgers University professor Beryl Satter's book, *Family Properties: Race, Real Estate, and the Exploitation of Black Urban America.* Professor Satter related a history of redlining that while denouncing presumed white supremacy. Coates has also written for *The Village Voice, Washington City Paper*, *Time* magazine,*The New York Times Magazine, The Washington Post, The Washington Monthly*, and *O*. Three of his nonfiction books: *The Beautiful Struggle, Between the World and Me*, and *We Were Eight Years in Power: An American Tragedy*.He has also written a Black Panther series and a Captain America series for Marvel Comics. His first novel, *The Water Dancer*, was published in 2019 and is a surrealist story set in the time of slavery, concerning a superhuman protagonist named Hiram Walker who possesses photographic memory, but who cannot remember his mother, but is able to transport people over far distances by using a power known as conduction.

Despite his personal negativism, he is living proof that the American Dream is alive and well, and he is a living refutation of the apocalypticism, resignation, indignation and hopelessness regarding the American experience that informs his misanthropic imagination.

Coates has been a magnet for conservative black critics who

50 Coates, Ta-Nehisi, "The Case for Reparations". The Atlantic, June 2014. See also Roig-Franzia, Manuel, "With Atlantic Article on Reparations, Ta-Nehisi Coates Sees Payoff for Years of Struggle," *Washington Post*, 18 June 2014.

have attacked Coates along several lines. The common criticism lies in the racial reductionism of Coates' vision and his hyperinflation of what he calls white supremacy as the single causal explanation for black oppression and suffering in the United States. He has called for blacks to disengage from civic life which his critics have hailed as morally irresponsible. He offered a very pessimistic analysis of the prejudicial nature of race relations without viable solutions. This, they claim, betrays the vision of a true moral intellectual, and also of an analytic journalist. He has refused to confront his youth when he was terrorized by the fears of his own suffering at the hands of violent blacks. That fear of his own race, his critics charge, he has transplanted to white society in general.

Reading Coates, they accuse, one gets the impression that the psychology of fear he attributes to black people is a projection of his own personal psychological make-up: he is deathly afraid of his own race, but, out of a sense of racial shame, finds it easier to blame white people for the endemic black-on-black violence to which he was systemically subjected to as a child, beginning with the beating inflicted on him by his own father. This is a rather unfair burden to download upon white people by a man who his personal demons. Some of the African-Americans who reject Coates see him as merely a loud-mouth spokesman of a neo-liberal emerging black elite. It is also true that the American political left, for a long time, had a very masochistic relationship with its left-leaning, anti-American black intellectuals such as Coates.[51]

Coates is deeply committed to a wholly amoral view of the world. More importantly, he denies that whites have the moral capacity or will necessary to foster strong positive moral sentiments about the lives of black people. Neither do Caucasians care about black suffering and misery. Even his most ardent liberal white supporters have expressed grave concern about his words. Many of them believe that Coates loathes them because they are white. He has clearly demonstrated how much he hates them as part of the ruling 'majoritarian pigs' he describes in *Between the World and Me*. He claims that these people who have created the policies and racial infrastructures majoritarian .rule have the doomed lives of black people. As an integral part of his wholesale indictment of white America as a country ruled by

51 Warren, Calvin L., "Black Nihilism and the Politics of Hope," *New Centennial Review* 15: 1 (2015), pp. 215-48.

majoritarian pigs, he has refused to show sympathy for the heroic white or even black firefighters who died in the World Trade Center in the aftermath of 9/11 attack. He writes that they were not human to him; rather, they were menaces of nature; they were the force, the comet, the storm which could, with no justification, shatter his body. It is obvious that his thought cannot progress upward so long as he maintains his loathing of supposed white prejudice against blacks.[52]

Ta-Nehisi Coates

Ta-Nehisi Coates, America's most pampered racist, the toast of academics, was born in 1975 is an American author and journalist, a national correspondent at *The Atlantic*, and writer for *The Village Voice, Washington City Paper*, and *Time* magazine. He has also contributed to *The New York Times Magazine, The Washington Post, The Washington Monthly*, and *O.* He has published three books: *The Beautiful Struggle; Between the World and Me;* and *We Were Eight Years in Power*: *An American Tragedy*. He was highly critical of President Barak Obama.[53]

His National Book Award-winning memoir, *Between the World and Me*[54], is a wealth of pseudo-Marxist legalisms in which 'black bodies' are the engines of commerce and culture on which a vast evil white conspiracy squats. The book is "a racist screed that masks its hatred in self-pity." In his book he talks about black bodies as sacred objects worthy of veneration. His fetishistic phraseology is now standard among members of the violent, racist Black Lives Matter movement, and has spread to the culture at large.

Between the World and Me by Ta-Nehisi Coates was published in 2014 in the wake of several highly public acts of police violence against black men and the death of nine black parishioners at a church in South Carolina at the hands of a white supremacist. The book explores race relations in contemporary America with a focus on the lived experience of the author, and a conceptual framework that locates the effects of racism on the black body, traceable both through history and in the contemporary context. The book is styled as a letter to the author's fourteen year old son and is broken into three chapters. This review offers a detailed summary of the main themes of the

52 Hill, Jason, "The Black Nihilism of Ta-Nehisi Coates," *Spiked*, 18 May 2018

53 Coates, Ta-Nehisi Paul. "Is Obama Black Enough?" *Time,* 2 February 2007.

54 *Between the World and Me,* One World publishers, 2015.

book, followed by an analysis. Ta-Nehisi Coates is regarded by many as the premier author of contemporary race relations in the United States.[55]

In his book Coates writes that the police officers and firefighters who died in the 9/11 terrorist attacks "were not human to me. Black, white, or whatever, they were menaces of nature; they were the fire, the comet, the storm, which could — with no justification — shatter my body." He has demanded that U.S. taxpayers who were never slave owners and whose ancestors gave their lives to end slavery pay reparations to the second- and third- and fourth-generation descendants of slaves who were never slaves themselves. He would prefer that laws not be enforced against African-Americans to avoid the alleged horrors of so-called racial profiling. He dismisses the threat posed by Islamists as irrelevant, claiming America has no right to judge terrorists "in a country built on theft, blood and slavery."[56]

Coates has been richly rewarded for his racist, anti-American screeds. He is the recipient of a $600,000 genius award, an editorial position at *The Atlantic*, and a lectureship at Massachusetts Institute of Technology even though he never graduated from college. He has proclaimed that President Donald Trump was a loathsome racist, although the only evidence he offered was that Trump was white. He wrote,

> It is insufficient to state the obvious of Donald Trump: that he is a white man who would not be president were it not for this fact. With one immediate exception, Trump's predecessors made their way to high office through the passive power of whiteness—that bloody heirloom which cannot ensure mastery of all events but can conjure a tailwind for most of them. Land theft and human plunder cleared the grounds for Trump's forefathers and barred others from it.

Anti-Jewish Activism

On 15 March 2021, the national president of the Zionist Organization of America, Morton A. Klein, along with two other officers, addressed a letter to officers of Penguin Random House, publishers of former President Barack Obama's book *A Promised Land,* complaining of its untrue and/or misleading statements about Israel. It not-

---

55 "Ta-Nehisi Coates," in Wikipedia.

56 Coates, Ta-Nehisi , "The Case for Reparations". *The Atlantic*, 20 June 2014. See also Roig-Franzia, Manuel, "With Atlantic Article on Reparations, Ta-Nehisi Coates Sees Payoff for Years of Struggle, *Washington Post,* 18 June 2014.

ed Obama's strong prejudices against Israel, which were evident during the eight years of his presidency, but holding those opinions to be within his right to free speech.[57]

One can find strong anti-Jewish sentiment s expressed among Obama's closest advisers and assistants. Among others, there is Joy-Ann Lomena Reid, born in 1968, in 2021 an MSNBC on-air personality. She was born Joy-Ann Lomena in Brooklyn, New York. Her father was a native of the Democratic Republic of Congo, and her mother a college professor and nutritionist from Guyana. She was raised Methodist. Her father was an engineer and usually absent from the family. After her parents divorced her father returned to the Congo and she was raised primarily in Denver, Colorado. Reid graduated from Harvard University in 1991 with a concentration in the visual art and documentary films.[58]

Ms Joy-Ann Reid has never been preoccupied with providing evidence of the claims of racism she habitually hurls at white Americans. The former Obama campaign press aide characterizes all conservatives as naturally racist, sexist, and oblivious to the needs of minorities and the poor. Previous blogs posted by Reid which date before she became famous revealed the broadcaster's bigotry as she sided with a genocidal regime dedicated to exterminating Jews, and embraced their proposed ethnic cleansing from Israel. As Bre Payton reported at the *Federalist,* in a post from *The Reid Report* dated December 5, 2005, Reid said that Mahmoud Ahmadinejad, then-dictator-president of Iran, was really onto something when he suggested that the "Zionist regime" of Israel should just relocate to Europe."God is not a real estate broker," the message reads. "He can't just give you land 1,000 years ago that you can come back and claim today."

In a post dated 16 July 2006, Reid attacked CNN's Wolf Blitzer for being excessively nice and understanding to Jews. Reid identified Blitzer, whose Jewish parents were Holocaust survivors,, as a "former flak for the American Israeli Public Affairs Committee (AIPAC)," after he was, in her opinion, insufficiently tough on Israeli officials during an interview."He doesn't even try to hide his affinity for his Israeli guests, or his partisanship for their cause, while turning instantly to prosecutorial mode when questioning any guest who has the dumb luck to be an Arab or Muslim in King Blitzer's court," Reid

57 Anti-Semite-in-Chief | Frontpagemag

58 "Joy-Ann Reid," in Wikipedia.

wrote. “It’s actually quite stunning how brazen Blitzer’s bias has become.”Of course, the canard that Jews are untrustworthy because they have “dual loyalty,” or more precisely, a higher, overriding loyalty to their fellow Jews –or, since 1948, to Israel—has been a popular anti-Semitic smear since Roman times.[59]

Posts written between 2007 and 2009 on Reid's former blog *Reid Report*, have been described by *The Nation* as employing “the trope of gay sex to mock politicians and journalists.”[60] She has become well-known in gay circles as homophobic.[61] Muslim Advocates and Representatives Ilhan Omar and Rashida Tlaib, two of the first Muslim women elected to Congress, have criticized several of Reid's remarks as Islamophobic and demanded an apology.[62]

Jamelle Bouie

Jamelle Bouie was born in Virginia Beach, Virginia and graduated from the University of Virginia in 2009 with a degree in political and social thought and government. He became a staff writer for online magazine *The Daily Beast* in 2013, writing about national politics and then moved to *Slate* magazine as its chief political correspondent in 2014. He joined *The New York Times* as a columnist in 2019. Bouie has written extensively on racial politics, including the Ferguson unrest, the Charleston church shooting, and the Black Lives Matter movement.[63]

Bouie became an expert at finding racism where no one else has seen it. Hours after the Route 91 Harvest music festival massacre in Nevada on 1 October 2017, an incident in which 58 persons were killed and almost 900 injured, he tweeted, “That Las Vegas authorities have ruled out terrorism at this early stage is another example of how the idea has all but been racialized.” Then he elaborated, tweet-

---

59"MSNBC Host Joy Reid Criticized Jews, Ariel Sharon in Old Blog Posts,” *The Times of Israel,* 9 June 2018; "Joy Reid Blog Post Attacked Wolf Blitzer for Being Too Soft on Jews,” *National Review,* June 2018; and "ZOA: MSNBC Should Fire Joy Reid for Perpetuating 'Sinister Anti-Semitic Canards'". *Jewish Journal*, 11 June 2018.

60 Kim, Richard, in *The Nation,* 27 April 2018.

61 "The Joy Reid Controversy, from Homophobic Blog Posts to a Hacking Claim, Explained,” *Vox*. 28 April 2018. See also "LGBT Advocacy Group Rescinds Award to Joy Reid,” CBS News, 27 April 2018

62 “Calls for Apology Grow over Joy Reid's 'Islamophobic' Remarks,” *Al Jazeera*. September 2, 2020.

63 “Jamelle Bouie,” in Wikipedia.

ing, “Essentially, by the definition currently in common currency, a white person cannot be a terrorist.”[64]

He compared those who voted for President Trump to the "angry, recalcitrant whites" who resisted the Reconstruction civil rights law enacted after the Civil War. Those laws were essentially eviscerated by the U.S. Supreme Court soon after enactment. His deep anti-Caucasian prejudices ran over during the first Trump election in 2016.“There’s No Such Thing as a Good Trump Voter,” Bouie wrote in his column on 15 November 2016: “People voted for a racist who promised racist outcomes. They don’t deserve your empathy.” In short, if one is white and/or voted for Trump, he deserves anything bad that happens to him.[65]

Bouie claimed that proof that President Trump is racist is his containment of the notorious transnational gang MS-13. The president’s speeches about the dangers of MS-13 and illegal aliens were specifically designed to “make white people afraid” of non-whites. “Trump wasn’t just connecting immigrants with violent crime,” Bouie said. “He was using an outright racist trope: that of the violent, sadistic black or brown criminal, preying on innocent (usually white) women.” Despite Bouie's rhetoric, MS-13 is known to prey almost exclusively on immigrants who are non-white.[66]

---

64 Bouie, Jamelle, "How Ferguson Changed America," *Slate,* 2 August 2015; and Clarke, Kinsey, "Jon Stewart, Jamelle Bouie, And Others Weigh In On The Charleston Massacre". NPR.org, 19 June 2015. See also Williamson, Kevin D., "Jamelle Bouie, Wrong as Usual," *National Review*, 28 May 2014.

65 Baragona, Justin, "Slate's Jamelle Bouie Says There Are No Good Trump Voters, Compares Them To Lynch Mobs," *Mediaite*, 15 November 2016; Wermund, Benjamin, "Slate Writer: Pro-Trump White 'backlash' Evokes End of Reconstruction," *Politico,* 9 November 2016; and Vernon, Pete, "Dancing around the Word 'racist' in Coverage of Trump," *Columbia Journalism Review,* 25 September 2017.

66 “Media sympathizes with MS-13, Lambasts Trump,” Fox News, 31 July and 26 September 2017.

Critical Race Theory

Critical race theory claims to be a theoretical framework in the social sciences that uses critical theory to examine society and culture as they relate to categorizations of race, law, and power. It began as a theoretical movement within American law schools in the mid- to late 1980s as a reworking of critical legal studies on race issues and is loosely unified by two common themes: First, CRT proposes that white supremacy and racial power are maintained over time, and in particular, that the law may play a role in this process. Second, CRT work has investigated the possibility of transforming the relationship between law and racial power, and more broadly, pursues a project of achieving racial emancipation and anti-subordination. Critical race theory is taught and innovated in the fields of education, law, political science, women's studies, ethnic studies, communication, and American studies. Many people believe the critical race theory to be a very important view to race and racism in America.

CRT is a theoretical framework which views society as dominated by white supremacy and categorizes people as 'privileged' or 'oppressed' based on their skin color," the PAC continued in a separate post. "It also teaches kids to hate America. Ask yourself who in their right mind would want this taught in public schools?" Critical Race Theory has been growing for over 40 years, and it has many deep problems. Therefore, this is long, and still it is not nearly complete. Advocates of Critical Race Theory rarely inquire if this is the way we should be dealing with race issues and racism in our society, or if we can genuinely do better.[67]

Critical Race Theory (CRT) is being funded by the U.S. Department of Education. The National Center for Education Research (NCER) claims it "supports rigorous research that addresses the nation's most pressing education needs, from early childhood to adult education." This institution is part of the Institute of Education Science (IES), an arm of the U.S. Department of Education (USDE). NCER issued a grant using IES funds (i.e., taxpayer funds) to North Carolina Central University's (NCCU) Research Institute for Scholars of Equity (RISE). NCCU is a traditional member of the United Negro Educational Fund. The award amount, $1,116,895. The purpose, to conduct "Mixed Methods Research to Improve Academic Outcomes

---

67 Delgado, Richard. *Critical Race Theory*. Temple University Press, 1999.

Among PK-20 African American and Latino/a Children, Youth and Young Adults."

The debate around race-based curriculum as the course load was brought to the center stage during both former President Donald Trump's administration and the Biden White House amid protests and riots surrounding the death of George Floyd. Scholars important to the theory include Derrick Bell, Patricia Williams, Richard Delgado, Kimberlé Williams Crenshaw, Camara Phyllis Jones, and Mari Matsuda. By 2002, over 20 American law schools and at least three law schools in other countries offered critical race theory courses or classes which covered the issue centrally.[68]

The base from which CRT builds is fundamentally Marxism with its emphasis upon the inevitability of the class struggle, which shows its origins with Marxist Angela Davis. CRT merely substitutes racial struggle for class struggle, whites versus people of color instead of poor versus rich. The whole assumes that those wielding power are exploiting those without power. In the name of equity, UCLA Law Professor and critical race theorist Cheryl Harris has proposed suspending private property rights, seizing land and wealth and redistributing them along racial lines. These ideas she advanced in a well-received article published in the *Harvard Law Review*.[69] Much of her research has concentrated upon establishing the interconnections between racial theory, civil rights practice, politics, and human rights. She has lectured internationally on issues of race and equality. She has served as faculty director for the Critical Race Studies Program at UCLA Law School, receiving the ACLU Foundation of Southern California's Distinguished Professor Award for Civil Rights Education.

Critical race planner Ibram X. Kendi, who directs the Center for Antiracist Research at Boston University, has proposed the creation of a federal Department of Antiracism. This department would be independent of, and thus unaccountable to, the elected branches of government, and would have the power to nullify, veto, or abolish any law at any level of government and curtail the speech of political leaders and others who are deemed insufficiently "antiracist." One practical result of the creation of such a department would be the

68 Crenshaw, Kimberle; Thomas, Kendall; and Peller, Garry. *Critical Race Theory: The Key Writings That Formed the Movement.* The New Press, 1996.

69 Harris, Cheryl I. (1993). "Whiteness as Property," *Harvard Law Review*, 106: 8 (1993), pp. 1707–1791

overthrow of capitalism, since according to Kendi, "In order to truly be antiracist, you also have to truly be anti-capitalist." Put another way, racism is the means and Marxism is the end. Ibram X. Kendi is an American author and historian located at American University. He won the 2016 National Book Award for Nonfiction for his book *Stamped from the Beginning: The Definitive History of Racist Ideas in America*, which was published by Nation Books. In July 2020, he assumed the position of director of the Center for Antiracist Research at Boston University, a study center which he moved from its previous association at American University in Washington.

Kimberlé Williams Crenshaw (1959--) is an American lawyer, civil rights advocate, and principal advocate of of critical race theory. She teaches at the UCLA School of Law and Columbia Law School, specializing in racial and gender issues. She is particularly interested in minority identities and how they relate to systems and structures of perceived oppression, domination, or discrimination. Her scholarship was also essential in the development of intersectional feminism, which examines the overlapping systems of oppression and discrimination to which women are subject due to their ethnicity, sexuality and economic background.

Crenshaw is known for the introduction and development of the concept of intersectionality, which is the theory which seeks to explain how overlapping or intersecting social identities, with particular emphasis on minority identities, relate to systems and structures of oppression, domination, or discrimination.[70] Having developed the theory of intersectionality, Crenshaw became the founding director of Columbia Law School's Center for Intersectionality and Social Policy Studies (CISPS) and the African American Policy Forum (AAPF). AAPF is a non-profit think tank and information clearinghouse, which focuses on "dismantling structural inequality" and "advancing and expanding racial justice, gender equality, and the indivisibility of all human rights, both in the U.S. and internationally." Its stated mission is to build bridges between scholarly research and public discourse in addressing inequality and discrimination.

One of the premises of critical race theory is that the colonization of the New World set the foundation for slavery and racism. The

---

70 Crenshaw, K. W., ""Mapping the Margins: Intersectionality, Identity Politics and Violence against Women of Color," in Bailey, A. and Como, C., eds. *The Feminist Philosophy Reader*, New York: McGraw-Hill, 2008, pp. 279–309.

basic assertions were advanced by Margaret Zamudio (, a professor at the University of Colorado. Margaret Zamudio, then age 76, a former University of Colorado at Boulder faculty member who made headlines a decade ago for drug use, and was instrumental in promoting CRT, best known for being fired from CU and suing the school, died on Christmas night in Laramie, Wyoming, and alcohol has been listed as a contributing factor in her death.[71] Regarding slavery, Zamudio noted that, "The colonization of the Americas, Africa, and the Asiatic world by the European powers set the foundation for contemporary racial inequality." Zamudio claimed that, "These colonial processes divided the world between conquered and colonizer, master and slave, white and non-white." Many of Zamudio's assertions are simply historically inaccurate. For one, slavery and racism have plagued the world long before America was discovered. Furthermore, slavery was not reserved to white masters and black slaves. In fact, in America, there were white indentured servants that labored side by side with black slaves. Professor Zamudio, along with the 1619 Project, made a number of claims that have been rejected by many historians, including the outrageously false claim that the Founding Fathers fought the American Revolution primarily to protect slavery. [72] Moreover, there were thousands of black masters who owned black slaves, including a director ancestor of the current vice-president Kamala Harris.

Patrisse Cullors (1983--) is an American artist and activist. Cullors created the #BlackLivesMatter hashtag in 2013. Other topics on which Cullors has agitated include abolition of conventional prisons and LGBTQ rights. Cullors has integrated ideas from critical theory, as well as social and Marxist movements around the world. She is the author of *When They Call You a Terrorist: A Black Lives Matter Memoir.* Cullors was born in Los Angeles, California, and grew up in Pacoima, a low-income neighborhood in the San Fernando Valley. She became an activist early in life, joining the Bus Riders Union (BRU) under the leadership of Eric Mann. At that time she attended a year-long organizing program led by the Labor Community Strategy Center where she learned about revolutions and revolutionaries, critical race theory, and social movements from around the world. Along with her friends Alicia Garza and Opal Tometi, Cullors founded

71 Washington Post, 28 January 2010.

72 Zamudio, Margaret, et al. *Critical Race Theory Matters Education and Ideology*. Routledge, 2010.

Black Lives Matter That movement grew out of disagreement with the jury's verdict in George Zimmerman's acquittal for the shooting of Trayvon Martin. In 2016, she married Janaya Khan who co-founded Black Lives Matter Toronto.[73]

Black Lives Matter co-founder Patrisse Cullors says only "radical shifts" can stop law enforcement violence. For her it is much more than holding individual officers accountable for their actions. Cullors has demanded the defunding of law enforcement and the reinvestment of the money usually allocated to it to be spent in black communities. To her that is the only way America can achieve justice for black Americans." The demand of defunding law enforcement becomes a central demand in how we actually get real accountability and justice," she says, "because it means we are reducing the ability of law enforcement to have resources that harm our communities."

Cullers claims that the demand of defunding law enforcement has become the central and non-negotiable central requirement that CRT has placed upon the political system. That demand is not just about taking away money from the police, it is about reinvesting those dollars into black communities. She asserts that these communities have been deeply divested from ,mainstream society. These are communities which have never felt the impact of having true resources allocated to them. The police for Cullers aill always represent an economy of punishment which has been chosen over an economy of care. For Cullers it is not possible for the entity of law enforcement to be a compassionate, caring governmental agency in black communities. According to her, training has done nothing but show the black community that law enforcement and the culture of law enforcement is incapable of changing.[74]

Cullors has made a career of condemning the 'white supremacy' of the housing market. In April 2021 investigative reporters from several organizations, including Na tional Public Raio (NPR) revealed Cullors owns a $3 million property portfolio. Cullors complained in an NPR interview and also on her Instag ram account about the low level of black home ownership. To NPR, she wrote: 'Thank you @npr for highlighting the history of racism inside of the housing market and

73 "How Two Black Women in L.A. Helped Build Black Lives Matter from Hashtag to Global Movement," *Los Angeles Times*, 21 June 2020. See also "Patrisse Cullors" in Wikipedia.

74 Defunding The Police Can Achieve 'Real Accountability And Justice,' Black Lives Matter Co-Founder Says | Here & Now (wbur.org) dated 3 June 2020.

why Black home ownership has always been a way to disrupt white supremacy.' The issues were addressed in an NPR documentary entitled "We Hold These Truths," which investigated how blacks have been systematically discriminated against by the real estate industry and government policy over decades. However, it became apparent that Cullors has not faced any such issues after it was revealed she owns four houses in desirable California neighborhoods, often where mainly white people live, worth a total of almost $3 million. Recently, the 37-year-old, who set up BLM with Alicia Garza and Opal Tometi back in 2013, has faced scrutiny over her $3 million real estate empire, and also why she requires four homes.[75]

Critical Race Theory (CRT) began as a highly obscure academic theory but has recently become completely a mainstream ideology lodged deep in societal thinking. The foundational Critical Race Theory scholars were Richard Delgado and Jean Stefancic. In their text *Critical Race Theory: An Introduction* they asserted that "First, that racism is ordinary, not aberrational—'normal science,' the usual way society does business, the common, everyday experience of most people of color in this country." Racism, for them, is at the heart of virtually every ill of society. Delgado and Stefancic wrote, "First, that racism is ordinary, not aberrational—'normal science,' the usual way society does business, the common, everyday experience of most people of color in this country."[76]

Richard Delgado held the John J. Sparkman Chair of Law at the University of Alabama and was one of the founders of critical race theory. Jean Stefancic has written about legal reform and social change, many with her husband Richard Delgado. Their book, *Critical White Studies: Looking Behind the Mirror,* won a Gustavus Myers award for outstanding book on human rights in North America in 1998. The pair edited *Critical Race Theory: The Cutting Edge* which questioned comfortable liberal premises, and leads the search for new ways of thinking about our nation's most intractable, and insoluble, problem: race. They have asked: can there be color-blind justice?

For them, racism is not prejudice based upon the belief that some race or races are superior, while others are inferior, to others. It

75 "Marxist BLM Patrisse Cullors bemoans racism inside the housing market," *Daily Mail,* 16 April 2021.

76 Delgado, Richard and Jean Stefancic, *Critical Race Theory: An Introduction*, p. 7.

is, instead, the system of belief that asserts that everything that happens in the social world and beyond, and which results in disparity of any kind, is based upon racial prejudice. Moreover, anything that works in the favor of racially privileged groups has occurred because of racial oppression of perceived inferiors. Racism means the "system" of everything that happens in the social world and beyond that results in any disparity that works in the favor of "racially privileged" groups (on average) or any "racially oppressed" person claiming they experience racial oppression. It is only a matter of time until someone with the proper worldview finds out how our entire nation and its resulting culture are "racist."

Such an assumption predisposes people who take up Critical Race Theory to be on the lookout for racism in every possible place until at last they find it. It is the task of a critical activists to look for the all problems, many of which are hidden and not evident at first glance, and find the racist origins which they assume must be present.

CRT has a legitimate and critical role in the workplace. One must discern whether one's co-workers have the correct world-view. If infected with perceived racism, they must be inoculated and then cured. Where it is most important is in out educational system. In schools, it will mean teaching all children to think in the approved way. School children must be ever vigilant and be looking always for racism in every adverse situation and failed interaction. In our personal relationships, it means that friends and even family members—especially our kids who have already been educated with Critical Race Theory ideas that have been incorporated in our schools—will eventually call each other out and reject one another, because tolerating racism is itself considered a form of racism that would have to be discovered and put to flight. The academic literature on "whiteness studies" is filled with the notion that everyone must be anti-racist.[77]

Another founder of Critical Race Theory, was a scholar at Harvard Law School, Derrick Bell, author of the "Interest-Convergence Thesis" which he made central to CRT. The idea of "interest convergence" is a form of material determinism, which adds a further dimension to CRT. As explained by Delgado and Stefancic,

> The second feature, sometimes called "interest convergence" or material

77 See, for example, Sullivan, Shannon. *Good White People: The Problem with Middle-Class White Anti-Racism.* SUNY series, Philosophy and Race. State University of New York Press, 2014.

> determinism, adds a further dimension. Because racism advances the interests of both white elites (materially) and working-class people (psychically), large segments of society have little incentive to eradicate it. Consider, for example, Derrick Bell's shocking proposal that *Brown v. Board of Education*—considered a great triumph of civil rights litigation—may have resulted more from the self-interest of elite whites than a desire to help blacks.[78]

Because racism advances the interests of both white elites materially, and working-class people psychically, large segments of society have little incentive to eradicate racism. Professor Bell is best known for having advanced the somewhat shocking proposal that *Brown v. Board of Education,* which put an end to racially segregated public facilities and schools, once considered a great triumph of civil rights litigation, resulted more from the self-interest of white elites than because of a desire to see racial justice triumph. In his writings, Bell employed a series of dramatic fables and dialogues to probe the foundations of America's racial attitudes and raise disturbing questions about the nature of our society. How have we failed to achieve racial equality, Bell asks--and why? What does this failure mean--for black people and for whites? Where do we go from here? Should we redirect the quest for racial justice? Bell desired to provoke discussion that will provide new insights and prompt more effective strategies for pursuing racial justice through CRT.

Since 1994 some black historians have espoused what has become known as Project 1619 which relates the story of black ancestors. It was on August 25, 1619 that a ship landed at Point Comfort, present day Fort Monroe in Hampton, Virginia, with the first enslaved Africans brought to English North America. A Dutch-operated privateer, *White Lion,* carried some twenty to thirty captives who had been enslaved during a joint African-Portuguese raid in the Kingdom of Ndongo, present-day Angola. The Dutch sold their cargo for food. Slavery was not yet legal in the colony when they arrived and would not become legal until 1661, so the Africans were treated as indentured servants who existed without a written contract

The 1619 Project became a long-form journalism project when taken over and developed by Nikole Hannah-Jones, writer for *The New York Times,* and *The New York Times Magazine*. The project was first published in *The New York Times Magazine* in August 2019 for

---

78 Delgado and Stefancic, *op. cit.*, p. 7.

the 400th anniversary of the arrival of the first enslaved Africans in the English colony. In 2019, T*he New York Times* launched ts seminal "1619 Project," which traces the consequences of slavery from its inception centuries ago to its modern-day implications for Black Americans. The project sets out to "reframe American history by considering what it would mean to regard 1619 as our nation's birth year." It has since become a part of CRT and some of the adherents of Project 1619 want to mandate inclusion of its basic texts into public school, and perhaps college, curricula, along side other earlier mandates, such as holocaust studies. Those who learn from it will realize that, at least for blacks, history began not with Christopher Columbus, the arrival of the Pilgrims, or with the Declaration of Independence, but in 1619.

Ms Hannah-Jones apparently earned only a M.A. degree and not a Ph.D., commonly associated with tenured and endowed faculty positions. Denied an endowed chair, she plans to sue the University of North Carolina. Jay Schalin, the director of policy analysis at the conservative James G. Martin Center for Academic Renewal, argued in a blog post on the group's website that "UNC's hiring Hannah-Jones signals a degradation of journalistic standards." "The real goal of The 1619 Project was not historical or journalistic, but political agitation," Schalin wrote. "And an angry, underhanded politics at that; Hannah-Jones admitted that her underlying intent is to get 'white people to give up whiteness.' That is, to make them regard their identities as something abhorrent."[79]

One of the strong Caucasian supporters of CRT is Matthew Desmond who is an American sociologist and the Maurice P. During Professor of Sociology at Princeton University. He received a Ph.D. in sociology from the University of Wisconsin-Madison. He was formerly the John L. Loeb Associate Professor of the Social Sciences at Harvard University. His principal work has revolved around attacks on capitalism, noting that it is an outmoded economic system that is no longer responsive, if it ever was, to human needs. It was founded upon exploitation and thrived because of slavery.[80] In his Pulitzer Prize winning *Evicted: Poverty and Profit in the American City*

---

79 Kruzel, John, "'1619 Project' creator Hannah-Jones weighs discrimination suit over tenure denial," Microsoft News, 28 May 2021.

80 Desmond, Matthew, "Why Work Doesn't Work Anymore," *New York Times Magazine*, September 16, 2018. See also Emirbayer, Mustafa and Matthew Desmond. *Racial Domination, Racial Progress: The Sociology of Race in America*. New York: McGraw-Hill, 2009.

(2017) he showed how mass evictions after the 2008 economic crash were less a consequence than a cause of poverty. In 2019 he joined the Project 1619 with his essay, "American Capitalism Is Brutal. You Can Trace That to the Plantation," part of the *New York Times Magazine* sponsorship of Project 1619.

In 2019, with the complicity of the *New York Times*, Hannah-Jones launched a project to re-examine the legacy of slavery in the United States, timed for the 400th anniversary of the arrival of the first slaves in Virginia. Hannah-Jones produced a series of articles for a special issue of *The New York Times Magazine* entitled "The 1619 Project." Her project "aims to reframe the country's history by placing the consequences of slavery and the contributions of black Americans at the very center of our national narrative." In the opening essay, Hannah-Jones wrote "No aspect of the country that would be formed here has been untouched by the years of slavery that followed."

Among those who found little historical authority for her assertions were historians Gordon S. Wood and Leslie M. Harris, who objected specifically to her asserting that "one of the primary reasons the colonists decided to declare their independence from Britain was because they wanted to protect the institution of slavery.[81] So Ms Hannah-Jones "clarified" some of the theories she had advanced so that by March 2020 she had altered the text to to read "for some of the colonists," a matter that is still debatable.

Credible historians have also dismissed her assertion in the 1619 Project that the nation was founded in 1619 with the arrival of enslaved Africans rather than in 1776 with the Declaration of Independence. Speaking to New York Times, Hannah-Jones said the suggestion of considering 1619 as a jumping-off point for interpreting U. S. history had always been so "self-evidently metaphorical that it went without saying."[82] To many, the work of Nikole Hannah-Jones (1976--), the mastermind behind the *New York Times*' 1619 Project, and instructor at the Hussman School of Journalism at the University of North Carolina on the 1619 Project, bespeaks the mindset of a zealot, not of a scholar.

CRT in Action

Examples of CRT in practice abound. In Cupertino, Califor-

81 *New York Times*, 20 December 2019; "Nikole Hannah=Jones," Wijkipedia.

82 *New York Times*, 9 October 2020.

nia, an elementary school forced first-graders to deconstruct their racial and sexual identities, and rank themselves according to their "power and privilege." In Springfield, Missouri, a middle school forced teachers to locate themselves on an "oppression matrix," based on the idea that straight, white, English-speaking, Christian males are members of the oppressor class and must atone for their privilege and "covert white supremacy."

When the Pew Research Center released data in 2013, which showed that the median net worth of black families was only $11,000 as compared with compared to $141,900 for white families, CRT immediately announced that the reason was that the white establishment had made in the United States prevented Black people writ large from being able to develop wealth and political influence. In the same vein, CRT alleges that even in the contemporary job market, academic research has indicated that black people with the same credentials as whites get fewer job opportunities. Perhaps most strikingly, they allege, research has shown that when a black American commits the same crime as a white American, the black man is often sentenced to a longer prison term. Black Americans are far less likely than whites to give police high marks for the way they do their jobs.[83]

In Philadelphia, an elementary school forced fifth-graders to celebrate "Black communism" and simulate a Black Power rally to free 1960s radical Angela Davis from prison, where she had once been held on charges of murder. And in Seattle, the school district told white teachers that they are guilty of "spirit murder" against black children and must "bankrupt [their] privilege in acknowledgment of [their] thieved inheritance." A teacher at the William D. Kelley School, a Philadelphia elementary school, ranked as one of the worst-performing schools in Pennsylvania, as a substitute curriculum had fifth grade students act out a Black Power rally in honor of radical Marxist Angela Davis as a part of the celebration of black communism. The fifth-grade teacher designed a social studies assignment "to celebrate the political radical Angela Davis, praising the 'black communist' for her fight against 'injustice and inequality.'"[84]

Among CRT advocates, the most hated police methodology is

---

83 DeSilver, Drew; Michael Lipka; and Dalia Fahmy, "10 things We Know about Race and Policing in the U.S.," Pew Research, 3 June 2020.

84 Berry, Susan. "5th Graders in Failing Public School Celebrate Angela Davis, 'Black Communism'" Breitbart, 11 February 2021.

the so-called broken windows theory. This is a relatively new approach to the containment of crime advocated by some conservative criminologists. It holds that visible signs of crime, anti-social behavior, and civil disorder create an urban environment which serves to encourage further crime and disorder, leading to instances of more serious crimes. The theory suggests that policing methods that target minor crimes, such as vandalism, loitering, and public drunkenness, help to create an atmosphere of order and lawfulness. Professors James Q. Wilson and George L. Kelling introduced the system which New York City police commissioner William Bratton and Mayor Rudy Giuliani put into practice. Initially praised as a comprehensive model of community policing, it purports to prevent major crimes by first criminalizing small signs of disorder. A major theme in CRT is abandonment of this system. Several BLM members have stated that discontinuance of broken-window criminology is a non-negotiable plank in the CRT platform. In practice, this doctrine has broadened police power and contributed to the contemporary crisis of policing that has been sparked by notorious incidents of police brutality and[1 killings. They argue that this form of policing has become one of the urgent issues of our time, and is the target of defunding movements.[85]

There are several reasons why CRT has thrived. For one, critical race theorists have constructed this argument: Any and all disagreement with CRT programming immediately becomes irrefutable evidence of a dissenter's "white fragility," "unconscious bias," or "internalized white supremacy." Only die-hard racists could possibly oppose the CRT syllabus. Diversity trainers can successfully make such outrageous assertions as "all whites are intrinsically oppressors" or "white teachers are guilty of spirit murdering black children". When confronted with disagreement, they adopt a patronizing tone and explain that participants who feel "defensiveness" or "anger" are reacting out of guilt and shame. Dissenters are instructed to remain silent, "lean into the discomfort," and accept their "complicity in white supremacy."

CRT has thrived in some areas as the sole voice, advanced as the only acceptable path to be taken, and promoted without opposition. For example, the Rochester Public Schools Board in Minnesota approved Black Lives Matter messaging under protected "government

---

85 Camp, J. T. and Heatherton, C., eds. *Policing the Planet.* New York: Verso, 2016.

speech," which officials say protects the school from being held liable for allowing those views while not allowing dissenting opinions. "[By] adopting the messages that you're adopting as government speech, you're saying these are the messages that we're communicating as a school district, and by doing that, we're not also creating a forum to allow other types of speech to enter the forum," the school board's attorney, John Edison, said. The phrases "brown lives matter," "indigenous lives matter, "stop Asian hate," and the pride flag are now also considered government speech. Under government speech, "it is the government itself that is speaking ... it can control what that message is. So, you don't have the same issue [of] people coming forward and saying that by expressing a certain message you have to allow others to be expressed, too. That concept does not apply when you're talking about government speech," according to Edison.[86]

The universities are, of course, on the cutting edge of CRT as to be expected. For example, in 2017, students and administrators at Evergreen State College hosted a "Day of Absence" in which they asked that white people leave the campus so that minority students could have their own space to participate in workshops and lectures on "race, equality, allyship, inclusion, and privilege." Cornell University when it listed in its course catalogue in 2021 a rock climbing course for "BIPOC," meaning it was designed exclusively for "black, indigenous and people of color. What it did not disclose was why Caucasians could not climb rocks. Iowa State University Sociology Professor Rita Mookerjee boasted that she tries to "limit my interactions with yt [white] people as much as possible" because of their "self-importance and performance [especially] during Black History Month."[87]

CRT advocates have successfully claimed that America was founded upon, and defined by, racism. Further, our founding principles, especially the U. S. Constitution, were born out of racist thinking. This has led to the highly erroneous conclusion that American political philosophy is inexorably inter-twined with racism. Thus, anything flowing from these racist first principles is necessarily evil and must be discarded and overthrown. What is more astounding is

---

86 Colton, Emma, "School makes Black Lives Matter official speech to protect against dissenting views," *Washington Examiner,* 4 May 2021.

87 Scarry, E. "Racial Segregation is the New Black," *Washington Examiner,* 6 May 2021.

that Americans across the political spectrum have failed to deny this assertion and defend American principles

In May 2021, Idaho's legislature banned public schools and universities from teaching critical race theory. In 2020, President Trump issued an executive order banning federal agencies from training sessions that included content related to the topic. In 2021, Florida Governor Ron DeSantis insisted that, "There is no room in classrooms for things like critical race theory." And other school districts in more conservative states are quickly moving to join Idaho.

In a recent nasty exchange, MSNBC host Joy Reid charged that parents who don't want critical race theory taught in schools are in fact racist themselves. While live on the air during one of her weeknight shows, *The ReidOut*. Reid discussed the growing movement in the U.S. to reframe how American history is taught and said that "some parents opposed to CRT aren't too pleased," before playing a video clip of an emotional mother expressing her opposition. "Just because I do not want critical race theory taught to my children in school does not mean I am a racist damn it," the unnamed mother said tearfully in front of a room with others and was met with clapping. Reid laughed at the mother's statement and said, "Actually, it does." Reid then added, "It's just another example of Republicans turning kids into a wedge issue just like their politically motivated attacks on transgender youth who just want to play sports."[88]

Slavery and the American Revolution

One of the most recent applications of CRT lies in the assertion that the United States of America was not only founded upon slavery, but that Europeans, realizing that slavery was doomed as an institution in most of Europe, emigrated to the new land where slavery would be legal into an indefinite future. Having come here to utilize inexpensive slave labor, they were not about to allow anti-slavery sentiments to interfere with the very institution which had produced capitalist riches. Thus, seeing the coming British liberation of slaves, the colonists, duped by secret pro-slave leaders, rebelled. Later, a modification of the supposition of support asserted that, even among

88 Marin, Julia, "MSNBC Host Joy Reid Says Parents Who Don't Want Critical Race Theory Taught in Schools Are Racists," *Newsweek,* 5 May 2021. See Also, Johnson, Marcus, "The Republican Push to Ban Critical Race Theory Reveals an Ugly Truth," *Newsweek*, 5 May 2021.

non-slave holders, there was general support for continuance of that peculiar institution, and thus support for a war to retain slavery.

Successful slave rebellions in the Caribbean slowly spread to the American colonies. In 1712 a few dozen armed Africans killed nine settlers in a Manhattan outhouse and in 1739 the Stono Rebellion erupted in South Carolina, killing 21 whites. These persistent rebellions demonstrated how dangerous and unstable the maintenance of the slave system would be. The profits from it were too handsome to resist, however, and the trade continued to accelerate despite the problems it created. This led to another predicament for London to worry about: the ratio of African slaves to white settlers. Spain had played a role in the Stono Rebellion because slaves believed that they could flee to Spanish Florida where they secure their freedom automatically. By this time, Africans were among the most important components of the Spanish Florida militia. Another major provocation from Spain came with an Edict in 1733 that promised to free all slaves who fled to Spanish Florida from the Carolinas.

The British responded to the Spanish threat, but without using armed Africans while developing the construct of whiteness. They created the colony of Georgia to be a white buffer between South Carolina, with its black majority slave population, and Spanish Florida. Those who fit the category of whiteness included Eastern Europeans, Italians, French, and Germans. Thus, the British had created the first apartheid state, as white settlers stole the land from the indigenous aborigine and worked it with enslaved Africans, all the while enjoying civil and political rights which they systematically denied to all those who were non-white.

One alleged proof of this assertion is the often cited offer made by the royal governor of Virginia, John Murray, styled Lord Dunmore, who issued a proclamation in November 1775, offering freedom to every slave who agreed to enlist in what Dunmore called his "Ethiopian Brigade." It apparently applied only to men who would join his army. As many as 800 slaves took Dunmore up on his offer, including a 35-year-old native of the African nation of Gambia, named Harry Washington who had absconded from Mount Vernon. "There is not a man among them [the slaves] here but would not leave us, if they believ'd they could make their Escape," Mount Vernon's overseer, Lund Washington, wrote to his cousin, George Washington.

Dunmore's proclamation served as a threat to slave holders

throughout the South. In "tampering with the Slaves," James Madison wrote a friend, Dunmore had hit on the Southern states' greatest weakness, "and if we shall be subdued, we shall fall like Achilles, by the hand of one that knows the secret." As it was, the British had no intention of freeing most slaves. Dunmore's proclamation applied only to the slaves of those who supported the Patriot cause. Slaves who ran away from Loyalist masters were still returned to their owners. While as many as 20,000 slaves took the opportunity to flee to British protection during the war, in truth only a relatively few obtained real freedom.[89]

Fox News contributor and former history teacher Leo Terrell said on Tuesday that the American Federation of Teachers president lied about the "importance of critical race theory" and that the American Revolution was predicated on preserving slavery. "It is very clear that the slave issue was discussed in American history but to make the premise that the American Revolution was fought on slavery is an outright lie. And I submit to you, that this union president, was afraid of losing her job if she said the wrong thing," Terrell told "Fox & Friends," adding he was "very upset" by AFT President Randi Weingarten's comments. "It is very insulting because what's at issue here is not only the credibility of American history, but lying to our school children about American history. This is what's so frightening about this critical race theory," Terrell said.

- The question of slavery as a major issue in the First War for Independence began in April 2021 on an installment of "The Story" when its host Martha MacCallum tangled with American Federation of Teachers president Randi Weingarten regarding her support of *The New York Times'* controversial "1619 Project" and its support of critical race theory which is being taught in classrooms across the country. MacCallum questioned Weingarten's push to implement a curriculum based on certain parts of the 1619 Project.[90]

The 1619 project is based on the belief that the first importation of the slaves to American shores in 1619 constituted the nation's true founding, "and that the reason for the American Revolution and the colonization was because people wanted to retain the system of

89 Horne, Gerald. *The Counter-Revolution of 1776: Slave Resistance and the Origins of the United States of America.* NYU Press, 2014.

90 Orlet, Chris, "GOP Still Wants to Pretend the Preservation of Slavery Wasn't a Major Reason for the American Revolution," *Counterpunch,* 3 May 2021.

slavery," MacCallum explained. Weingarten, who is a self-described history and social studies teacher defended this nonsensical belief which is totally without factual merit. She claimed that "from everything I can see and understand from the data that I see, 1619 was the year that the first slave boat came from Africa to the United States. So that's a point in history that I think we should be teaching." "That's a very simplistic take on it," MacCallum fired back. "The Story" host explained that the project indoctrinates children to believe that "the country was founded on the basis of wanting to preserve slavery."

MacCallum told viewers. "In fact, scholars say there's no evidence that colonists were motivated by that in coming to the United States. So it would be wrong as an historian to want to teach them something that is not true, because that is the basis that sets up all of these other tenants that lead to teaching kids that we live in a systemically racist country." Weingarten claimed that she had "several conversations" with 1619 Project founder and that she had not arrived at the same conclusion from her work as MacCallum had.

For his part in the on-going discourse, Terrell, a civil rights attorney, said the teachings of critical race theory imply that teachers have been lying to children for decades. "In the American Revolution, we fought against the British for our independence, not to preserve slavery. That is a lie, and yes, that union president is afraid. I hope she is listening. She is afraid to tell the truth because no one believes that the American Revolution was fought to preserve slavery."[91]

Slavery and the Old South

- Slavery retarded real growth in the Old South by absorbing southern savings, preventing the accumulation of non-human capital and holding back the growth of manufacturing. More specifically, historians contend that capital was "frozen" in the form of slave labor, making it unavailable for other forms of investment. Half of the South's assessed worth was tied up in slaves and close to half in land itself. Although the South earned as much as $60 million a year in the 1850s from cotton, tobacco and rice exports, almost all investment went back into slaves and land, leaving little for manufacturing.79 A poor transportation network also hindered southern modernization.

91 Halon, Yael and Joshua Q. Nelson, ""Leo Terrell blasts teachers union president's 'lies' about American Revolution, critical race theory," Fox News, 12 May 2021. See also *Washington News Post,* 12 May 2021.

There was a distinct lack of main lines connecting cities to markets in the West, and the manufacturing base was very small compared with that of the North. In *A House Dividing: Economic Development in Pennsylvania and Virginia Before the Civil War,* historian John Majewski writes that the central problem was Virginia's slave economy. The slave system discouraged the growth of an investor class that could provide funds for transportation projects, or the growth of a consumer class to provide passengers for such projects.[92] Majeski also argued that "A slave society, no matter how much wealth it produced, could not compete against a northern economy that harnessed the power of ordinary households left free to invent, to improve, to invest, and to consume."[93]

In the mid-1800s, the Industrial Revolution was radically transforming the northern United States and Europe. But the Industrial Revolution bypassed the American South. In 1850, the South produced only 10 to 11 percent of the nation's industrial output. The South produced less than New Hampshire and only about one-third as much as Massachusetts. Rhode Island produced about as much industrial goods as the entirety of the southern states. In 1860, output per person the Old South's plantation-based economy hindered industrialization. In 1850, the South produced only 10 to 11 percent of the nation's industrial output was $19 in the South, versus $149 for New England.[94] Additionally, several neo-Marxist scholars have argued that the slave system served to encourage aristocratic conservative rule which resisted the growth of capitalism.

Much of the present damning perspective on the Old South and slavery is but a modern updating of Hinton Rowan Helper, (1829—1909). Hinton was the only prominent American Southern author to attack slavery before the outbreak of the American Civil War. In 1857 he published his best known work,.*The Impending Crisis of the South: How to Meet It.* Many rank this book second only to Harriet Beecher Stowe's *Uncle Tom's Cabin* as an influence on the abolitionist movement. The book was a combination of statistical charts and provocative prose. Helper concluded that slavery hurt the Southern economy by blocking industrialization which the main reason why the

92 5 Majewski, John. *A House Dividing: Economic Development in Pennsylvania and Virginia Before the Civil War.* Cambridge University Press, 2000.

93 Ibid., p. 11. See also op. 172.

94 Bateman, Fred, and Weiss, Thomas, *A Deplorable Scarcity: The Failure of Industrialization in the Slave Economy.* University of North Carolina Press, 1981.

South had progressed so much less than the North. Helper used the Census of Manufactures of 1830 and compared it with the same census in 1850. The gap between industrialization in the South and that in the North was huge and growing rapidly. Helper claimed to speak on behalf of the majority of Southern whites of moderate means.[95]

What's Wrong with CRT?

One critique of Critical Race Theory can be summarized as follows. First, it teaches that racism is present everywhere. It is to be found in every aspect of life, every relationship, and every interaction and therefore has its advocates are mandated to look for it everywhere. It relies upon an idea stated as "interest convergence" according to which white people only give black people opportunities and freedoms only when it is also in their own interests. Because of its constant witch hunts and investigations, it acts in opposition to free societies, seeking to dismantle them and replace them with a politically correct system which is opposed to what its advocates condemn as racism. CRT treats race issues as "socially constructed groups," so there are is no place for individuals within Critical Race Theory.

CRT discusses two divergent ways of approaching living. In Caucasian societies there is a concern for science, reason, and evidence, that is, a "white" way of knowing and acting. Opposed to that are storytelling and lived experience which constitute a black alternative, which, anti-CRT voices claim, injure and retard everyone, but especially black people. CRT thus rejects all potential alternatives, like colorblindness, as forms of racism, reserving to itself the only allowable game in town, an ideology usually called totalitarianism. Anyone who dares to disagree does so only because such persons are racists and white supremacists. Woe unto those people who disagree but are black.[96] Here CRT makes recourse is to Franz Fanon and his *Black Skin, White Masks*.

---

95 DeBow, James D. B. *Compendium of the Seventh Census*. Government Printing Office, 1854, showed that Hinton was in error at least as often he was correct in his use of the 1860 Census and the 1860 Census of Manufactures. DeBow did not write a refutation, but provided a much more accurate picture of what these censuses showed. Lefler, Hugh T., "Hinton Rowan Helper: Advocate of a White America," *Southern Sketches*, 1 (1935), argued that Helper twisted and deliberately misinterpreted data to suit his purpose.

96 Lindsay, James, "Eight Big Reasons Critical Race Theory Is Terrible for Dealing with Racism," *New Discourses*, 12 June 2020.

Critical race scholars are frequently discontented with liberal views of freedom and free speech as a framework for addressing America's racial problems. Delgado and Stefancic were quite critical of any liberals believe in the sufficiency of color blindness and neutral principles of constitutional law" to set matters aright.[97] One criticism of the various movements upon which Critical Race Theory is based was advanced by Robin DiAngelo and set in book form by Ozlem Sensoy who noted that while CRT initially advocated a type of liberal humanism, which included individualism, freedom, and peace, it rather quickly turned to a *rejection* of liberal humanism. The ideal of individual autonomy that underlies liberal humanism (the idea that people are free to make independent rational decisions that determine their own fate) was viewed as a mechanism for keeping the marginalized in their place by obscuring larger structural systems of inequality. In other words, it [free society] fooled people into believing they had more freedom and choice than societal structures actually allow.[98]

In schools, it will come to mean that teaching our children to think this way, to always be seeking out racism in every situation and interaction, will be a new way of living. In our personal relationships, it means that friends and even family members, and especially our children who have already been educated with Critical Race Theory ideas that have been incorporated in our schools, will eventually call out one another because tolerating racism is a form of racism that would have to be discovered and eradicated. If Mommy is a racist you have to turn her in.

If someone with alleged "racial privilege" (including white, Asian, Hispanic, Arab, Indian, and lighter-skinned black people) should decide to become an anti-racist in accordance with CRT's demand, the Interest-Convergence Thesis would say they only did so to make themselves look good, protect themselves from criticism, or to avoid confronting their own racism – and not out of heart-felt desire to do what is just and right.

In May 2021 Republican Governor Kevin Stitt of Oklahoma supported legislation banning "critical race theory" in public schools. As a result he was ousted from a commission created to commemorate the 100th anniversary of the 1921 Tulsa Race Massacre. This was

97 Delgado and Stefancic, *op. cit.*, p. 21.

98 *Sensoy, Ozlem. Is Everyone Really Equal? An Introduction to Key Concepts in Social Justice Education.* Teachers College Press, 2011., p. 5

punishment for his having signed legislation that would ban the teaching of some race and racism concepts in public schools. Oklahoma House Bill 1775 bans any instruction of the concept that "meritocracy or traits such as a hard work ethic are racist or sexist or were created by members of a particular race to oppress members of another race," and stipulates that college students cannot be required to engage in "mandatory gender or sexual diversity training or counseling." Governor Stitt defended his decision to sign the bill, saying, "Now more than ever, we need policies that bring us together, not rip us apart," he said earlier this month. "Not one cent of taxpayer money should be used to define and divide young Oklahomans about their race or sex."

In a separate statement, issued after the dismissal, Phil Armstrong, the project director of the Centennial Commission, in a separate letter blasted Stitt for his support of the legislation, asserting that "HB 1775 chills the ability of educators to teach students, of any age, and will only serve to intimidate educators who seek to reveal and process our hidden history," he wrote. "You know that. You seemingly disregarded and dismissed this chorus of voices aligned against HB 1775."[99]

In May 2021 Montana Attorney General Austin Knudsen issued an opinion labeling critical race theory and some anti-racism programs taught in schools as "discriminatory" and said they violate federal and state law. That decision bans the activities, which are also used for employee training. Knudsen issued his opinion after the Superintendent of Public Instruction Elsie Arntzen requested a legal opinion as a guide. Thus, Montana became the latest state to decry critical race theory as an attempt to pit racial groups against each other and teach that certain groups are responsible for injustices of the past. Knudsen's opinion, binding in public institutions in Montana, states that certain activities that fall under the umbrella of critical race theory teaching violate the U.S. and state constitutions.

The American Civil Liberties Union of Montana and the Montana Federation of Public Employees both immediately attacked Knudsen's decision as did some faculty at public universities. ACLU of Montana executive director Caitlin Borgmann accused them of trying to "impose an alternate version of American history — one that erases the legacy of discrimination and lived experiences of Black and

99 Dorman, John L. "Oklahoma Gov. Kevin Stitt Ousted from Tulsa Race Massacre Commission," *Business Insider*, 16 May 2021, insider@insider.com

Brown people." It continued,"Our country needs to acknowledge its history of systemic racism and reckon with the present-day impacts of racial discrimination — this includes being able to teach and talk about these concepts in our schools,"

Knudsen's office attacked such ideas as grading students differently based on race; forcing people to admit privilege or reflect on their racial identities; assigning fault, blame or bias to a race; and offering training or assignments that force students or employees to support concepts such as racial privilege. It was Knudson's opinion that chools and government and public workplaces could lose state funding and could be liable for damages from lawsuits if they offer critical race theory training or activities,said in a statement. "Committing racial discrimination in the name of ending racial discrimination is both illogical and illegal," Knudsen said in a statement. "Montana law does not tolerate schools, other government entities, or employers implementing CRT and anti-racist programming in a way that treats individuals differently on the basis of race or that creates a racially hostile environment."[100]

One most unfortunate result of CRT has been a campaign seen first in San Diego, California, which targets pregnant black women, telling them that racism could hurt their babies even before they are even born. Public officials have been spending tax money on what conservatives have called 'divisive and misleading' billboards which argue that racial discrimination is behind higher rates of miscarriages and maternal deaths among black women. The billboards, sponsored by Black Legacy New SD, include such claims as 'Our black babies are nearly 60% more likely to be premature due to discrimination' and 'Racism hurts your baby long before they're born'. Critics claim that these statements are not supported by data and could discourage women from seeking medical care.

The campaign was funded and approved by Governor Gavin Newsom, reportedly to address disparities in the health outcomes of black babies and mothers. Statistics from the National Center for Health Statistics shows that black babies were more likely to be born prematurely between 2017 and 2019 – at a rate of 14% nationally and 12.2% in California, but provides no cause for that disparity. White

---

100 Eichardson, Valerie, "Montana AG bans critical-race theory programs," *Washington Times,* 27 May 2021. See also Associated Press, "Montana's Top Prosecutor Bans Critical Race Theory Programs," 27 May 2021.

babies were born prematurely 9.2% of the time nationwide and 7.7% in California. The numbers for Hispanics are 9.8% and 9.1%.[101]

CRT teaches that all white people are inherently racist, that blacks cannot be racist because they have no power, and that free-market capitalism must be jettisoned because it is a tool of white oppression. The *Examiner* has called Ibram X. Kendi, Critical Race Theory's trendiest faux-intellectual in large because of his position that holds to truly be anti-racist, one also has to be opposed to capitalism. President Joe Biden's educational specialists cite "the toxic, malevolent work of the huckster Kendi" as authoritative. They also promulgate the *New York Times*' widely discredited "1619 Project," which ludicrously argued that the desire to keep and spread slavery was at the "very center of the United States' national narrative."

As one read the news daily one sees constant reaction against CRT-based education in the public schools. Where there is action there is counter-action and reaction to the counter-reaction, and the chain can go one to nearly infinite length, producing a giant volume of literature, apologetics, advocacies, and revisions, and condemnations. What has yet to be established is this: does CRT bring us together? Does it seek to destroy legitimate history be rewriting it in a style reminiscent of George Orwell's 1984? Will it prevent ugly racist events and prejudices?

---

101 Tingle, Rory, "Officials slammed for 'divisive and misleading' racism billboards, "Dailymail.com, 16 May 2021,

Critical Race Theory: Reaction

CRT has already infected the public-school systems with its ultra-left wing ideology. Examples are numerous and horrendous. Think tank leader Christopher Rufo has written about some of them. "In Seattle, the school district told white teachers that they are guilty of 'spirit murder' against black children and must 'bankrupt [their] privilege in acknowledgment of [their] thieved inheritance.'"

Biden's appointees at the Department of Education advocate making Critical Race Theory an essential part of federal grant awards for several "American History and Civics Education" programs. In doing so, they have effectively created a back-door mechanism to make it the basis for more widespread mandates through the main law governing all federal actions related to K-12 schools. Biden's American Families Plan would increase Washington's control of preschool, child care, community college, and four-year colleges by providing strings-attached subsidies to government-approved programs. This approach stifles innovation, limits the choices available to families, and unfairly shifts the cost burden to those who do not use the programs.

The critical race theory battle in Virginia heated up as "woke" parents and teachers have started directly attacking critics of the controversial movement, including by threatening lawsuits. Ian Prior, executive director of Fight for Schools PAC and a Loudon County parent, recently received a cease-and-desist order from a fellow parent trying to silence him for speaking out against CRT by threatening legal action. The cease-and-desist letter accused Prior of "misrepresenting" the Anti-Racist Parents of Loudoun County which supports CRT. Prior claimed that his name was being targeted by members of the anti-racist parents group. Prior asserted that the letter sent to his home was a clear intent to silence him while pushing the CRT agenda.[102]

No critic of critical race theory has been more forthcoming and vocal than the *Washington Examiner*. Call CRT a neo-Marxist ideology that espouses overt black racism in the name of anti-racism, it has consistently denounced this approach to racial harmony a grave danger to America. In effect, CRT teaches that racial identity is at the center of modern life and that the United States was founded on, and remains a pernicious embodiment of, racism. Its very soul supposedly

---

102 Laco, Kelly, "Angry 'woke' parents and teachers are trying to silence critics of critical race theory," Microsoft News,29 May 2021.

is imbued with racism. CRT emphasizes division instead of unity, race-centric consciousness instead of Martin Luther King's ideal of color-blindness, and economic "equity" (that is, Marxist economics) rather than equality before the law.

Parents React

Parents rarely become involved in educational matters in the public schools, so initially it was surprising to see the powerful parental reaction against CRT. But across the nation, groups of parents, many actually frightened by CRT teaching tenets, are using both the courts and the ballot box to oppose its inclusion in public school curricula.[103]

In Texas the state's Attorney General Ken Paxton on Tuesday praised parents for pushing back against the teaching of the quasi-Marxist critical race theory in the nation's schools, urging more people to speak out and arguing it's the "only way we save our kids" from leftist indoctrination.[104]

Shawn McBreairty, a parent of twin girls, said he was banned from their graduation over objections to critical race theory being taught in their school, telling 'The Faulkner Focus' that 'we need education, not indoctrination.'[105] A Rhode Island mother of two Nicole Solas on possibly facing a lawsuit for seeking records on critical race theory.[106] Under the headline of "Mom fights anti-white training in daughter's kindergarten class," opposed the teaching of CRT as a form of racism in kindergarten: Nicole Solas told the story that her school district threatens to sue her for requesting public records regarding CRT.[107] In another case of parental disapproval of CRT, a black man, Kory Yeshua and his daughter were going viral in a video opposing critical race theory."[108]

---

103 Slisco, Alica, "Americans Terrified to Oppose Critical Race Theory," *Newsweek*, 25 May 2021.

104 Ozimek, Tom, "Parents Should Oppose Critical Race Theory to 'Save Our Kids' from Left-Wing Indoctrination: AG Paxton," *The Epoch Times*, 5 May 2021.

105 "Maine father fights back after being banned from graduation over critical race theory objections," Fox News 1 June 2021

106 "Rhode Island mom 'wants more answers' on critical race theory," Fox News, 2 June 2021.

107 Fox News, 4 June 2021

108 "Dad-daughter duo speaks out against critical race theory," Fox, 3 June 2921.

States Banning CRT

During his last months in office, former President Trump ordered federal agencies to stop racial sensitivity training sessions, including those based on so-called critical race theory. The President noted that CRT holds, in part, that racism is a social construct ingrained in American life and laws. President Biden has since rescinded that order by his predecessor, but the push to ban the teaching of racial justice theories has now moved to the states. Four states — Tennessee, Idaho, Oklahoma, and Arkansas— have already placed limits on how race can be addressed in the classroom and 16 states in all are looking to limit the way teachers discuss racism in school.

In the spring 2021 Idaho Governor Brad Little signed a bill authored by Republican state lawmakers that aims to outlaw teaching critical race theory and other social justice concepts in the public schools. Many school officials and long-time teachers said CRT attempted to treat a non-existent problem. In early January 2021, the president of the libertarian Idaho Freedom Foundation, urged lawmakers to especially target the state's higher educational institutions, notably Boise State University and University of Idaho, from where had come the concept of CRT indoctrination in the state's public school system.[109]

In Tennessee, sixty-eight House Republicans voted for House Bill 580, which Gov. Bill Lee signed into law, precisely because they saw critical race theory as a Marxist derivative which is both divisive and discriminatory. In sponsoring that legislation, the Republicans asserted that CRT "teaches our children that each of them is either inherently racist or inherently oppressed based on nothing but the color of their skin." This is a "highly objectionable idea to be forcing" upon second graders. Additionally, they claimed, CRT teaches that America's institutions are "designed solely to create and maintain social, economic and political inequalities between the privileged and the minoritized."[110] The law now prohibits state educators from teaching that "an individual, by virtue of the individual's race or sex, is inherently

---

109 Dawson, James, "Idaho Governor Signs Bill To Ban Critical Race Theory In Schools," National Public Radio, 1 May 2021. See also McIntosh, Scott, "Idaho task force on critical race theory: Serious examination or political witch hunt?," *Idaho Statesman,* 3 June 2021.

110 Faison, Jeremy, "We Tennessee lawmakers banned critical race theory in school to protect children," *The Tennesseean,* 2 June 2021. Faison, a member of the state legislature, wrote this as an op-ed opinion piece.

privileged, racist, sexist, or oppressive, whether consciously or subconsciously." Democratic lawmakers opposed the new law, saying that teachers will be fearful of teaching their students how racism shaped the current state of the country. A school found to be in violation of the law could have its funding withheld.[111]

Oklahoma Governor Kevin Stitt signed a bill into law banning the teaching of critical race theory in public schools and universities. "Now more than ever, we need policies that bring us closer together – not rip us apart. As governor, I firmly believe that not one cent of taxpayer money should be used to define and divide young Oklahomans by their race or sex," said Stitt.[112] The measure prohibits all public schools from teaching students that "one race or sex is inherently superior to another" and that "an individual, by virtue of his or her race or sex, is inherently racist, sexist or oppressive." The legislation passed rapidly through both chambers of the Oklahoma Legislature. Democratic lawmakers largely opposed the bill. Some of the bill's sponsors argued that it sought to mend nonexistent problems in the state's education system.[113]

Texas Republican state Rep. Steve Toth firmly believes that a curriculum that teaches young people about systemic racism is itself a form of racism. Toth is the primary author of House Bill 3979, which seeks to ban the teaching of "critical race theory," an educational movement that seeks to contextualize recent and historical events in a framework of systemic racism, in public schools. "This bill is a direct reflection of the 1964 Civil Rights Act," Toth told Yahoo News in a phone interview this week. "It echoes Dr. King's wish that we should judge people on the content of their character, not their skin." Toth's bill, which has passed in both chambers of the Texas legislature and is headed to Governor Greg Abbot's desk for signature into law, states that social studies and civics teachers are not allowed to discuss the concept that "one race or sex is inherently superior to another race or sex," or the idea that "an individual, by virtue of the individual's race or sex, bears responsibility for actions committed in the past by other members of the same race or sex." The bill also states that teachers cannot be compelled to talk about current events, and if they do, they

---

111 Oshin, O., "Tennessee governor signs measure banning critical race theory instruction," The Hill, 25 May 2021.

112 *Washington Examiner.,* 5 June 2021.

113 *Tulsa World*, 7 June 2021.

must "give deference to both sides." While supporters say this provision promotes objective teaching, critics counter that it limits honest conversation around the deep-rooted issues surrounding the history of race and racism in the U.S. "The more people learn about critical race theory, whether Republican or Democrat, the more they oppose it," said Toth, who noted that he is also a preacher that God led him to write this bill limiting the teaching of what he termed "an offshoot of critical theory and Marxism."[114]

BLM Leadership and CRT

The founder of Black Lives Matter (BLM) in St. Paul, Minnesota, recently released a video in which he called out the group's "ugly truth," by which he meant their positions on family and education. "In 2015, I was the founder of Black Lives Matter in St. Paul," said Rashad Turner, who now leads the pro-school choice group Minnesota Parent Union. "I believed the organization stood for exactly what the name implies, Black lives do matter. However, after a year on the inside, I learned they had little concern for rebuilding Black families," he added. Turner's video which was published on YouTube in May 2021, highlighted how the group's website stated that it wanted to "disrupt the nuclear family structure." Also, he noted, "And they cared even less," Turner added, "about improving the quality of education for students in Minneapolis. That was made clear when they publicly denounced charter schools alongside the teachers' union." He continued, "I was an insider in Black Lives Matter and I learned the ugly truth – the moratorium on charter schools does not support rebuilding the Black family. But it does create barriers to a better education for Black children." Turner's comments touched on an ongoing criticism of BLM – namely that its goals and political positions are much more left-wing than the name might suggest.

The group has acquired heightened popularity in the wake of prominent police encounters that sparked ongoing protests in recent years. Politicians and other leading figures have adopted the slogan as well. Recent events, however, have intensified scrutiny of its leader and her ideas. Co-founder Patrisse Cullors came under fire after it was revealed she bought four homes for more than $3 million. The self-described "Marxist" was also seen in a resurfaced video favorably

114 Francis, Marquis, "Author of Texas bill to ban critical race theory says Martin Luther King Jr. would approve of it," Yahoo, 4 June 2021

comparing a book to "red book" propagated under Mao Zedong.

The BLM curriculum also engendered controversy over ideas the organization was promoting in schools. Cullors is stepping down from her role as executive director of the activist group's central foundation amid questions about her finances. She told the Associated Press in May 2021 that she was leaving the position to focus on other projects, including the release of her second book and a television deal with Warner Bros. She held the top post at Black Lives Matter Global Network Foundation for more than five years. The activist said she had created "the necessary bones and foundation" at the organization and felt the "time is right" to leave. She asserted that her exit was planned for more than a year and was unrelated to scrutiny regarding her personal finances. "Those were right-wing attacks that tried to discredit my character, and I don't operate off of what the right thinks of me," Cullors said.[115]

The Loudoun County Virginia School Controversy

Loudoun County Public Schools of Loudoun County, Virginia, serves over 80,000 students ranging from kindergarten through high school in Virginia, just outside of Washington, D.C. In March, Loudoun County made national headlines over its discouragement of connecting children's author Dr. Seuss to Read Across America Day over "strong racial undertones" written and illustrated in some of his works. In may 2021, an elementary school physical education teacher Byron "Tanner" Cross was placed on leave after he gave a speech to the Loudoun County School Board over his refusal to "affirm that a biological boy can be a girl and vice versa." That action prompted a lawsuit filed on behalf of Cross, who cited his Christian convictions for his resistance to address students by their preferred names and pronouns. The suit was filed by Alliance Defending Freedom, an Arizona-based legal nonprofit group focusing on religious liberty.[116]

The Loudoun County School Board (LCPS), adopted a uniform equity curriculum, but it does have a "Culturally Responsive Framework." According to documents provided by LCPS, the purpose of the Culturally Responsive Framework is: "To create and guide sup-

115 Dorman, Sam and Barrabi, Thomas, "Former BLM leader sounds off on group's 'ugly truth'," Fox News, Microsoft News, 1 June 2021

116 Soellner, Mica, "Virginia parents sue school board over allegedly chilling students' free speech" *Washington Examiner,* 2 June 2021.

port of student-centered learning environments with a critical focus on culturally and linguistically diverse students that have been marginalized by inequitable systems. Eric Williams, Superintendent of Loudoun County Public Schools, said 'LCPS calls for all students, staff, families, and other members of our community to engage in the disruption and dismantling of white supremacy, systemic racism, and hateful language and actions based on race, religion, country of origin, gender identity, sexual orientation, and/or ability.' One teacher who advocated CRT was quoted as saying, "A culturally responsive framework also creates and guides culturally responsive teaching by, 'using the cultural knowledge, prior experiences, frames of reference, and performance styles of ethnically and racially diverse students to make learning encounters more relevant to and effective for them.'" Another LCPS official was quoted as saying, "Our equity group programs and our professional development for teachers is not about bringing one student down or elevating another student. Our equity efforts are about providing a world-class education for all of our students."[117] In general, LCPS refused to make public statements or to talk with news media, especially Fox.

The clash over CRT and equity learning has put LCPS school board meetings in the national spotlight. The previous superintendent recommended that the teachers and staff read Ibram X. Kendi's book *How To Be An Antiracist,* a fact that John Beatty, LCPS school board member and a candidate for Congress in Virginia, has made quire public. In March, video footage posted online showing an LCPS high school teacher appearing to berate a student for not acknowledging the race of two girls seen in a presentation slide went viral. Despite this, Ziegler insists he is not aware of any circumstances where a teacher has crossed the line when interacting with students. He says the back and forth captured in the video took place in a "college-level" English class, although obviously in high school and involving adolescent children.

One night, soon after the story spread nationally, the LCPS school board held an "equity workshop" to discuss training and student outreach being done in schools. The meeting did not include public comment. According to one parent, who has two middle school-aged daughters in LCPS, "the best that it can do is pit people

117 Mastrangelo, Alana, "Loudoun County Parents Rally to Recall School Board Members Pushing Critical Race Theory," *Breitbart*, 4 June 2021.

against each other. . . ."[118]

A group of Virginia parents filed a federal lawsuit against the Loudoun County School Board, citing allegations that it violated students' free speech rights. The plaintiffs, represented by the Chicago-based Liberty Justice Center, targets the school board's "bias reporting" system that encourages students to report on people's perceived biases anonymously. Defendants also argued against having only students of color and those who "expressly attest" to being allies of historically oppressed groups be eligible to participate in the schools' Equity Ambassadors Program. "Our kids have the right to develop their own opinions, free from indoctrination and school-sanctioned bullying. Instead of opening young minds, Loudoun County school leaders are policing them. This is not education; it is coercion," said one parent of a Loudoun County high school student who was also founder of Parents Against Critical Theory.

A senior attorney at the Liberty Justice Center, called Loudoun County's policies "extreme and divisive." "Not only are Loudoun school leaders telling students what they can and can't say, they are imposing controversial political views on students and punishing those who don't agree,"[119] He continued, "Every student has a right to express his or her views and to engage in a respectful, robust conversation about real issues without fear of retribution."[120]

A child's first teacher is their parent, but in Loudoun County, some parents say that's no longer the case. One outraged parent, who also was a black man, was quoted as saying, "Critical race theory basically enforces or introduces an idea that the sins of our great- grandparents are still here with us, and there's nothing we can do about it. He is one of a growing number of parents banding together to support Fight For Schools, a political action committee opposed to CRT. The group is spearheaded by Ian Prior, a former Trump administration DOJ official and father of two children in Loudoun County public schools. "They'll talk about it with different words, like equity or culturally responsive learning, but those are really the implementation tools of critical race theory," says Prior. "What you see is constant references to White privilege, White supremacy, White fragility, and re-

118 Leach, Matt, "Virginia parents organize to fight critical race theory learning in classrooms," Fox News/ Microsoft News, 2 June 2021.

119 *Washington Examiner*, 30 May 2021.

120 Soellner, Mica, "Virginia parents sue school board over allegedly chilling students' free speech" *Washington Examiner,* 2 June 2021.

ally focusing on kids not as individuals with their own skills, talents, dreams and goals, but instead looking at kids through an identity group lens," he says. Concerns over critical race theory in schools has sparked controversies across the country. "Critical race theory, is not something that is relatable on the K-12 level, it's not something that is taught in our schools or presented to our students," says LCPS Interim Superintendent Scott Ziegler. According to LCPS, The Equity Collaborative, a group that offers "equity coaching," was hired in 2019 to perform a "systemic equity assessment." Loudoun County parents have repeatedly denounced the school board and also have tried to recall its members, Their lawsuit represents a significant escalation and growing shift in strategy among CRT opponents. Because CRT training session frequently make sweeping claims about racial groups, they, by their own actions, have raised concerns about potential civil rights violations that can only be addressed in courts. According to this lawsuit, the Loudoun schools explicitly indicated that white students were disqualified from serving as equity ambassadors. Before they were removed from Loudoun's website, an FAQ section and information packet designated the positions for children of color.

The minors who are plaintiffs, were listed anonymously in the suit, and purportedly could not have met LCPS' criteria for the ambassadorships by membership in the Caucasian race. Moreover, these children would not describe their "views as 'social justice' as LCPS uses that term." In response to an FAQ about a white youngster potentially serving, the web posting said: "Thank you for your interest but this opportunity is specifically for students of Color. However, students at each school have an option of creating an affinity group for students of Color who all share a similar racial identity and they may also include allies."[121]

Two leading scholars on the topic of critical race theory discussed their views on the controversial concept and why they believe it is being unfairly characterized by opponents. Kendall Thomas, a law professor at Columbia University, and Marvin Lynn, a professor at Portland State University, chose to defend the beginnings of CRT, its educational goals, and the motivations of those whom they believe intentionally seek to distort its true substance.[122]

---

121 Dorman, Sam, "Virginia parents sue school district over alleged racial discrimination, free speech violations," Fox News 3 June 2021

122 "University professors hit back against opponents of critical race theory" Fox

Black Privilege and White Privilege

` The concept of white privilege has been studied by theorists of whiteness studies seeking to examine the construction and moral implications of 'whiteness'. There is often overlap between critical whiteness and race theories, as demonstrated by focus on the legal and historical construction of white identity, and the use of narratives (whether legal discourse, testimony, or fiction) as a tool for exposing systems of racial power. Academic disciplines, such as history and cultural studies, have become primarily responsible for the formative scholarship of critical whiteness studies .Peggy McIntosh, of whom more later, defined white privilege: It is "The unquestioned and unearned set of advantages, entitlements, benefits and choices bestowed upon people solely because they are white. Generally white people who experience such privilege do so without being conscious of it. "Political activists and writers have built on Ms McIntosh's original essay by adding to and modifying the original list to highlight how privilege is not merely about race or gender, but that it is a series of interrelated hierarchies and power dynamics that touch all facets of social life: race, class, gender, sexual orientation, religion, education, gender identity, age, physical ability, passing, etc.[123]

The ideology of white privilege asserts that in the United States there exist systems of power, such as government, law enforcement, education, financial systems, which have been developed through a white culture lens, rewarding those who can adapt to white culture and punishing those who do not. It teaches that especially in those communities with few people of color, white people do not necessarily see their spaces as racialized, white privilege transcends the interpersonal stories we share with neighbors, family, friends and co-workers. Institutionalized power shapes and controls access to resources. Understanding requires that white people explore their stories in light of history, culture, power and economics in order to create a more equitable and just society.[124]

The origins of the so-called anti-White Privilege movement can be traced to communist thinking. Perhaps the leading theorist to write on this topic was Theodore "Ted" Allen. He was a communist

---

News, 1 June 2021

123"White Privilege," Alberta Civil Liberties Research Centre.

124 Kendall, Frances. *Understanding White Privilege*. Routledge, 2006.

party member, a labor organizer, and eventually a researcher and teacher on labor organizing at the Communist Party-founded Jefferson School of Social Science. Based on his experience working to educate the working class about Communism, and drawing from the work of W.E.B. Dubois, Allen became concluded that the white working class would never rebel as long as it benefited from the a white-skin privilege. Allen developed the theory that the capitalist system had evolved as an artificial, but deeply-rooted, method of control by divide the white working class from the black working class, thereby precluding the possibility of a united proletariat. White workers could save themselves only by purging themselves of their privilege. Only then could the New Left succeed where their predecessors had failed. [125]

The National Museum of African American History and Culture, created and funded by U.S. taxpayer dollars, displays prominently the following definition: "White Privilege. Since white people in America hold most of the political, institutional, and economic power, they receive advantages that nonwhite groups do not. These benefits and advantages, of varying degrees, are known as white privilege. For many white people, this can be hard to hear, understand, or accept—but it is true. If you are white in America, you have benefited from the color of your skin."

Assisting Allen in this effort was another leading Marxist theorist, another former Communist party member, Noel Ignatiev, also known as Noel Ignatin. Working together they effected a split between the Students for a Democratic Society (SDS), and the Revolutionary Youth Movement (RYM). Eventually, the RYM would also fracture into The Weather Underground and Revolutionary Youth Movement II, which would later evolve into the New Communist Movement. But the concept of White-Skin privilege was instrumental to all of these organizations. Whereas the Weather Underground sought to destroy their white privilege using Maoist-style struggle sessions and by carrying out violent terrorist acts, the more practical Allen and Ignatiev focused on more traditional tactics.

Using various front organizations, such as the Harper's Ferry Organization and the Sojourner Truth Organization, Allen and Ignatin and their followers adopted the strategy targeting alleged white privilege in the workplace, while pretending to support black workers.

125Allen, Theodore. "Can the White Workers Be Radicalized" 1967 tract.

Meanwhile, they would re-educate white workers, shaming them for taking advantage of their black brethren by basking in their racial privilege. They urged groups to lead strikes and other disruptions against perceived racial injustice in the workplace. Most particularly, they opposed meritocracy in hiring, claiming it to be essentially racist. While these cadres were never large, their tactics were influential, and their ideas even more so. Ignatiev moved on to teach at Harvard where he became one of the leading proponents of the concept of "White Privilege" and the burgeoning field of critical race theory.

Some will trace the concept of White Privilege to W.E.B. DuBois in his 1935 *Black Reconstruction in America* (1935), wherein Du Bois introduced the concept of a "psychological wage" for white laborers. This special status, he wrote, divided the labor movement by leading low-wage white workers to feel superior to low-wage black workers. Du Bois identified white racial supremacy as a global phenomenon, affecting the social conditions across the world by means of colonialism. Du Bois explained:

> It must be remembered that the white group of laborers, while they received a low wage, were compensated in part by a sort of public and psychological wage. They were given public deference and titles of courtesy because they were white. They were admitted freely with all classes of white people to public functions, public parks, and the best schools. The police were drawn from their ranks, and the courts, dependent on their votes, treated them with such leniency as to encourage lawlessness. Their vote selected public officials, and while this had small effect upon the economic situation, it had great effect upon their personal treatment and the deference shown them. White schoolhouses were the best in the community, and conspicuously placed, and they cost anywhere from twice to ten times as much per capita as the colored schools. The newspapers specialized on news that flattered the poor whites and almost utterly ignored the Negro except in crime and ridicule.[126]

One of the more important components of White Privilege was developed by Professor Roderick Harrison of Howard University who concluded that "wealth is a measure of cumulative advantage or disadvantage" and "the fact that black and Hispanic wealth is a fraction of white wealth is proof of a history of discrimination. Dr. Harrison based his conclusion largely on a Pew study that showed the signifi-

---

126Du Bois, W. E. B. *Black Reconstruction in America, 1860–1880*. New York: Free Press, 1995 (reissue of 1935 original), pp. 700–701

cant disparity of wealth.[127]

The White Privilege aspect of critical race theory has advanced under the tutelage of academics, such as Cheryl Harris[128] and George Lipsitz.[129] Such scholars have asserted that "whiteness" has historically been treated as a form of property rather than as a racial characteristic. Whiteness became an object which possessed intrinsic value which must be protected by social and legal institutions. Laws and mores concerning race were designed to legally separate the different races. These laws have served the purpose of retaining certain advantages and privileges for Caucasians. Because of this, academic and societal ideas about race have tended to focus solely on the disadvantages suffered by racial minorities, overlooking the advantageous effects that accrue to whites.[130]

One important expose of white privilege was described through the lens of Peggy McIntosh's groundbreaking essay "White Privilege: Unpacking the Invisible Knapsack." Originally published in in magazine form in 1988, the essay helps readers recognize white privilege by making its effects personal and tangible. For many, white privilege was an invisible force that white people needed to recognize. It was being able to walk into a store and find that the main displays of shampoo and panty hose were catered toward white hair type and skin tone. It was being able to turn on the television and see people of your race widely represented. It was being able to move through life without being racially profiled or unfairly stereotyped. This idea of white privilege as unseen, unconscious advantages took hold. It became easy for people to interpret McIntosh's version of white privilege—fairly or not—as mostly a matter of cosmetics and inconvenience. Those interpretations overshadow the origins of white privilege, as well as its present-day ability to influence systemic decisions. They overshadow the fact that white privilege is both a legacy and a cause of racism. And they overshadow the words of many peo-

---

127 "Study Says White Families' Wealth Advantage Has Grown." *New York Times,* 18 October 2004. See "Study: Housing Bust Hit U.S. Minority Households Especially Hard" PBS NewsHour

128Harris, Cheryl I. "Whiteness as Property," *Harvard Law Review*. 106: 8 (1993), pp. 1709–95.

129 Lipsitz, George. *The Possessive Investment in Whiteness: How White People Profit From Identity Politics*. Philadelphia: Temple University Press, 2006.

130 See Lucal, Betsy. "Oppression and Privilege: Toward a Relational Conceptualization of Race," *Teaching Sociology*. 24: 3 (1996), pp. 245–55.

ple of color, who for decades recognized white privilege as the result of conscious acts and refused to separate it from historic inequities. She argued that whites are carefully taught not to recognize white privilege, just as males are taught not to recognize male privilege.[131]

Attacking white privilege became so fashionable, and was so used and abused, that it lost any real content. Labor historian Eric Arnesen reviewed books, journal articles, and academic papers purporting to be whiteness studies and produced in the 1990s, and found that the concept of whiteness was used so broadly during that time period that it served no useful purpose.[132]

As a part of his support of BLM's anti-white privilege campaign, President Joe Biden, as a part of his COVID-19 stimulus plan seeks to forgive agricultural loans made to farmers and ranchers who are black, native American, Hispanic, or Asian, but not to those who are white. A dairy farmer in Wisconsin who is physically disabled has sued the Biden administration over a COVID relief program, arguing the program is racist. Adam Faust, who runs a herd of 140 Holsteins on his family farm in Chilton, joined other plaintiffs in the lawsuit filed last week in Green Bay, alleging the loan forgiveness program illegally discriminates against them. At issue is the $4 billion program tucked into the Biden administration's proposed giveaway. The lawsuit argues that because plaintiffs are ineligible to even apply for the program solely due to their race, they have been denied the equal protection of the law. The U.S. Department of Agriculture issued a statement saying it was reviewing the lawsuit with the U.S. Department of Justice, but that the USDA plans to continue to offer loan forgiveness to 'socially disadvantaged' farmers.[133]

A more recent exponent of subtle white privilege is found in liberal racism. It manifests itself in various apparently harmless ways, such as: An individual assumes that any one minority individual represents an entire cultural/racial group. That assumption is usually combined with the belief that this individual/culture is "traditional."

---

131 "White Privilege: Unpacking the Invisible Knapsack" first appeared in *Peace and Freedom Magazine*, July/August, 1989, pp. 10-12. That article was a publication of the Women's International League for Peace and Freedom, Philadelphia, PA.

132 Arnesen, Eric, "Whiteness and the Historians' Imagination". *International Labor and Working-Class History*.60 (2001), pp. 3–32.

133 Griffith, Keith, "Wisconsin dairy farmer sues Biden admin over 'racist' relief plan," *Daily Mail*, 6 May 2021.

A person may assume that a single creative work represents an entire minority culture, or even to contain culture. Persons from a dominant culture assumes that minority groups or individuals can teach the dominant majority about the minority culture, while correcting the dominant person's mis-perceptions about persons of color. Thus, there is the expectation that indigenous representatives should teach people about all or specific indigenous cultures and histories. For example, liberals may hold the expectation that all black individuals should be able to teach non-blacks how to be anti-racist. Such liberal minded persons expect to receive affirmation from minority cultures that they are “not racist” or to “use” those in the less privileged position as proof that they are not racist. It is often stated in this way: "I have a friend who is _____ therefore...[134]

Criticism of perhaps unconscious liberal white privilege is said to occur in a variety of ways. Some liberals act as though persons of color are not there, in effect, making them invisible by ignoring them or refusing to recognize a person of color as a real American. Some well-intentioned liberals will refuse to engage in confrontational or challenging dialogue with people of color, presumably out of politeness, or perhaps because they feel that their potential opponents would be unworthy. Some have a fear of giving critical feedback to people of color. Others unrealistically deny obvious differences. Others feel comfortable around people of color who talk and act most like white people. A few will insult minorities by comparing perceived instances of oppression, thus denying or minimizing the impact of racism. Perhaps the most insulting is feigned color-blindness: “I don’t even think of you as black.” Similar is the espousing the liberal sentiment of “We’re all the same under the skin.”[135]

Background Thoughts

For many decades, historians have argued concerning the capture of Africans who were purchased in the thriving slave trade. Did European traders did, or did they not enslave anyone. One major assertion has been that Caucasians simply purchased Africans who had already been enslaved. Presumably, many such slaves might otherwise have been put to death for alleged crimes. Thus, apologists

---

134 Burton, M. G. *Never say Nigger again!: An Antiracism Guide for White Liberals*. Nashville, TN: James C. Winston Publishing, 1994.

135 Collins, M. *Responding to Diversity*. Muttart Foundation, 2006.

claimed, the slave trade actually saved lives. Are such claims represent a gross distortion of the facts? It certainly is true that some independent slave merchants did in fact stage raids on unprotected African villages and kidnap and enslave Africans.

Still, evidence points to most professional slave traders having set up bases along the west African coast where they purchased slaves from Africans. At one time, American history taught about the run-sugar-slave trade that thrived in colonial days. Merchants bought sugar with slaves, distilled that sugar into rum, and traded rum for more slaves. Rum was the key since, having obtained rum and consumed it, those who had traded slaves for rum wanted more on the next trip. But it would be a misnomer to assume that there were not other items bartered in the slave trade, for there were certain exchanges for firearms, lead, and gunpowder as well as and other goods, such as cloth, iron pots and pans, and knives.

Well before the end of the seventeenth century, England, France, Denmark, Holland, and Portugal all had established slave trading posts on the west African coast. Of course, there had been a slave trade within African tribes and nations prior to the arrival of Europeans. Brutal black-on-black slavery had been common in Africa for thousands of years because the phenomenon of enslavement extends back thousands of years, but not just among blacks, and not just in Africa, but among all peoples, as we have seen in earlier chapters. However, the substantial European demand for slaves caused a growing number of Africans to be enslaved by their own people, often because of petty debts or alleged criminal or religious offenses. Africans gathered even more slaves following raids on other tribes' villages. An increasing number of religious wars broke out with the goal of capturing slaves. European firearms and other weapons expedited the capture of slaves.[136]

Many black slaves were allowed to hold jobs outside the plantations. While it is true that in most of the American colonies slaves were not legally permitted to own property or businesses, they could earn money and often did so, to the extent that some slaves were able to purchase their own freedom as well as the freedom of family members. Slaves frequently learned trades, even such potentially danger-

---

136Mintz, Steven. *African-American Voices: A Documentary Reader, 1619-1877.* Wiley, 2009. See also Rodriguez, Junius P. *Historical Encyclopedia of World Slavery.* Santa Barbara: ABC-CLIO, 1997.

ous skills as gunsmithing.[137] In addition, free blacks owned slaves. Some free blacks bought and sold other black people, and did so at least since 1654, continuing to do so right through the Civil War. .[138]

Even the native aborigine were permitted to own black slaves in addition to the enslaved members of other Amerindian tribes who had been captured or purchased. On recent scholar placed the number of enslaved people held by Cherokees at around 600 at the beginning of the nineteenth century and around 1,500 at the time of their westward removal in 1838-9. Additionally, Creeks, Choctaws, and Chickasaws owned approximately 3,500 additional slaves at about the same time. In 1837, Cherokee Joseph Vann, expelled from his land in Georgia during the era of Amerindian removal, took with him at least 48 enslaved black people along with him to the Oklahoma Territory. By the 1840s, Vann was said to have owned hundreds of enslaved black laborers.[139] If an enslaved man had a child with a Native woman that child could inherit any slaves and their children.[140]

On the other hand, enslavement of the native aborigine was not uncommon at the beginning of European colonization in North America. In 1637, a group of male Pequot Indians, having risen up against English colonists in Connecticut and been defeated, were sold

---

137The earliest record of a black learning gunsmithing was on 5 July 1727, "Ordered that David James, a free Negro, be bound to Mr. James Isdel, who is to teach him to read ye Bible distinctly, also ye trade of a Gun Smith, that he carry him to ye Clerk's Office & take Indentures to that Purpose." in Virginia. In South Carolina, gunsmith Peter Francis Desverneys was granted the right to vote to vote following his heroic service to the Patriot cause in the American Revolution.

138African-American historian John Hope Franklin wrote "The majority of Negro owners of slaves had some personal interest in their property. . . . There were instances, however, in which free Negroes had a real economic interest in the institution of slavery and held slaves in order to improve their economic status." Franklin, John Hope. *An Illustrated History of Black Americans.* Time Life, 1970. See also Franklin, J. H. "The New Negro History," *Journal of Negro History*, 43 (1957).

139Krauthamer, Barbara. *Black Slaves, Indian Masters: Slavery, Emancipation, and Citizenship in the Native American South* . University of North Carolina Press, 2015.

140DKrauthamer, Barbara. *Black Slaves, Indian Masters: Slavery, Emancipation, and Citizenship in the Native American South* . University of North Carolina Press, 2015.avis, J. B., "Slavery in the Cherokee Nation," *Chronicles of Oklahoma,* 11: 4. (1993). See also Onion, Rebecca. "America's Other Original Sin," *Slate,* January 2016

to plantations in the West Indies in exchange for African slaves.[141] Since they were less troublesome, the tribe's women were enslaved in colonial homes in New England. In 1741, a band of Cree, Assiniboine, and Monsoni warriors, arrived in Montreal with a group of recently captured and enslaved Sioux Indians. The French colonists were delighted to purchase these slaves for use in domestic and agricultural labor.[142]

Instances of Amerindian enslavement in the Colonial period were illegal so no paper trail was left. But historians have offered a few estimates. Reportedly, thousands of Amerindians were enslaved in Colonial New England. Another historian claims that between 1670 and 1715, more native aborigine were exported into slavery through Charleston, South Carolina, than Africans were imported into South Carolina in the same time period. Another historian estimated that some two million to fout million Amerindians, from both the North and the South, may have been enslaved over the centuries that the practice prevailed. That is a much larger number than had previously been estimated, although it was not on the level of the African slave trade.[143]

Anti-Slave Thought in Early America

Contrary to assertions emanating from black militants, there was a strong undercurrent of anti-slavery thought in American history. Many Americans adopted the philosophical and ethical standards of the Enlightenment with its ideals of freedom and liberty. There also was a strong Christian objection to slavery, beginning with the Society of Friends (Quakers) and *Unis Fratram* (Moravians) who firmly believed that all men were equal before God. The Society of Friends produced the first statement against slavery in Colonial America, written in 1688. On 18 February 1688, Francis Daniel Pastorius of Germantown, Philadelphia County, Pennsylvania, drafted the *Germantown Quaker Petition Against Slavery*, a two-page condemnation of the practice of slavery. His congregation sent the document to the governing bodies of all Quaker churches with the intention of ending

---

141Newell, Margaret Ellen. *Brethren by Nature: New England Indians, Colonists, and the Origins of American Slavery*. Cornell University Press, 2016.

142Rushforth, Brett. *Bonds of Alliance: Indigenous and Atlantic Slaveries in New France.* University of North Carolina Press, 2014.

143 Reséndez, Andres. *The Other Slavery: The Uncovered Story of Indian Enslavement in America.* Mariner Books, 2017.

slavery within the Quaker community.

In founding Georgia, James E. Oglethorpe insisted that slavery was to be banned. The struggle between Georgia and South Carolina over the issue of slavery led to the first debates in the English Parliament over the issue of slavery between 1740 and 1742 .In the late 1700s, the same sentiments were voiced variously by the Methodists, Presbyterians, Evangelical Anglicans and Unitarians. Slavery was utterly wicked in the eyes of these Christians, a terrible stain on those who promoted it and on governments who permitted it. An important contribution was was John Wesley's *Thoughts on Slavery* (1774). Wesley had spent time in Georgia observing slavery first-hand.

The Society for the Relief of Free Negroes Unlawfully Held in Bondage became the Pennsylvania Abolition Society, the first American abolitionist organization, was formed on 14 April 1775, in Philadelphia, primarily by Quakers. The society suspended operations during the American Revolutionary War, but reorganized in 1784, with Benjamin Franklin as its president. In 1775 the well known pamphleteer of the Revolution, Thomas Paine, wrote *African Slavery in America*, urging its abolition.

In 1777, the territory of Vermont became the first polity in North America to prohibit slavery. While not actually freeing any slaves, the law required that slave-masters remove slaves from Vermont. The first state to begin a gradual abolition of slavery was Pennsylvania, in 1780. All of the other states north of Maryland began gradual abolition of slavery between 1781 and 1804, based on the Pennsylvania model and by 1804, all the Northern states had passed laws to abolish it. Some slaves continued in involuntary, unpaid "indentured servitude" for two more decades, and others were moved south and sold to new owners in slave states.

A new and well-researched article has advanced the theory that during the years immediately following the American Revolution, it was common for Southern elites to express concerns about the morality or long-term viability of slavery. This point has been made before, especially with regard to Thomas Jefferson and many of the other Virginia Founding Fathers and Patriots.

Thomas Jefferson had lamented the impact of slavery on the moral character of planters: "There must doubtless be an unhappy influence on the manners of our people produced by the existence of slavery among us. The whole commerce between master and slave is a perpetual exercise of the most boisterous passions, the most unre mitting despotism on the one part, and degrading submissions on the other."[144] Regarding slavery, in his *Notes on the State of Virginia* (1782), Jefferson wrote, "Indeed I tremble for my country when I reflect that God is just; that his justice cannot sleep forever..." In September 1814 Thomas Jefferson wrote to his friend to Thomas Cooper, "There is nothing I would not sacrifice to a practicable plan of abolishing every vestige of this moral and political depravity."

James Madison noted the tension between slavery and revolutionary ideals in a little known work, *Vices of the Political System of the United State*s, "Where slavery exists the republican Theory becomes still more fallacious."[145]

George Washington first stated concerns about slavery in economic terms. Later, he added moral objections. Washington condemned the slave economy for the agricultural depression of the revolutionary war period caused by soil exhaustion and overproduction of cash crops: "I never ride to my plantations without seeing something which makes me regret having continued so long in the ruinous mode of farming, which we are in." In 1786, Washington wrote, "I never mean (unless some particular circumstance should compel me to it) to possess another slave by purchase: it being among my first wishes to see some plan adopted by the legislature by which slavery in the Country may be abolished by slow, sure, & imperceptible degrees."[146]

In 1782, a new Virginia law loosened restrictions on freeing slaves, prompting a surge of manumissions by the state's slaveholders. Between 1780 and 1800, Virginia's free black population rose from about 3,000 to more than 20,000. To many it has been unclear, however, whether such expressions of anti-slavery sentiment were genuine, especially given the failure of so many slave owners to emancipate their slaves. The number of free blacks as a proportion of the black population in the upper South increased from less than 1 percent to nearly 10 percent between 1790 and 1810 as a result of voluntary manumission. Still, that "peculiar institution," as pro-slavers called it, remained solid in the South, and regional customs and social

---

144 Jefferson's Views on Slavery – Thomas Jefferson's Poplar Forest

145 Quoted in *The Papers of James Madison*. W. Hutchinson et al., eds. University of Chicago Press, 1962, 1: 257

146 Washington's Changing Views on Slavery · George Washington's Mount Vernon; See also W. W. Abbot , ed. *The Papers of George Washington, 19 May 1785-31 March 1786*. University Press of Virginia, 1994, volume 1.

beliefs evolved into a strident defense of slavery in response to the rise of a stronger anti-slavery stance in the North. In 1835 alone, abolitionists mailed over a million pieces of anti-slavery literature to the various Caucasians in the South

In a new paper, the authors show that there was a change in elite rhetoric about slavery, initiated by Whig politicians in the mid-1830s seeking a campaign issue in the South, in which anti-slavery rhetoric became linked to attempts by abolitionists to foment slave unrest, making anti-slavery an unsustainable position for the region's politicians. Before that development, the authors contend, some planters believed that slavery might some day be abolished for both humanitarian and economic reasons. After the growth of the abolition movement, the slavers abandoned most concerns. The current writers argue that the change in slave owners' beliefs about the probability of abolition in the mid-1830s should have been reflected in slave prices at auction and test that claim using evidence from the New Orleans auction market.[147]

According to one study, there were approximately 319,599 free blacks in the United States in 1830, meaning that approximately 13.7 per cent of the total black population in the United States was free. A significant number of these free blacks themselves owned of slaves. That study concluded that the census of 1830 included 3,775 free blacks owning 12,760 slaves. Indeed, free blacks could even buy and own the services of white indentured servants in Virginia. Free blacks owned slaves in Boston by 1724 and in Connecticut by 1783. The study also found that by 1790, 48 free blacks in Maryland owned 143 slaves.[148]

In the economic sphere, slavery imposed long-term costs in excess of the private returns. For example, slaves provided the labor on plantations, but in order to force them to work, plantation owners had to provide significant controls and oversight. Additionally, the states had to provide for slave patrols to prevent slave insurrections and someone had to bear the cost of hunting down fugitive slaves.

---

147 Grynaviski, Jeffrey D. and Michael Munger, "Did southerners favor slavery? Inferences from an analysis of prices in New Orleans, 1805–1860," *Public Choice,* 159: 3/4 (2014), pp. 341-361.

148Halliburton Jr., R., "Free Black Owners of Slaves: A Reappraisal of the Woodson Thesis," *South Carolina Historical Magazine,* 76: 3 (1975), pp. 129-42. See also Gates, Henry Louis, Jr. "Did Black People Own Slaves?" *The Root*, 4 March 2013.

The cost of policing became a major deterrent to slavery, which is why economists as early as Adam Smith considered that slaves would unavoidably be less efficient than free workers. Additionally, owners bore the costs of maintaining slaves who were disabled or too aged and infirm to work.[149] Slave owners provided cradle to the grave care, including whatever medical care there was, and care for the children. A recent study suggests that, since many costs were borne by the state, the annual subsidy for enslavement paid by all free citizens was at least one dollar.[150]

Just as slave owners had the ability to shape their laws, they had the ability to set the parameters of any discussion and, as such, possessed a strong advantage in imposing their preferred explanation and propositions. In a way, they increased the costs of holding an egalitarian ideology in ways which still persisted into the Reconstruction, and beyond. Slavery became a race issue rather than a labor issue, as distinctions between indentured or contract servitude and involuntary servitude were expanded. Some have argued that views on slavery, and the prevalence of slave-owning, appear to have shown sharp changes at "critical junctures," with increases in support for slavery appearing in times of social and political stress.

Whereas, in the early days of the American republic, slavery was seen as a necessary evil which would have, eventually, to be eradicated, this view gradually changed to encompass one in which slaves were considered lesser human beings who were not responsible enough to be free. The literature that supports perpetual slavery for some, especially African descendants, did not appear until after the emergence of abolitionist societies. Espoused by white politicians like John Caldwell Calhoun, and ultra-conservative writers, such as George Fitzhugh (1806-1881),[151] pro-slave advocates argued that, for the nation to survive, slavery must be supported, and slaves restrained. For whatever reasons, many Southerners changed their minds, and embraced slavery after about 1835.

Prior to the Civil War, intellectual elites, even in the North

149 Wright, Robert E. *The Poverty of Slavery: How Unfree Labor Pollutes the Economy*. New York: Palgrave Macmillan, 2017.

150Hummel, Jeffrey Rogers. "Deadweight Loss and the American Civil War: The Political Economy of Slavery," Ph.D. dissertation, University of Texas at Austin, 2001

151Fitzhugh, George. *Cannibals All! or, Slaves without Masters* (1857) has to be one of the most pessimistic studies of humankind ever written.

held pro-slavery views. Their defense of slavery forthrightly claimed that bondage ennobled the African natives. Politicians, clergy, and social critics claimed that slavery contributed to their economic development, Christianized their souls that otherwise would be damned, protected them from the perils of the jungle, brought them culture and civilization, assured them of daily nutritious meals, and generally contributed to their happiness.[152]

Black Privilege

A necessary, perhaps, popular assumption of Black Lives Matter is that people of color can not be racist because they lack power. Moreover, by definition, racism applies only to Caucasians and can not be attached to blacks/ Racism transcends prejudice because it is a system of advantage based on race and people of color do not have sufficient institutional power to oppress others. As with every other racist idea, the powerless defense underestimates black people and overestimates white people. Racism remains such a destructive force in American life.

Black privilege simply means that black people enjoy certain prerogatives and advantages that their Caucasian counterparts do not. As an example of a perk that blacks that he could not one can name a wide variety of things associated with black history: Black History Month, specific modules in educational course work that identify only black contributions; black cultural centers; and black textbooks. In America cannot even talk about whiteness. If ones attempts to embrace being white, one is immediately portrayed as being a racist. If we had a White History Month, that would be viewed as a racist.

The term is being deployed especially in conservative circles as a rhetorical counterattack to the growing use of the term "white privilege." It's part of a larger transformation. If one uses one of the several search engines on the net to locate the phrase "black privilege," and one steps into a universe where whites struggle daily against the indignities heaped upon them because of their skin color. There are books and articles which charge black privilege, such as *Black Skin Privilege and the American Dream,* and I*t's Past Time to Acknowledge Black Privilege*. White commentators describe how blackness has become such a "tremendous asset" that some whites are

152 Tise, L. E. *Proslavery: A History of the Defense of Slavery in America: 1701-1840.* University of Georgia Press, 1987.

now trying to "pass" as black. There is even a "Black Privilege Checklist" listing some of the perks blacks enjoy that whites cannot.

Black Privilege in Journalism

The *Wall Street Journal*, Associated Press and most other news outlets have begun capitalizing the "B" in black when describing people. The "w" in white will remain lower-cased, however, to make sure white folks remain properly chastised. "White privilege" indeed. The National Association of Black Journalists (NABJ) says "white" should be capitalized as well, and Fox News, CNN, and a few others say they will also do so. The remainder of the media, however, will capitalize only B in black. The Associated Press (AP) made the change to "B" on Juneteenth but only recently announced that "W" would not follow. In reporting on its own decision, the AP noted, "The AP said white people in general have much less shared history and culture, and don't have the experience of being discriminated against because of skin color." So the AP is going to discriminate against white people in news coverage to teach them a lesson. AP's vice president for standards, was almost explicit in saying so: "We agree that white people's skin color plays into systemic inequalities and injustices, and we want our journalism to robustly explore these problems. But capitalizing the term white, as is done by white supremacists, risks subtly conveying legitimacy to such beliefs."[153] To many conservatives, this is all part of the Marxist cultural revolution of identity politics.

Chicago Mayor Lori Lightfoot, a black woman, is in a permanent relationship with a Caucasian woman. Lightfoot's latest decision, that to exclude white journalists as much as possible, is most strangely, but thoroughly, racist. There is no other way to describe it. And "progressive" racism like that must be stamped out the same as any other strain. Lightfoot has decided she will discriminate against reporters based on skin color, only offering one-on-one interviews to nonwhite reporters. Her justification is that Chicago media outlets are too white, and so "in order to progress, we must change." But this isn't progress. Racism will never be progress. And there is no other way to describe Lightfoot's decision than that it is explicitly racist. It doesn't matter what kind of woke nonsense about "equity" you try to qualify this decision with. It is racism by any definition, boiling down

---

153 Jackson, Nate, "Black Privilege in the Media," *Patriot Post*, 21 July 2020.

the entire life and career accomplishments of every member of the Chicago media to their level of melanin. Moreover, this performative woke racism is designed to earn her progressive praise and drown out coverage of her abysmal leadership.[154]

While Mayor Lightfoot determines who is too white for her to talk to, the *Sun-Times* list of homicide victims lists 185 black victims, along with 23 Hispanics. The *Chicago Tribune* tracker states that 596 black people have been killed in Chicago in the last 365 days, along with 66 Hispanic victims. Lightfoot is a perfect representative of progressive racism. Pretend you care about equity by making a flashy show of discrimination while ignoring real issues in the communities for which you claim to be fighting. Instead of taking realistic steps to counter the catastrophic rise in the crime rate, Mayor Lightfoort has chosen to blame incipient racism which she calls a health problem and for which she is diverting $10 million in public funds. In response, Alderman Raymond Lopez, also a Democrat, described the violence plaguing the city's 15th Ward and beyond. He slammed Democratic Mayor Lori Lightfoot, whose law enforcement policies and focus on systemic racism are doing little to stop the mostly gang-related violence, prompting a vitriolic outburst from the mayor.[155]

Just because this kind of racism has become mainstream among progressives and leaders of the Democratic Party does not mean it should be shrugged off. It is still grotesque and anti-American and always will be. It is used not to achieve "equity" but to fuel hatred and division. This racial obsession views everyone as unthinking drones, products of one's racial group and little else. It's a primitive idea that has no place in a civilized society. Lightfoot's racism should be called what it is. She should be made to answer for it. And then she should be asked why it is that she is focused on the skin color of journalists while black and other nonwhite residents are being gunned down in record numbers in the streets of Chicago, under her watch.[156]

---

154 Vaki, Caroline, "Chicago mayor defends her decision to grant interviews exclusively to people of color," The Hill, 12 June 2021. Lightfoot bragged that she had started a "long overdue conversation about diversity in newsrooms in coverage."

155 Dowling, M., "Dem. Alderman says it's gangs, not racism, causing Chicago violence," *Independent Sentinel*, 20 June 2021.

156 Faria, Zachary, "'Progressive' racism is still racism, and it should not be tolerated or shrugged off," *Washington Examiner,* 18 May 2021.

Politically Correct Teaching

Political correctness is a term used to describe language, policies, or measures that are intended to avoid offense or disadvantage to members of particular groups in society. According to Merriam-Webster, the simple definition of "politically correct" is "agreeing with the idea that people should be careful to not use language or behave in a way that could offend a particular group of people." In public discourse and the media, the term is generally used as a pejorative with an implication that these policies are excessive or unwarranted. Since the late 1980s, the term has been used to describe a preference for inclusive language and avoidance of language or behavior that can be seen as excluding, marginalizing, or insulting to groups of people disadvantaged or discriminated against, particularly groups defined by ethnicity, sex, gender, or sexual orientation.[157]

More and more over recent years the term "politically correct" has seemingly taken on a life of its own, in part because of the emergence of social media. When someone says the wrong thing, intentionally or accidentally, the trial begins immediately in the court of public opinion, within the court room of Facebook, Twitter, Instagram or any of the dozens of other social media apps. We learn quickly to not be on the wrong side of a hashtag. On social media sites such as Twitter, hashtag is a word or phrase preceded by a hash or pound sign (#) and used to identify messages on a specific topic.

Political conservatives have rebelled against political correctness. Senator Ted Cruz exclaimed, "Political correctness is killing people." Dr. Ben Carson lamented, "And this is how they [the left] frighten people and get people to shut up, that is what the PC culture is all about, and it's destroying this nation." Many attribute Donald Trump's rise in popularity due to a backlash against PC language with several newspapers and magazines labeling it "Trumps War on Political Correctness." To many the concept of being politically correct, in and of itself is good. The question is whether the idea of not wanting to offend people has spun out of control.

Many charismatic and evangelical Christians have our own special version of political correctness and what constitutes offense, called "Biblically correct." According to that term, speech and press must correspond to specific interpretations of religious tradition. Mat-

157 "Political Correctness," in Wikipedia.

ters considered sinful in the Bible, such as homosexuality, cannot be handled in a way corresponding to secular correctness. In Biblical terms, marriage is a contractual arrangement, ordained by God, between a man and a woman only, so they would not allow for same-sex marriages. Abortion is not a woman's "right" but "murder of the yet to be born." One of the earliest substitutions of politically correct terms for those deemed offensive to at least a small group involved assigning dates for various events. Before Christ (BC) and Anno Domini (AD) have now become Before Common Era (BCE) and Common Era (CE) which have been deemed more appropriate and less offensive. It has been my experience that known and major publishers have returned my book manuscripts with the demand that I change BC and AD to BCE and CE. Because the word of God is unalterable and immutable, so it always was and always will be. Thus, their values will inevitably clash heavily with secular political correctness.

When teaching history one must set criteria regarding inclusion and exclusion, presentation of the subject as good or evil, and how to treat problems with moral lapses. If a supposed accomplishment is filled with, or based upon, demonstrable lies, should that per be ignored or exposed. Surely, one would not present Adolf Hitler and Joseph Stalin |objectively" without regard to the banality of their evil – or would one? Schools and other public institutions have long reacted against denial of the Holocaust which was directed against European Jewry. For whatever strange reason, there has not been similar outrage expressed over denial of other acts of genocide, such as happened in Turkey directed against the Armenian minority in 1915.

When one memorializes historic figures, must one demand that such persons have an absolutely clean (that is, politically correct) record? In my own experience, my beloved and esteemed colleagues denied emeritus status to a dedicated teacher and researcher because of his extracurricular "diving shows." Baseball has refused to induct into its Hall of Fame Pete Rose, who had more hits than any other player in major league history, because of his betting on the outcome of some sports contests. Should monuments be removed that honor Martin Luther King, Jr., who, according to Boston University, plagiarized portions of his doctoral dissertation. Late in 1987, a graduate student working on the project to publish the collected papers of Martin Luther King discovered that King had plagiarized huge parts of his doctoral dissertation. Clayborne Carson, the director of the project, decided to suppress this fact, thus setting in motion one of the most sordid tales of academic dishonesty and race-based special pleading in recent memory.[158] In nearly any other imaginable case, the university concerned would have revoked the degree.

While abuses against minorities have been real, and most have been stopped, some white Americans feel under attack as well. This has led to a conversation about whether "reverse racism" exists in America, and whether there is discrimination against white people from minorities. The idea of reverse racism is a highly divisive factor in American race relations, especially since many whites political correctness as having created a double standard. Over half of the US population says the language of others too easily offends Americans. In fact, 80% of Americans think that political correctness is a problem. Some say that the pervasive outrage against political correctness and many Americans' perceptions that their communication was being restricted by others helped usher in the Trump era, in which he resented and rejected political correctness. Some white Americans believe that a political correctness double standard exists, limiting what they can say though it is permissible for non-whites to reprimand the Caucasian race for past transgressions. This double standard can also exist in the cultural realm as well, with artists and entertainers being favored for their race rather for their talent. The result influences how society views racial interactions.[159] Racial tensions in America are high, and some white people feel under attack, that their voices to speak out have been limited, and that government policies favor minorities

Racial Disparity in Schools

How people explain the gaps in education that exist today among various racial and ethnic groups? When the Brookings Institution asked, "How much of the difference in test scores between white students and black students can be explained by discrimination against blacks or injustices in society?" Nearly half (44%) of respondents chose "None." Only 10% chose "A great deal." [160]

Black students are three times more likely to be suspended or expelled than their White peers, according to the U.S. Department of

---

158 "Boston U. Finds Plagiarism by Dr. King." *New York Times,* 11 October 1991.
159 Stutts, Jordan, "Des Reverse Racism Exist in America?" *The Perspective*, 2020.
160 The banality of racism in education (brookings.edu)

Education.[161] And in the American South, racial disparities in punitive discipline are even greater. A 2015 report from the University of Pennsylvania Center for the Study of Race and Equity in Education found that 13 Southern states (Alabama, Arkansas, Florida, Georgia, Kentucky, Louisiana, Mississippi, North Carolina, South Carolina, Tennessee, Texas, Virginia, and West Virginia) were responsible for 55% of the 1.2 million suspensions involving Black students nationwide. These states also accounted for 50% of expulsions involving Black students nationally, according to the report, titled "Disproportionate Impact of K-12 School Suspension and Expulsion on Black Students in southern States." The finding most indicative of racial bias is that in 84 Southern school districts, 100% of students suspended were Black.[162]

Pushing children out of class increases the chances that they will have contact with the criminal justice system.[163] A 2016 study published on children and suicide suggested that punitive discipline may be one of the reasons suicide rates among Black boys are rising.[164] Black third graders are half as likely as White third graders to paticipate in gifted and talented programs

The fundamental assumption is that the Amer education system is systemically racist in myriad ways. The racism shows in ways ranging from unequal funding for schools, to a school-to-prison pipeline which disproportionately affects students of color, to the fact that white women in education make up the majority of teachers, which can engender oppression against female students of color.[165]

Racial Equity in Education

The Virginia Department of Education is seeking to eliminate

161 "Data Snapshot: School Discipline." Civil Rights Data Collection. U.S. Department of Education Office for Civil Rights, Mar. 2014.

162 Smith, Edward J., and Shaun R. Harper. "Disproportionate Impact of K-12 School Suspension and Expulsion on Black Students in Southern States." University of Pennsylvania Center for the Study of Race and Equity in Education, 2015.

163 Raufu, Abiodun., "School-to-Prison Pipeline: Impact of School Discipline on African American Students." *Journal of Education & Social Policy,* 7: 1, (2017).

164 Sheftall, Arielle H., et al. "Suicide in Elementary School-Aged Children and Early Adolescents," *Pediatrics*, 138: 4 (2016),

165 Kendall, Mikki, "We Need To Talk About Racism In Education ," *The Establishment,* 21 December 2016.

its accelerated math programs below 11th grade, citing "equity" as one of the catalysts for its changes to the mathematics curriculum. The change was presented in early April 2021. As currently planned, this initiative would eliminate all math acceleration prior to eleventh grade. That is not an exaggeration, nor does there appear to be any discretion in how local districts implement this. As it stands now a spokesman for the Virginia Department of Education (VDOE), said: "We have students who take Algebra I in middle school and then move through Geometry, Algebra II, and advanced math courses in high school."

Staff in the Virginia Mathematics Pathway Initiative (VMPI) listed equity in math education as one of the reasons they are initiating changes. "Many children can and are finding success in the structures that exist in our schools. However, we must consider changes to support improving the learning opportunities for all students," said Jennifer Allard, a high school mathematics specialist at Fairfax County Public Schools. "Many of our students do not have access to the mathematics that they will need either in their personal or professional adult lives. The issue of inequity in mathematics education makes it essential for us to initiate serious discussions among a variety of stakeholders to achieve the critical mass necessary to catalyze change in school mathematics."

The new initiatives would take place during the 2025-2026 school year, after the next revision of mathematics standards of learning by the state Board of Education. "The initiative as currently proposed allows for student acceleration before the 11th grade and for the traditional sequence of courses leading to calculus and other advanced courses," a spokesman told the *Washington Examiner.* "The content of Algebra I, Geometry, and Algebra II would not be eliminated by VMPI. Rather, the content of these courses would be blended into a seamless progression of connected learning. This would encourage students to connect mathematical concepts and develop a deeper understanding of each concept within its context and relevance. And again, students would still be able to accelerate through the content based on their ability and achievement."[166]

Oregon's math teachers were urged to sign up for the "Pathway to Math Equity Micro-Course," created by the Oregon Depart-

166Soellner, Mica, "Virginia to drop advanced math courses before 11th grade, citing 'equity'" *Washington Examiner*, 23 April 2021.

ment of Education. The creators of the course argue that "White supremacy culture infiltrates math classrooms" because students are "required to 'show their work' in standardized, prescribed ways," and the "focus is only on getting the right answer."[167] Not to be outdone, the California Department of Education decided to follow Virginia's and Oregon's lead and eliminate the advanced 2021 mathematics framework. It made that decision to end accelerated math opportunities for gifted students due to racial disparities in "gifted" math programs. In California between 2004 and 2014, 32% of Asian American students were in gifted programs, compared with 8% of Caucasian students, 4% of black students, and 3% of Latino students. Because of this racial inequality there must be a new framework devised for teaching mathematics. In response to these apparent inequities, the framework recommends doing away with the accelerated math track the state's middle school students can currently choose. Under the current system, gifted math students could take both Math 7 and 8 in 7th grade, allowing them to take Algebra 1 in 8th grade. This track puts such students on a pathway to take Calculus by 12th grade, setting the stage for them to take more advanced math courses in college. The framework argues California's public schools should do away with grouping students by ability, instead "districts and schools must confront the structural inequities of tracking and ability grouping, and to strengthen their efforts to support all students learning along a common pathway."[168]

Alex Haley and the Plagiarism of *Roots*

Can a work that was clearly and admittedly plagiarized still be considered a useful teaching tool? Having determined that the literature in question was produced under the most devious circumstances, should it be kept or discarded? The case which we are considering transpired completely within a time frame which considered plagiarism to be absolutely wrong. *Roots* was reportedly written by Alex Haley. This was a most unusual case if only because the book had many positive cultural impacts which came into question once the plagiarism was revealed.

167McIntosh, David, "Parents sick of critical race theory and more need alternatives," Fox News, 4 June 2021.

168Lee, Michael, "California seeks end of advanced math courses in name of social justice," *Washington Examiner*, 5 May 2021.

The book related the story of an Africa who was captured by his own people, sold to slavers, and subsequently enslaved in the United States. The story follows the slave and his several descendants through generations. The fact that Haley related it as the true account of his ancestors from Gambia up until the present time made it a compelling historical narrative. The book made a huge impact. Many black Americans could relate to the story as what might have been the case with their own ancestors. In 1977 ABC turned it into a mini TV series, one the most watched television events of all time. During the year after it was published it made an impressive cultural impact and was widely discussed in the media and academically.

Almost immediately, Harold Courlander, then a 70-year old author from Bethesda, Maryland, contended there were substantial similarities between *Roots* and his own earlier novel, *The African* (1967). The greatest difference was between a story sold as being allegedly a true tale versus pure fiction with an historical background.

Courlander sued in Federal District Court in Manhattan for more than half the profits of *Roots*. As the trial was about to reach a climax with summations by the opposing lawyers, they issued the following statement: "The suit has been amicably settled out of court. Alex Haley acknowledges and regrets that various materials from *The African* by Harold Courlander found their way into his book *Roots*. Haley settled a lawsuit by acknowledging that his world-renowned book *Roots* (1976), along with its multi-episode television retelling, contained some material from a relatively unknown novel about slavery that was published nine years earlier. Haley had won a Pulitzer Prize for what he claimed to be a work of non-fiction. The last minute out-of-court settlement ended the six-week trial of a suit. Under the agreement to settle, the amount of money that will be paid to Mr. Courlander and his publisher, Crown, was not disclosed. But the nature of the case made it seem likely that the amount was substantial.[169] Later, there reports of a $650,000 settlement which Haley was forced to pay Courlander.

While there are some major differences between the two books, Courlander and several expert witnesses testified that Haley, at a minimum, had used *The African* as source material both for his 1976 book and the 1977 TV miniseries, which was seen by about 140

169 Lubasch, Arnold H., "Roots Plagiarism Suit is Settled," *New York Times,* 15 December 1978.

million viewers. Haley's plagiarism was quite evident. Moreover, the plagiarism case brought into focus Haley's claims that the book was a historical account of his own family's odyssey from Africa to the United States. The unfortunate result of this was that a story that gave valuable insights into the black slave experience was wholly discredited. Although the story was proven to be fictional and heavily plagiarized, it did play an important role in drawing cultural attention to the lives of descendants of slavery.[170]

Investigative journalist Philip Nobile writing in the *Village Voice* in the early 1990s did an expose of *Roots* and Haley. Nobile called it one of the great literary hoaxes of modern times. Nobile also exposed the fact that Haley had a ghost writer work with him on *Roots,* a *Playboy* magazine editor named Murray Fisher. In his article Nobile called Roots an elegant and complex work of fiction that was made up as the writers progressed. For example, the character whom Haley identified as his ancestor, the slave named Toby could not possibly have been Kunta Kinte. Toby was in America in 1762, years before the ship Haley claims abducted him arrived. Toby also could not have been Haley's ancestor, because he died eight years before Haley claims that Toby's daughter (and Haley's fictitious ancestor) Kizzy was born. [171]

The Story of Yakub

As taught by the Nation of Islam (NOI), Yakub was a black scientist who lived some 6,600 years ago. Using selective breeding (called grafting in this narrative) the scientist began the creation of the white race of people. Yakub performed his experiment on the island of Patmos, where the Biblical John had written the Book of Revelation. Nation of Islam theology equated that Yakub with the biblical Jacob.

In chapter ten, Malcolm also relates the myth of Wallace D. Fard, the founder of the Nation of Islam, who was supposedly a prophet of Allah, a divinity on earth. Fard was reportedly born in 1877 and disappeared mysteriously in 1934.[172] The story of Yakub originated in the writings of Wallace Fard Muhammad in his doctrinal work entitled *Lost Found Moslem Lesson No. 2*. A biographer ex-

---

170 Dugdale, John. "Roots of the Problem: the Controversial History of Alex Haley's Book," *The Guardian*, 9 February 2017,

171 "Roots of Alex Haley's Fraud, *New York Daily News*, 12 April 1998.

172 "Wallace D. Fard - American religious leader," in Encyclopedia Britannica. See also "Wallace D. Fard," in Wikipedia.

plained Fard's religious teaching:

> The black men in North America are not Negroes, but members of the lost tribe of Shabazz, stolen by traders from the Holy City of Mecca 379 years ago. The prophet came to America to find and to bring back to life his long lost brethren, from whom the Caucasians had taken away their language, their nation and their religion. Here in America they were living other than themselves. They must learn that they are the original people, noblest of the nations of the earth. The Caucasians are the colored people, since they have lost their original color. The original people must regain their religion, which is Islam, their language, which is Arabic, and their culture, which is astronomy and higher mathematics, especially calculus. They must live according to the law of Allah, avoiding all meat of 'poison animals', hogs, ducks, geese, possums and catfish. They must give up completely the use of stimulants, especially liquor. They must clean themselves up – both their bodies and their houses. If in this way they obeyed Allah, he would take them back to the Paradise from which they had been stolen – the Holy City of Mecca.[173]

Fard's successor Elijah Muhammad expanded upon, and further developed, this myth in several writings. Elijah's "The Making of Devil" chapter in his book *Message to the Blackman in America* is the most expansive version of the Yakub story.[174]

Malcolm X expended a large section of chapter ten in his auto biography[175] in relating *Yacub's History* which he accepted on faith as being absolutely true. his story relates the origins of man, who was black. The fall of man takes place when Yacub, an evil scientist, creates a race of white devils. These white men eventually seize power and enslave the black race. According to the myth, it was prophesied that in six thousand years, that is, in the twentieth century, the black race would rise up and regain control of the world.[176]

The major figure, Yakub, was said to have been born in Mecca at a time when thirty percent of the original people who were black were "dissatisfied." Yakub was a member of the Meccan branch of

---

173 Beynon, Erdmann Doane (1938). "The Voodoo Cult among Negro Migrants in Detroit," *American Journal of Sociology*. 43: 6 (1938), pp. 894–907 at 900-01.

174 Elijah Muhammad, *Message to the Blackman in America,* Elijah Muhammad Books, 1973.

175 Alex Haley, *The Autobiography of Malcolm X*, First Ballentine Books, 1992, p. 192

176 Malcolm X, Benjamin Karim. *The End of White World Supremacy: Four Speeches by Malcolm X*, Arcade Publishing, 1989, pp. 53–54.

the Tribe of Shabazz. He had acquired the nickname "big head", because of his unusually large head and his personal arrogant nature. At the age of six, he discovered the law of attraction and repulsion by playing with steel magnets. That insight led to a plan to create new people. He "saw an unlike human being, made to attract others, who could, with the knowledge of tricks and lies, rule the original black man."

By the time he was eighteen years old, Yakub had exhausted all knowledge available in the universities of Mecca. He then discovered that the "original black man" contained both a "black germ" and a "brown germ". With 59,999 followers, he traveled to an "isle in the Aegean Sea called Pelan," which Muhammad assures his readers was Patmos. He immediately established a despotic regime and set about breeding out the black traits. By murdering all dark colored babies, Yakub created a brown race which took two hundred years. Although Yakub died at the age of 152, his devoted followers carried on his work. After 600 years of practicing careful eugenics, Yakub's disciples created the white race was created. The brutal conditions of their creation determined the evil nature of the new race: "by lying to the black mother of the baby, this lie was born into the very nature of the white baby; and, murder for the black people was also born in them—or made by nature a liar and murderer."[177]

This new inferior race traveled to Mecca from whence they were exiled to West Asia [Europe], having been stripped of everything except their language. Allah took direct action to keep them out of Paradise. Soldiers[angels?] patrolled the border armed with swords, to prevent the devils from escaping. For many centuries they lived a barbaric life, surviving naked in caves and eating raw meat.

Eventually, Moses drew out of their caves and "taught them to wear clothes". Moses tried to civilize them, but eventually gave up and blew up three hundred of the most troublesome with dynamite. However, this devious race had learned to use "tricknology" to usurp political power and were thus able to enslave the black population. This dominant race brought the first slaves to America. According to *The Autobiography of Malcolm X*, all the races other than the black race were by-products of Yakub's eugenic experiments. Yakub created the "red, yellow and brown" races by "bleaching" them. The

177 Kambiz GhaneaBassiri, *Competing Visions of Islam in the United States*. Greenwood Publishing Group, 1997, pp. 146ff.

noble black race included Asian peoples, considered to be shared ancestors of the Moors. Whites" were the Europeans. Some of the new white race "tried to graft themselves back into the black nation, but they had nothing to go by." As a result, they became gorillas. "A few were lucky enough to make a start, and got as far as what you call the gorilla. In fact, all of the monkey family are from this 2,000 year history of the white race in Europe." According to NOI doctrine, Yakub's progeny were destined to rule for 6,000 years before the original black peoples of the world regained dominance, a process that had begun in 1914.[178]

In the concluding passage of his autobiography, written after his separation from the Nation of Islam, Malcolm criticizes this belief from the point-of-view of orthodox Islam, and he denounces Elijah Muhammad. This story still constitutes the central myth of the Black Muslim faith. The story has caused disputes within the NOI during its history. Under its current leader Louis Farrakhan, the NOI continues to assert that the story of Yakub is true, claiming that it is consistent with, and compatible with, modern history and science.[179]

College Meritocracy as Racism

Because standardized testing has failed to provide politically and racially desired results, it must be suspended according the a small, but highly vocal, group of academics and their supporters. Indeed, some education officials like Alison Collins, vice president of the San Francisco Board of Education, have declared meritocracy itself to be essentially racist.[180] Alison M. Collins is an American community activist, real estate consultant, and a former educator. Collins has served as one of seven elected commissioners on the San Francisco Board of Education since January 7, 2019. During her tenure, she came into national attention for changing the merit-based admission policy at Lowell High School. Additionally, she reportedly made racist comments about Asian-Americans in a series of tweets in 2016. She accused them of benefiting from, but not supporting, CRT.[181] The

---

178 Fardan, Dorothy Blake. *Yakub and the Origins of White Supremacy,* Lushena Books, 2001. Quotes are from *Yakub: The Father of Mankind.*

179 Gates, Henry Louis, "Farrakhan Speaks," *Transition: An International Review*, Summer 1996, pp. 140–167;

180 "San Francisco School Board Commissioner calls merit-based education "racist," sparking debate," *Newsweek*. 4 February 4, 2021.

181 Melendez, Lyanne and Larsen, Kate, "SFUSD Board Vice President Alison

tweets led to Collins being stripped of her title as Vice-President of the Board on March 25, 2021. Subsequently she filed an $87 million lawsuit against the school district and board on March 31, 2021.[182] Reportedly, she holds a master's degree in education from San Francisco State University. It has been reported that her father was one of the first black professors at UCLA. They demand that some other method to determine admissions must be found.

In early 2020 University of California President Janet Napolitano announced that the ten schools in the system will no longer base admissions on standardized tests, joining a "test-blind" admissions movement nationally. The problem is that when standardized tests are used it is possible to determine that someone with a high score has been passed over in favor of another person whose test score was inferior. Without standardized testing, it would be difficult to prove the weight given to race in admissions. Those seeking greater diversity in admissions have long opposed the use of standardized tests as disfavoring minority applicants, claiming that standardized tests are vehicles designed to maintain white supremacy.[183]

Dr. Napolitano created a Standardized Testing Task Force in 2019 to evaluate the use of standardized testing as the key to college admissions. Many anticipated that the task force would recommend the cessation of standardized testing. The task force did find that while 59 percent of high school graduates were Latino, black, persons of color, or Native American, only 37 percent were admitted to one or another of the California universities. Noteworthy is the fact that the Task Force did not find standardized testing to be unreliable or call for its abandonment, however.

It concluded that "test scores are currently better predictors of first-year GPA than high school grade point average, and were equally valid at predicting first-year retention, University GPA, and graduation. Moreover, the amount of variance in student outcomes explained by test scores has increased since 2007. The test scores are predictive for all demographic groups and disciplines. In fact, test scores are better predictors of success for students who are Underrep-

---

Collins apologizes for offensive tweets aimed at Asian Americans," ABC7 San Francisco, 24 March 2021.

182 Knight, Heather, "Alison Collins wants $87 million for damage to her career," *San Francisco Chronicle*, 8 May 2021.

183 "California Report Gives Boost to College Admissions Tests," https://www.usnews.com/news/education-news/ 5 February 2020.

resented Minority Students, who are first generation, or whose families are low-income. In short, test scores remain the best indicator for continued performance in college and thus were completely valid.[184]

The Task Force clearly had failed to produce the result which Dr. Napolitano and others wanted. The study, having failed to yield the fore-ordained and politically correct answer, left the critics of standardized testing with no alternative: they simply rejected the concept and announced a cessation of the use of such scores in admissions. The system will go from two years of "optional" testing to a "test-blind" system until or unless it develops its own test. It should be clear that ending standardized testing will have a notable impact on legal challenges to the use of race in college admissions.[185] Last November, Californians in referendum rejected a resolution to restore affirmative action in college admissions.

The California Task Force's report was buttressed by an Ivy League study. Reports indicate that significant differences remain on such scores, particularly for Asian students. *The Harvard Crimson* reported that "Asian-American applicants to Harvard earned an average SAT score of 726. White applicants earned an average score of 713, Native American and Native Hawaiian applicants an average score of 658, Hispanic American applicants a score of 650, and African American applicants a score of 622." Yet, during that same period, "Asian-Americans saw the lowest acceptance rate of any racial group."

In the earliest decision on affirmative action in education, the U. S. Supreme Court ruled that affirmative action was constitutional, but it invalidated the use of formal racial quotas. was a landmark decision by the Supreme Court of the United States. It upheld affirmative action, allowing race to be one of several factors in college admission policy. However, the court ruled that specific racial quotas, such as the 16 out of 100 seats set aside for minority students by the University of California, Davis School of Medicine, were impermissible.[186] The Supreme Court has issued a series of 5-4 decisions that have ruled both for and against such race criteria admissions, but

---

184 Gross-Sable, Eve, "Report recommends retention of UC standardized testing admissions requirement," *Daily Bruin*, 29 May 2001. See also Watanabe, Teresa, "SAT should be suspended for UC admissions, Napolitano says," *Los Angeles Times*, 11 May 2020.

185 Turley, Jonathan, "Will ending tests really end racism in college admissions?," The Hill, 29 May 2021.

186 *Regents of the University of California v. Bakke*, 438 U.S. 265 (1978),

even justices supporting such systems have expressed reservations. The author of the 2003 majority opinion in *Grutter v. Bollinger,*[187] Associate Justice Sandra Day O'Connor, said she expected "that 25 years from now, the use of racial preferences will no longer be necessary to further the interest approved today." Chief Justice Rehnquist, joined by Justice Scalia, Justice Kennedy, and Justice Thomas, argued the Law School's admissions policy was an attempt to achieve an unconstitutional type of racial balancing.[188] Outrage at the *Grutter* decision sparked a move to ban racial preference by amending the state constitution to disallow such affirmative action. In another landmark decision of the United States Supreme Court concerning affirmative action and race- and sex-based discrimination in public university admissions, in a 6-2 decision, the Court held that the Fourteenth Amendment's Equal Protection Clause does not prevent states from enacting bans on affirmative action in education.[189]

Results of Politically Correct Education

Governmental policies, largely resultant from political agendas advocated by vocal minorities, have put pressure on universities not to select the best candidates, normally thought of as those with the highest grades and the best scores on standardized tests, but instead to select the candidates from social backgrounds that fitted the government's preferred background' profile. Should there be an offspring of a lone parent who is a black lesbian with a wooden leg then that person advances to the top of the list. Conversely, the child bo rn to married parents who abide in a nice home with a new auto in the garage , there is likely to be little or no opportunities. Some medical and other professional schools are very alarmed by this silly policy and have asked why the country should not have the best possible candidates to be the physicians, lawyers, judges, and other professionals of tomor-

---

187 539 U.S. 306 (2003), *Grutter v. Bollinger* was a landmark case of the Supreme Court of the United States concerning affirmative action in student admissions. The Court held that a student admissions process that favors "underrepresented minority groups" does not violate the Fourteenth Amendment's Equal Protection Clause so long as it takes into account other factors evaluated on an individual basis for every applicant.

188 Devins, Neal, "Explaining Grutter v. Bollinger". *University of Pennsylvania Law Review.* 152: 1 (2003), pp. 347–383.

189 *Schuette v. Coalition to Defend Affirmative Action*, 572 U.S. 291 (2014),

row.

Politically correct educational system is betraying our children. Moreover, a politically correct syllabus is seeing them leave school in such an ignorant state that they are hopelessly ill equipped to cope in an adult world. One in four pupils leaves high schools functionally illiterate. Universities have found it necessary to offer remedial teaching in basic subjects. Some even actually award college credits for passing courses that teach what should have been learned before graduation. Colleges have found that some pupils who received, but evidently did not earn, four As cannot compete in introductory college level arithmetic. Like it or not, irrespective of legislation and angry protests, there will always be good schools and bad schools, and superior and inferior students, and traditionally it made great sense to select those with greatest intelligence to go to the the very schools.

Many modern educators assert that 50% of children should go to universities. Thus, watered down community college classes teach what should have been on tenth and eleventh grade syllabi. A lot of children are just enrolled meaningless degree courses, instead of difficult subjects such as mathematics or physics. College credit is actually awarded for sheer nonsense or for what are essentially vo-tech classes. And when the children leave such colleges, they find it difficult, if not impossible, to secure jobs in the subject area in which they graduated – or indeed any jobs at all. The only thing they have to show for the time spent at University is a huge debt.

Traditional teaching methods that were tried and tested over many years have been abandoned and replaced by the most recent politically correct ideas. New systems of learning have clearly failed to convey to students how to read, write and spell. Failed new curricula have left a generation of children severely handicapped to operate in civilized society. Teacher training, backed by the National Educational Association (NEA), along with its various state affiliates, seek to create and implement the latest methodologies, which do not stress the traditional output of increased academic skills. Rather, they seek to attain politically correct goals. Mathematical and spelling skills which were once honed by practicing them out loud have disappeared. Children have grown into adults totally relying upon calculators and spelling checkers to do this work for them. One of the primary reasons for all this stems from the idea that children must be socialized first. A politically incorrect child is far worse than an illiterate one. The object of reading Heather Has Two Mommies is not learning to read, bu t rather learning to accept a new lifestyle. If, in becoming politically correct, one also learns to read, it is just a desirable, but unnecessary, side effect.

It becomes far more important to inculcate the correct mental attitudes and settle politically correct thought patterns than to teach the basic subjects. Educational systems are the last place where freedom of speech and thought are protected. Expulsion is a penalty as frequently applied to wrong (politically incorrect) speech and acts than to what are traditionally considered wrongful acts. Normal penalties are frequently reinforced by adding the additional penalty of "hate crime." In clashes between traditional Scripture-based morality and the new politically acceptable standards, college students are taught to ignore tradition and become acceptably modern.

One reason the term "politically correct" is increasingly being used in our political discourse is because it is a formidable, and often highly successful, strategy to ridicule not only an idea but the person who communicates the idea. Moreover, the accusation deftly distracts from the content, kills civil debate and creates a delusional perception that the person engaging in "politically correct" discourse is honest, authentic and brave while the politically incorrect person is intolerant, prejudiced, weak, bigoted, cowardly and, at an absolute minimum, overly sensitive.

Denouncing someone as politically incorrect is also dangerous because it can become a subtle warning to those who point out offensive and biased language and/or behavior that they are overreacting and limiting others' so-called "free speech." There is the great risk that progress in our society will be stifled because some few are being overly sensitive. Thus, charges of bigotry and bias have the great potential to move society backwards. It is only when we remove the concept of political correctness from our conversations that we can approach people with the critical thinking skills and maturity necessary to hear opinions that we passionately disagree with. Must one, before speaking, not only verify the accuracy, but also consider if a listener might be offended? One wag stated it this way: You were correct in your answer, but I shall rule against you because one of your classmates was offended by your answer.

The term political incorrectness a way to dodge a question instead of answering directly. Political incorrectness has been employed by those who are opposed to, and especially fearful of, viewpoints they cannot refute. It goes without saying that no one of good sense would delve into what is truly politically or socially incorrect. We might consider three different but related issues. First, political correctness is used to describe the goals of those advocating a more pluralistic, multicultural, race-, gender-, and class-sensitive curriculum., and political incorrectness is defined as those who oppose such ideas. Second, certain ideas are branded politically incorrect for insisting that intellectual inquiry reflects, to some degree, the values and interests of the inquirer and that aesthetic judgments are always intertwined with moral and political ones. Third, people are frequently labeled politically incorrect for opposing policies designed to minimize sexual and racial harassment on campuses.

The English language was also considered to be full of male-dominating patterns which must be hunted down and utterly destroyed. Utterances like "Every teacher plans his lessons" once referred to teachers in general, and words with the stem "man" (e.g., mankind, chairman) were used to denote both sexes. Politically correct feminists pounced upon the nasty male chauvinism, criticizing these items as sexist. Thus, all patterns referring to men only were called "sexist, old-fashioned" and highly pejorative language. Sexist language was opposed by "modern nonsexist or inclusive language" that suggested gender equality and neutrality. Inclusive language suggested avoiding the use of male pronouns in the cases when the gender of a person is unknown. Utterances like "Every student has to pass his exams" were replaced by "All students have to pass their exams" which, of course, proved to be grammatically incorrect (singular every student, followed by plural their). Enter "Every student has to pass his or her exams." However, it would still be preferable to say " Every student has to pass their exams" which violates traditional rules of subject-verb agreement because it conforms to new rules of gender neutrality. General terms containing the segment man, such as mankind and man-made, were made inclusive by using synonyms such as humankind and artificial. Later, the names of jobs and occupations were revised to become gender neutral. There are other ways to avoid sex markers: flight attendant (replacing terms steward and stewardess), sales person (never salesman), police officer (not policeman) and chairperson or chair (not chairman). However, adding being seems to be carrying it a bit too far, as in chairbeing, salesbeing.[190]

The politically correct use of terms for races and ethnic groups is challenging. Many years ago I was completing a book with a major New York publisher and used the term "Amerindian" to describe the native aborigine of United States and Canada. The publisher was unfamiliar with that term, but after doing thorough research rewarded me amply for bring on the cutting edge of political correctness.

In my international law class we had a discussion regarding who bombed Pearl Harbor on 7 December 1941. After much discussion the class voted on Japanese, seeing other terms such as Japs, Nips, and even Niponese, as insulting. If one recalls television, Jerry Lewis, who I never found funny, just obnoxious, made a career of making fun of Orientals. In casting Mr. Moto the Japanese detective, Hollywood used make-up on Jewish star Peter Lorre. Likewise, in casting Charlie Chan the Chinese detective Hollywood chose, first Swedish Warner Oland, then another Caucasian Sidney Toler. There was always a bit of race baiting in these films. In casting the big budget *The Good Earth* (1937) Director Sidney Franklin chose Jewish Paul Muni as the lead and the infamous Hays Code then required his screen wife to also be Caucasian, so Franklin picked Louise Ranier. World War II brought the inevitable highly negative stereotyped Japanese soldier. In the John Wayne oater *El Dorado* (1966) James Caan insultingly mimics an Oriental.

It is politically correct, perhaps quite desirable, to say "persons of colored" but never "colored persons" despite the existence of the National Association for the Advancement of Colored People (NAACP). Likewise the once-correct term Negro, which still exists in United Negro College Fund, is nearly as insulting as the forbidden N-word. I found it necessary to do some fancy explaining when I taught about Marcus Garvy in my American political philosophy class, since he founded the United Negro Improvement Association (UNIA). In my graduate student days one heard "Afro-American" and, especially given my horrible hearing, it took me too long to realize that was out and the correct term was "African-American," a term I now hear far less frequently than a few years ago.

In *Gone With The Wind* (GWTW) in 1939 any of several insulting terms could have been used for the black characters. Instead, GWTW used "darkies" a term I have not heard for some time and re-

---

190 Zabotkina V. I. *New Lexis of Modern English*. Moscow: Vysshya Shkola, 1989.

ally do not know how acceptable it is currently. In a compulsory sensitivity training session at my university of employment, the training officer related that we must not use that term African-American with her since she hailed from Jamaica and it would be inappropriate, so one must call her black which was not at all descriptive of her color.

As we have seen, political correctness refers to language that avoids offending persons of various genders, races, sexual orientations, cultures, or social conditions. The most commonly stated goal of political correctness is the elimination of verbal discrimination and negative racial and ethnic stereotyping. The demand that people respond positively to political correctness has become ever more controversial as greater demands are made. In its extreme form, it has become the source of criticism and satire. It is clear that political correctness cannot change the underlying feelings that lead to discrimination and social marginalization. Political correctness is now one of the most common battlegrounds in the cultural and political war between American conservatives and liberals.

Consider this: one rarely, if ever, hears a white person use the forbidden N-word and a Caucasian is not even allowed to pronounce it in a conversation but one cannot watch a black comedian or listen to a black rapper without hearing the word constantly. It seems that some blacks, including some who complain most, use the N-word so often that it might just be the most used descriptive term in their vocabulary.

Distant Learning and Race

The latest ploy suggests that one way to avoid racial profiling and discrimination is to advance the cause of distant learning. The argument seems sound enough. Teachers who do not see students cannot act against them in some way attached to the student's race. The recent pandemic has provided a way to test that hypothesis. Students were isolated away from bullying and prejudiced classmates for a reason that even remotely had nothing to do with race. In early June 2021 the *New York Times* ran an op-ed opinion column by journalist RiShawn Biddle[191] arguing that remote learning in public schools should be extended as an option for students indefinitely, especially

191 Biddle, RiShawn, "Don't Kill Remote Learning. Black and Brown Families Need It," *New York Times,* 7 June 2021. See also his homepage, Welcome to the Home of RiShawn Biddle

because minorities were most in favor of it throughout 2020. Biddle, a black educator, is editor of Dropout Nation, self-described as the leading outlet covering and commenting on education and school reform. Biddle argued against announcements made by politicians such as the New York City mayor, Bill de Blasio, and Gov. Phil Murphy of New Jersey that remote learning will not be available for the next year are bad news for a majority of the country's black, Latino and Asian students and their parents who wish to keep virtual learning as an option. Eliminating remote learning, which many of these families support, exacerbates already-existing educational and health care inequities. New York City and other districts should figure out how to keep remote learning as an option.

What were the results of such isolation? The *Washington Post* reported in October that the achievement gap between white students and minority students in Washington, D.C., public schools significantly widened for the pandemic-time year. The early literacy data showed that the achievement gap between White students and students of color widened during the pandemic. At the beginning of the 2019-2020 academic year, forty-five percent of black students and seventy-three percent of white children in kindergarten through second grade who took the early literacy assessment met expectations. At the beginning of the current academic year, the number of black children who met the literacy benchmarks dropped by fourteen percentage points, to thirty-one percent. For White students, it dropped six percentage points, to sixty-seven percent. Latino students dropped twelve percentage points, from forty-two percent of students passing the exam to thirty percent.[192]

As with nearly all the latest so-called educational improvement schemes, it actually perpetuating the very problems which it claims to fix. In reality, remote learning has largely proven to be catastrophic for academic development and it was even worse for minority students. If it is systemic racism which has already putting minorities at a disadvantage, as Biddle claims, why would anyone want to exacerbate that problem with ineffective remote learning?

192 Scarry, Eddie, "If Democrats care about racial equity, they should make sure remote learning never happens again," *Washington Examiner*, 7 June 2021.

Cancel Culture

Cancel culture has become a social phenomenon which has been more widely written about, discussed, and argued over than any other socio-political topic. Everyone uses his own definition, contradicting others, causing confusion, arousing anger, inviting scorn, spawning moral outrage, and stifling debate. Some psychology researchers view cancel culture as synonymous with social media activism, but are loathe to fully explain the psychology behind it. Defining a concept carefully and delineating its domain and boundaries would seem to be an essential and indispensable early step in the study of any subject, but especially cancel culture, because a good definition provides the foundation for a shared understanding and brings one to clarity and insight.

Allowing for the ramifications of cancel culture on individuals and institutions it is imperative to seek a working and useful definition. As a beginning, we may view canceling as an individual's volitional act of publicly rejecting and actively pursuing harm against a perceived transgressor. There are two parties necessary to bring to fruition every canceling episode: the person who cancels and the entity, whether individual person, group, or organization which is to be canceled. Canceling requires the one who is engaged in canceling to follow three psychological processes: First, he must be able to identify, or at least become aware of, a transgression and then to decide that it is so significant that he must act. Second, he must experience strong negative emotions regarding the situation. Third, he must act in a punitive way to bring his idea of justice to the situation.[193]

The phrase cancel culture has existed for decades, the past several years has seen cancel culture become an increasingly politicized topic. Americans are deeply divided over the definition and meaning of the term. To many it means simply a method of withdrawing support for public figures or companies, something every consumer has an absolute right to do. Academics had discovered other distinct descriptions of the term cancel culture: First, people canceling anyone they disagree with; Second, consequences for those who have been challenged; Third, an attack on traditional American values; Fourth, "a way to call out issues like racism or sexism; and Fifth, a misrepresentation of people's actions.

---

193 Dholakia, Utpal, "What Is Cancel Culture?," *Psychology Today*, 27 July 2020

Some 150 academics, writers and activists, representing both the political Left and Right condemned cancel culture in a letter in *Harper's Magazine* in 2020. It was cited in a 2020 antitrust hearing by representative Jim Jordan who demanded to hear from each technology executive whether he believed cancel culture was good or bad.

The debate over cancel culture has intensified in recent months, including opinions expressed in the *New York Times*. That newspaper fired its editorial page editor after he published an op-ed opinion article authored by Sen. Tom Cotton (R-Ark.), which called on the military to respond to protests in the U.S. over racial equality The Times claimed that Cotton's article had prompted several people of color on the *Times*'s staff to say the piece put them in danger.[194]

Congressman. Jim Jordan (R-Ohio) gained national attention when he called cancel culture the "most dangerous thing happening in the country today." The Republican lawmaker had been angered by the Democrats stripping Representative Marjorie Taylor Greene (R-Ga.) of her House committee assignments in response to her allegedly politically incorrect and insensitive social media posts. Jordan said that "no one's condoning the remarks that she's made" but slammed any effort to hold her accountable. This action clearly constituted "the worst of cancel culture. If we don't stop it now, every single American is at risk, and that's what concerns me," he argued. The Republican House leadership has criticized Greene's rhetoric but stopped short of removing her from the committees she sits on.[195]

Cancel culture has become one of the most divisive terms in America, stoking a moral panic and even sparking calls from Republican lawmakers to make it illegal. Some conservative Republicans have argued that the cancel culture can destroy a person's career or reputation based on past events in which that person participated, or past statements that person has made, even if their beliefs or opinions have changed.

With the rise of social media, the #MeToo movement and recent reckonings on racism, many forms of accountability have been labeled as cancel culture. Some critics of such opinions say those defending cancel culture are merely upholding toxic power structures.

One vitriolic attack on cancel culture argued that cancel cul-

---

194 Associated Press, 22 July 2020.

195 Harvey, Josephine, " Cancel Culture 'Most Dangerous Thing' Happening Today," *Huff Post*, 4 February 2021. Fox News, 3 February 2021.

ture is actually great for America. It means that the self-important, self-indulgent, bloated, and buffoonish legacy media and legacy entertainment industries are imploding. They have reached the red giant phase. Out of ideas, out of fuel, they can do nothing but consume themselves, swelling with impotent rage until, one day in a flash, they collapse and become white dwarfs: lifeless reminders that a star once was there. It will be all over for them, but entertainment and culture in America will flourish.[196]

President Donald mentioned cancel culture during his Fourth of July speech at Mount Rushmore in 2020, calling it one of the left's "political weapons." He continued, "One of their political weapons is 'cancel culture' — driving people from their jobs, shaming dissenters, and demanding total submission from anyone who disagrees," he said. "This is the very definition of totalitarianism, and it is completely alien to our culture and our values, and it has absolutely no place in the United States of America."

Dethroning Politically Incorrect People

Two years after merging with the John Marshall Law School, the University of Illinois-Chicago announced it would be removing the name of the longest-serving chief justice of the United States due to Marshall's slave ownership and pro-slavery actions. On July 1,2021, the school's name will be changed from UIC John Marshall Law School to the University of Illinois Chicago School of Law. The vote to change the name was approved by the University of Illinois Board of Trustees, and the Legacy Law School Corporation and the Foundation Legacy Corporation, who were in charge of the school before its acquisition by the UIC.

The vote came after months of investigation by a task force which gathered input from students, faculty, staff and alumni in addition to conducting research on the proposed name change. This task force concluded, "Despite Chief Justice Marshall's legacy as one of the nation's most significant U.S. Supreme Court justices, the newly discovered research regarding his role as a slave trader, slave owner of hundreds of slaves, pro-slavery jurisprudence, and racist views render him a highly inappropriate namesake for the Law School."[197]

---

196 Gelernter, Dan, "Cancel Culture's Newest Victims," *American Greatness*, 9 March 2021.

197Klapper, Rebecca, "University of Illinois Removes Justice John Marshall's

John Marshall (1755-1835) was the fourth chief justice of the United States Supreme Court, and served from 1801 to 1835. He was noted for creating the principle of judicial review, previously only hinted at by Alexander Hamilton in the *Federalist Papers*. Judicial review is the principal check which the Supreme Court has in our system of checks and balances. This idea allows the highest federal court to strike down federal and state laws which had been formulated contrary to the constitution. Other important decisions deal with citizenship; established the supremacy of the federal government in dealing with the Amerindian tribes; defined the nature of contracts; that the Supreme Court could hear appeals from state courts in criminal lawsuits; and establishing the rule of *jus solis*, place of birth, rather than parentage. His decision in regard to interstate commerce allowed the high court much later to sustain the Civil Rights Act (1964). He clashed with President Andrew Jackson, who he regarded as a dangerous demagogue, over removal of the Native Americans their lands in Georgia, and regarding destruction of the national bank.

The statue of former Supreme Court Chief Justice Roger Brooke Taney remains in storage in Baltimore County with no immediate plans more than two years after it was removed from the State House in downtown Annapolis. The bronze statue, which had been placed outside the original front entrance to the State House in 1872 will remain, a part of the state's art collection until a decision is made on what to do with it. The statue of Taney was removed in the early morning hours of Aug. 18, 2017. It was one of many Confederate or pro-slavery statues removed across the country.

Maryland Gov. Larry Hogan who had previously supported keeping the Taney statue at the State House in 2015 had called removing monuments to the Confederacy "political correctness run amok." In response to political pressures, and in the name of political correctness, the governor changed his mind. "While we cannot hide from our history — nor should we — the time has come to make clear the difference between properly acknowledging our past and glorifying the darkest chapters of our history," Hogan said in a statement at the time. "With that in mind, I believe removing the Justice Roger B. Taney Statue from the State House grounds is the right thing to do, and we will ask the State House trust to take that action

---

Name From Law School Due to Slave Ownership," *Newsweek*, 25 May 2021.

immediately."[198]

Protesters were angry at Justice Taney because it was he who authored the infamous 1857 Dred Scott decision and ruled black Americans were not people under the U.S. Constitution, although that decision was perfectly sound law under the U.S. Constitution as it then existed. The Taney Court, second in importance in Supreme Court history to the John Marshall court, firmned up and firmly planted many of Marshall's rulings. decided cases in a variety of areas, with three major groups dominating his Court: the rights and responsibilities of corporations, (2) the legal status of slavery; and (3) the Commerce Clause of the U.S. Constitution. Taney's most important and lasting decision was the *Charles River Bridge* case was sustained Chief Justice John Marshall's decision in *Gibbon v Ogden,* explaining, defining and expanding federal control over interstate commerce. Scott v Sanford was his most controversial decision and that is what caused to row over the retention of his statue.

In 2015, the Roman Catholic Church declared that Junipero Serra (1713-1784) was a saint, which resulted vandals toppling statues and desecration of his gravesite at the Carmel Mission, where his remains are buried. In 2017, a statue of Serra in a park across the street from the San Fernando Mission was vandalized, with its hands painted red and the word "murderer" written across it. In 2018, Stanford University removed Junipero Serra's names from its university buildings. The Board of Supervisors of Ventura County, California, are planning to remove the likeness of Father Junipero Serra from the Ventura County seal. Serra was a Spanish priest who founded a mission in Ventura but who is accused by Native American groups of abusing their ancestors. Ventura had already removed Father Serra's statue, alleging that the Catholic missions Serra founded throughout California in the late 18th century abused Native Americans, including local Chumash. Serra defenders argued that the statue should remain, saying the allegations are unsubstantiated and that Serra frequently intervened with Spanish authorities in defense of Native Americans. The Ventura City Council decided last week to remove the statue, which was on public property outside City Hall, and put it

---

198 DuBose, Brooks, "Two years after its removal from Annapolis, Taney statue sits in storage," *Capital Gazette,* 30 September 2019. See also Brown, DeNeen L., "Removing a slavery defender's statue: Roger B. Taney wrote one of Supreme Court's worst rulings," Washington Post, 18 August 2017.

in storage with the ultimate goal of moving it to Mission San Buenaventura, one of the missions Serra founded.[199]

Black activists have been fighting to remove for years to remove the statue of Confederate General Robert E. Lee statue from Monument Avenue in Richmond. Critics of its removal used many arguments against its removal, beginning with the charge of erasing history to defend its presence. So protesters relied upon self-help and covered it with graffiti, turning it into a symbol of black protest.

We shall be looking at more cases of statue removal and especially desecration later in the text.

Book Boycott

The *Index Librorum Prohibitorum*, or *The List of Prohibited Books* was a publication delineating published works which were deemed heretical or which advanced ethical stances which were contrary to morality promulgated by the Roman Curia, and which books Catholics were forbidden to read without specific ecclesiastical permission. The first list of the kind was published in Catholic Netherlands in 1529 and other areas followed this example. Both Protestant and Catholic authorities reasoned that only control of the press, including a catalog of prohibited works, coordinated by ecclesiastic and governmental authorities could prevent the spread of heresy. Pope Paul IV, who reign as pope between 1555 and 1559, established the universal *Index of Prohibited Books* which banned thousands of book titles and blacklisted publications, including many of the works of Europe's greatest intellectuals. To be included, a publication had to be more than just theologically offensive; it had to be considered dangerous to the morality of the faithful or a direct challenge to the Church. The stated aim of the list was to protect the faith and morals of the faithful by preventing the reading of theologically, culturally, or politically disruptive books. The twentieth and final edition of the *Index* appeared in 1948. Pope Paul VI formally abolished the *Index* in 1966.

Modern society has now created a new Index, a list of books and other publications, and motion pictures, that are politically incorrect and are thus sexist or racist or somehow a threat in some other

---

199 Harris, Mike, "Controversial Serra statue removed from in front of Ventura City Hall early Thursday, *Ventura County Star*, 24 July 2020; Morrison, Seren, "Who Was Father Junipero Serra? Statues of California Missionary Removed," *Newsweek*, 22 June 2020.

way. Where the authority of popes was well established in Europe in the sixteenth century when the Roman Index was created, it is hard to determine by what recognized authority the politically incorrect index of the twenty-first century was created. Yet, in its own way, this modern index is every bit as powerful as was the Roman Index in its time.

Ebay will no longer list certain Dr. Seuss books, and the Dr. Seuss Foundation has decided to "recall" six titles. The man known as Dr. Seuss was born Theodor Seuss Geisel. He became one of the best-known authors in the world. He penned several beloved classics like *The Cat in the Hat, Green Eggs and Ham* and *How the Grinch Stole Christmas*. The two most popular of the six titles to be banned are 1950's *If I Ran the Zoo* and the 1937 book *And to Think That I Saw It on Mulberry Street,* which was the first children's book published under the Dr. Seuss name. *If I Ran the Zoo* follows a young boy imagining a hunting expedition to the fictional land of Zomba-ma-tant where locals "wear their eyes at a slant." Other pages also show the "African island of Yerka," featuring squat African tribesmen with large hoops through their noses. *And To Think That I Saw It On Mulberry Street* has its young protagonist imagining an increasingly fanciful street parade that includes "a Chinaman who eats with sticks," a "Rajah, with rubies" and two fur-clad figures being pulled by a reindeer. By 2015, over 650 million copies of his books have been sold worldwide.

Upon closer examination of Dr. Seuss it was unveiled that he had engaged in a long history of publishing racist and anti-Semitic work, going all the way back to the 1920s. As a student at Dartmouth College, Dr. Seuss once drew black boxers as gorillas and perpetuated Jewish stereotypes, according to a study published in the journal Research on *Diversity in Youth Literature*. That study, published in 2019, examined 50 books by Dr. Seuss and found that 43 out of the 45 non-white characters were depicted in an unfavorable or negatively stereotyped manner.[200]

Both a much beloved book and a highly successful television program, *Little House on the Prairie* (1935), penned by Laura Ingalls Wilder is now on the forbidden list. Running from 1974 through 1983, the televised version was highly rated and remains popular in re-runs. Although most historians consider it to show accurately life

---

200Watts, Amanda, and Leah Asmelash, "6 Dr. Seuss books won't be published anymore because they portray people in 'hurtful and wrong' ways," CNN, 3 March 2021.

on the Midwestern plains in the mid- to late nineteenth century, it has fallen under the politically correct axe because of its treatment of the Osage native aborigine. The fact that settlers and Amerindians really did interact as discussed in the book is immaterial.

Rudyard Kipling's books have made the forbidden list because of their strong emphasis on British racial and cultural superiority. The odyssey of *Kim* (1900), an Anglo-Irish lad, suggests that British colonialism just might have been a good thing. Kipling's *Jungle Book* has suffered a similar fate, partly because of guilt by association, and partly because of supposed racist underlying themes. The poem *Gunga Din* (1890) is the most hated of Kipling's works because of its racism despite the fact that, at the end, Kipling tells us that Din was a better man than he. The story was made into a first rate motion picture in 1939 with Ben Jaffe outstanding as Din.

One of the surprise entries on the politically incorrect list was William Styron's *The Confessions of Nat Turner*, who led a slave revolt in Southampton County, Virginia, in which some sixty whites were killed. Nat (1800-1831) was born on Benjamin Turner's plantation. Benjamin Turner allowed Nat to be instructed in reading, writing, and religion. He became a fiery, perhaps inspired, preacher who claimed God had chosen him to lead the other slaves from bondage. The militia gathered and quickly suppressed the insurrection. Fifty-six blacks were accused of participating in Nat Turner's rebellion and were executed. An additional 200 others were beaten, injured, maimed, or killed by angry mobs or white militias. Styron's book was a phenomenal success, winning a Pulitzer Prize for fiction and placing second on the list of the bestselling novels of 1967. Following immediately after its initial success, the book began drawing heavy criticism from African-American scholars and critics. Some black critics like Styron's portrait of Turner which they claimed depicted Nat as a bumbling would-be revolutionary. Some claimed Styron characterized the wealthy southern plantation owners much too kindly. Others disliked like his treatment of inter-racial sexual attraction. Protesters created an angry anthology, *William Styron's Nat Turner: Ten Black Writers Respond.* Nonetheless it has remained in print and is still recommended by less militant blacks.

Never as popular in the United States as in Western Europe, *Babar the Elephant* (1931), authored by Jean de Brunhoff was generally viewed as a sort of animals' rights story. Babar was a popular

French children's fictional character who first appeared in *L'Histoire de Babar*. Some writers, have argued that, although superficially delightful, the stories are politically and morally offensive for and were produced to justify French colonialist ideas. One must plow deep to find imperialist themes.

Crime and Punishment (1866) by Fyodor Dostoyevskii has been ranked by many critics as the greatest novel ever written, and, if not the absolute greatest, certainly it ranks in the top ten. Camouflaged by a mass of Christian theology and agonizing introspective thoughts, Dostoyevsky conveys dark nihilistic thoughts and messages and thus became the first politically incorrect author of modern times: Among many criticisms is one which asserts that committing a crime can alleviate self-doubt and obviate of the boredom of daily life. Despite criticism by petty reviewers, this novel is likely to live on as long as humans read classical literature.

Journey to the End of the Night (1932) by Louis-Ferdinand Céline is, correctly, the most controversial work on the politically incorrect list. Wholly nihilistic, it reflects a pessimistic view of the human condition in which suffering, old age and death are the only eternal truths. Life is miserable for the poor, futile for the rich, and hopes for human progress and happiness are illusory. To some reviewers, hate is a central theme of the novel. Man suffers from an original sin of malicious hatred, but there is no God to redeem him. Hate gives the characters their concrete, if illusory, reason for unhappiness. No single group or race is singled out so neither racism nor sexism is an issue. While it is not a pleasant novel, is that a sufficient reason to ban?

A recent book that has come under close scrutiny is Traveller, a narration by Robert E. Lee's horse. when Traveller hears men of the Old South cheering about going to war, the horse assumes that War is a place on the map, a destination somewhere up North where everything will be wonderful and glorious. When he finds himself surrounded by humans who are killing one another, he asks a veteran warhorse why they would do such a thing. There is no objection, of course, to an anti-war novel. The problem comes in the fact that it is generally favorable to General Lee who was fighting to keep African-Americans in chains. He was a traitor who tried to tear his own country apart. Some protesters are necessarily offended by the notion of Lee's life story could be the subject of a popular romance. After some considerable effort in degrading other books on Lee, attacking his statues, and attempting to remove his final resting place as a place of honor, suddenly a new threat to Cancel Culture has appeared on the market.

John Michael Crichton, M.D. (1942 – 2008) was an American author and filmmaker whose books have sold over 200 million copies worldwide, and over a dozen have been adapted into films. His literary works are usually within the science fiction displaying a great knowledge of high technology. He came under the Counter Culture's microscope when Crichton dared to attack the presumed science that underwrites the theory of global warming. He testified on the subject before Congress in 2005. His novel *State of Fear* not only attacked, but humiliated, so-called climate science. In this book, Dr Crichton rejects the notion that humans might be responsible for global warming, one of the mainstay beliefs of the political Left.

Irrespective on contents, should a book be banned simply because of the character its author? A book first offered as a true narrative, but later reclassified as fiction in 1991 because of evidence that the author had actually made up most of the story, *The Education of Little Tree*, tells the story of a boy who is orphaned at five and goes to live with his Cherokee grandparents, who instill in him a love of the land and of his Native American ancestors and their ways. Oprah Winfrey once recommended the book on her website and many libraries found ir a popular selection. Then it was revealed that the author, listed as Forrest Carter was actually Asa Earl Carter, a notorious racist and one-time leader of the Ku Klux Klan. Indeed, even for his time c.1925 to 1979, Carter's racism was horrifying. All of this makes it astounding that such a man could produce such a beautifully written novel that is a hymn to the idea that mankind should live in harmony with the natural world and the spirit world.

It is possible to bowdlerize some books considered politically and socially offensive. *Dr Dolittle* (1920), by Hugh Lofting has undergone corrective surgery, with its original derogatory terms for, and depiction of, certain ethnic groups, both in written form and in its illustration skillfully excised. Editions published in the United States sometimes had alterations made from the 1960s. The book went out--of-print in the 1970s despite the fact that in 1967 Hollywood had produced a highly popular film version using full color and significant production values, starring Rex Harrison in the title role. In 1986, to mark the centenary of Lofting's birth, new editions were published which had such passages rewritten or removed. Offending illustrations were either removed (and replaced with unpublished Lofting originals) or altered.

In most cases of book banning, the reporting on the subject is often too cowardly to tell us exactly what in these six books was offensive, but we are given to understand that they contained anti-wokeness. Banning the sale of books on a media such as eBay or Amazon carries with it implications of totalitarian tactics such as Nazi book burning. Does it really make much difference whether a book is destroyed or its sale is disallowed?

Politically Incorrect Movies

Turner Classic Movies (TCM) has decided to "reexamine" what it called some eighteen "troubling and problematic" films of the past. There is no question that blacks were depicted shamefully in many early moving pictures. For the most part, those with the nastiest characterizations would constitute no loss to moving picture history, many of which were produced at so-called Poverty Row studios with the cheapest possible production values. Some talented black actors, like Stepin Fetchit (Lincoln Theodore Monroe Andrew Perry) and Mantan Moreland, were cast in the most brutal possible and openly racist roles. There were very few parts available for black actors. Hattie McDaniel, probably the first black to sign on radio, for her part as a slave-servant in *Gone with the Wind* (1939) won her the Oscar for Best Supporting Actress, the first African American actress to win an Academy Award. In other movies she was cast in stereotyped roles.

Among TCM's questionable films are *My Fair Lady*, and *Psycho,* both of which are now considered deeply sexist or racist or both. *Gone with the Wind*, along with several other high quality movies, such as *Band on Angels*, raise some questions although they generally accurately depict a real historical period. Most odd of all on TCM's lits is *Guess Who's Coming to Dinner*, which is explicitly and aggressively anti-racist and certainly was bold and brave for its day.

The fact that TCM's list encompasses only eighteen movies shows how little the woke brigade knows about movies. One can consider more than 200 movies that the modern Left would find offensive for one reason or another: Women in traditional roles, some of whom seem to be even happy about their condition; mockery of other and diverse cultures; treatment of non-white races and minorities as inferior;

and mockery of other beliefs and opinions. The situation of blackface routines, such as Fred Astaire's extraordinary homage to the African American dancer Bill Robinson, require review and study.[201]

Gone with the Wind was one of several motion pictures that correctly and accurately depicted the Civil War era in the the American South. Another memorable movie that pointed out most brutally the hypocrisy of many Northerners was *Band on Angels* (1957) filmed with the same high production values as *Gone with the Wind*. Should these and similar films be destroyed? Or shown only after an intense politically correct introduction? Had GWTW been written by a man, it might be ranked alongside *The Red Badge of Courage* as one of the greatest American war novels. However, having been written by a woman, it has generally been categorized as a romance novel.

Disney some years ago removed *Song of the South* (1946) from the American market. The kindly story-teller Uncle Remus tells a young boy stories about trickster Br'er Rabbit, who outwits Br'er Fox and slow-witted Br'er Bear. Many consider the performance of James Basket (1904-1948), who appeared 40 years older than his character, to have been extraordinary, and was certainly the highlight of his otherwise undistinguished career. Beautifully combining animated with live characters, it was a retelling of tales from Joel Chandler Harris (1848-1908), a Caucasian, born in utter in utter poverty who published his first collection of folk poems and proverbs in 1881, featuring a black folk tale artist, Uncle Remus. Br'er r Rabbit was the black man who, although far less powerful, regularly outwitted Br'er Fox and Br'er Bear, representing whites. Presumably because the white owned the poor cabin Uncle Remus lived in and did order him to leave, the film was condemned a s racist. It ignored the triumphs of Br'er Rabbit (blacks) and the fact that the children deeply loved Uncle Remus who taught them much which their white parents had not. It also taught a lesson of friendship among rich white children, black youngsters, and impoverished Caucasian kids.

The Love Guru (2008) is frequently ranked as the single most offensive (politically and socially offensive) movie ever made. Hindus are the object of many jabs. The American Hindu community asked to to view the film prior to its general release; Paramount agreed, but reneged. Pretending to be an American buddy comedy

---

201 Gelernter, Dan, "Cancel Culture's Newest Victims," *American Greatness*, 9 March 2021.

film, directed by Marco Schnabel in his directorial debut, and written and produced by Mike Myers, the film was a financial flop and was universally panned by critics. Rotten Tomatoes gave the film an approval rating of 14%, based on 174 reviews, with an average rating of 3.32 out of 10. The film did poorly at the box office, grossing a total of $40.8 million worldwide, against its $62 million budget. It is frequently seen on television. It seems to be utterly without redeeming artistic merit and the racially based humor is wholly misplaced.

Often noted as the second most offensive modern film, *Soul Man* (1986) was an American comedy directed by Steve Miner and written by Carol L. Black. A Caucasian, played by C. Thomas Howell, who cannot afford to attend Harvard Law School after being cut off by his rich father decides to overdose himself on tanning pills so as to be able to apply for a scholarship reserved for African American students. This could well have been a film that attacked the prejudices that black students in the United States faced in the 80s (and still face today), and it does scratch the surface of the debate at times, as Mark Watson discovers that his fellow students are less lenient than he imagined when it comes to accepting African Americans at the school. The film became embroiled in controversy due to depicting a white actor in blackface, prompting protests against its release. Presumably, it was designed to parody the granting of financial aid on account of race rather than academic qualifications. Despite the controversy and negative reviews from critics, *Soul Man* was a commercial success, grossing $35 million on a minuscule $4.5 million budget. The film centers around the single allegedly humorous racial situation. Soime supporters asserted that the film was rather innocuous and had attracted negative attention only because black film director Spike Lee, who admittedly never saw the film, made an issue of the racism, which actually many viewed as anti-racism.

Breakfast at Tiffany's (1961) starred darling Audrey Hepburn so all must be correct, right? Mickey Rooney's portrayal of Japanese man Mr Yunioshi is fully blown racist. Decked out with ridiculous buckteeth, Rooney's cringe-worthy, stereotypical performance as Yunioshi really would have offended had it been played by an Asian actor, never mind a white man with yellow-face makeup. Despite the scene being brought to the attention of the modern media in 1993, Rooney maintains that people loved Mr Yunioshi. Honorable mention here goes to Jerry Lewis (Joe Levitz, Jr.) for his frequent nasty characterization of orientals.

There were, and are, films that genuinely offend. Forced racial "humor" has frequently been a trademark of Hollywood. Bottom line is: should Americans emulate totalitarian states such as Hitler's Nazi Germany and burn the offending materials? One answer is that much, if not all, of what Hitler reveled in destroying was true art and should have been preserved whereas there is genuine trash that should be destroyed being based on lies and prejudices. My own first choice for destruction is *Mission to Moscow* (1943) based on Ambassador Joseph E. Davies' memoirs, directed by first line director Michael Curtiz, and starring Walter Huston and Ann Harding. The movie relates how the great Stalin, with the noble assistance of "great humanitarians" Litvinov, Vyshinsky, and Molotov, all so much brighter than Franklin Roosevelt, have advanced Russia to the greatest possible heights despite sabotage and opposition from totalitarian Trotsky.

Survey Results

In September 2020, Pew Research Center undertook a major survey to reveal how many Americans feel about the term cancel culture. It began with an assumption that cancel culture had considerable power to hold people accountable. According to the Pew Research Center, which released the findings, it had conducted a survey of more than 10,000 US adults. The survey asked respondents to define cancel culture in their own words. It found many were confused or uncertain about its meaning and application. Despite its dominance in national discourse, a large number of respondents said they are not familiar with the issue. A majority – 56% – of those responding say they have heard little or not too much about cancel culture, including 38% who have heard nothing at all about it.

Familiarity with the term varies with age. While 64% of adults under 30 say they have heard a great deal or fair amount about cancel culture, that share drops to 46% among those ages 30 to 49 and 34% among those 50 and older. Overall, 44% of Americans say they have heard at least a fair amount about the phrase, including 22% who have heard "a great deal".

Pew also surveyed people for their broader thoughts on the act of calling out others on social media, asking whether this kind of behavior is more likely to hold people accountable or punish those who do not deserve it. More than half – 58% of US adults – say in general calling out others on social media is more likely to hold people accountable, while only 38% say it is more likely to punish people who don't deserve it.[202]

In another poll, this one conducted by Politico/Morning Consult 46 percent of registered voters surveyed agreed that cancel culture "has gone too far," while 10 percent said it has not gone far enough. Another 18 percent said it has neither gone too far nor not far enough, and slightly more than a quarter of respondents, 26 percent, said they didn't know or didn't have an opinion.

This survey offered a rather standard definition of cancel culture using dictionary.com's definition: "the practice of withdrawing support for (or canceling) public figures and companies after they have done or said something considered objectionable or offensive."

Nearly half of respondents, 49 percent, said they believe cancel culture has had a negative effect on society, while 27 percent said they think it has had a positive impact. Forty percent responded that they have participated in cancel culture, and about one in ten respondents said they participate in it "often."

Political party affiliation had much to do with responses. About half of Democrats and a third of Republicans reported that they shared their disapproval of a public figure on social media after the figure did something controversial. Age played a factor, according to the poll, with those belonging to Gen Z and Millennials being most-likely to approve of cancel culture, while Gen Xers and Baby Boomers were more likely to disapprove.

A total of 55 percent of voters ages 18 to 34 reported participating in cancel culture, while 32 percent of voters over 65 said the same. Respondents' disapproval of a public figure also depended on when their public statements were made. For those from a year ago, 54 percent said a controversial statement would "completely" or "somewhat" change their opinion of the individual, while 29 percent said it would "change a little bit" or "not change at all." For statements from 15 years ago or more, that breakdown flipped: 26 percent said the statement would "completely" or "somewhat" change their opinion, while 53 percent reported it would "change a little bit" or "not change at all." The poll surveyed 1,991 registered voters between

---

202 Paul, Kari, "Survey of 10,000 Americans reveals what adults think of 'cancel culture'," *The Guardian,* 18 May 2021.

July 17 and 19. The margin of error amounted to 2 percentage points.[203]

Despite its association with social justice movements, social canceling is agnostic to political affiliation, ideology, or another property. Nor is it limited to celebrities or well-known companies, or to certain forms of perceived transgressions. Anyone can cancel, and anyone can be canceled for any reason as long as enough people think that the target has transgressed and they are willing to act punitively on their beliefs.

Cancel culture is never based upon a balanced assessment of the transgression or any absolute criterion of wrongdoing. Rather, cancel culture is a visceral response which relies on one particular shared understanding of the transgression filtered through the lens of a political or a social ideology. It sees only one side of the story, and does not seek to comprehend opposing or contrarian viewpoints. Thus, every canceling campaign is necessarily grounded in some type of bias. The lack of tolerance for opposing views, the restriction of free speech by coercion or censorship, and the disproportionate punishment given to the canceled entity are separate processes, marshaled in support of punitive action. They may influence how the social canceling process unfolds and its outcomes, but more often than not, they are environmental factors that vary from one instance to the next.[204]

---

203 Coleman, Justine, "Poll: Plurality of voters say 'cancel culture' has 'gone too far'," The Hill, 22 July 2020.

204 Dholakia, Utpal, "What Is Cancel Culture?," *Psychology Today*, 27 July 2020

Reparations for Enslavement

Reparations for slavery is the application of the concept of reparations to victims of slavery and/or their descendants. There are concepts for reparations in legal philosophy and reparations in transitional justice. Throughout history reparations for slavery have been both given by legal ruling in court and/or given voluntarily by individuals and institutions. Reparations can take numerous forms, including: individual monetary payments, settlements, scholarships, waiving of fees, and systemic initiatives to offset injustices, land-based compensation related to independence, apologies and acknowledgments of the injustices, token measures, such as naming a building after someone, or the removal of monuments and renaming of streets that honor slave owners and defenders of slavery.[205]

BLM and their allies argue that, so evil was slavery, that it established political and economic structures which created deleterious effects which have lasted to this day, and will continue to have such negative impact into the foreseeable future. Some of the harmful effects can evidently be eradicated by cash payments to descendants of the original slaves.

Demands for reparations reach into the trillions of dollars. Some advocates favor direct cash payments by the U.S. government to blacks, while others favor support for organizations and other initiatives aimed at assisting blacks. Activist lawyer Dr. Robert Brock, for example, wants the government to pay $500,000 to every slave descendant. Given that the large majority of the 35 million African Americans have a slave ancestor, that would amount to more than $15 trillion and require a surtax of roughly $50,000 on each non-African American man, woman and child in this country. The median family income is not even that high. One estimate, cited in a Harper's magazine article, puts the reparations total at $97 trillion, based on 222,505,049 hours of forced labor between 1619 and 1865, "compounded at 6% interest through 1993."[206]

205Alfred L. Brophy, The Cultural War over Reparations for Slavery, *DePaul Law Review* 53 *2004) pp. 1181-1213. See also Coates, Ta-Nehisi, "The Case for Reparations," *The Atlantic*, 1 June 2014.

206 Parker, Jay, "Reparations or Rip Off?" Issues & Views, www.issues-views.-com/index. php?print=1&article=2005

Reparation Payments for Historic Enslavement

Maureen E. Ruprecht Fadem, who teaches English at Kingsborough Community College, part of the City University of New York (CUNY), describes herself as a scholar-activist whose work centers around colonialism, empire, race, racism and the residual impact of slavery. She wrote her recent book[207] to provoke a reckoning with the ways enslavement has tainted race relations in the U.S. and calls for reparations to repair the emotional, social and political damage it has caused. Such reparations, Fadem argues, would be the logical culmination of Morrison's literary campaign. Fadem, following Morrison's lead, argues that reparations for slavery are an essential component of making the U.S. more equitable. It is also the only acceptable method of eradicating the brutal slave past. Her argument utilizes Toni Morrison's 1987 novel, *Beloved,* to highlight the necessity of grappling with the brutality of "that peculiar institution," as slavery was once known. Both support monetary reparations for those whose genealogies include enslaved fore-parents as a foundational first step, but also advocates the building of monuments to pay homage to those forced into servitude.[208]

What Morrison laid out in fiction had been outlined much more fully in a non-fictional work by Boris Bittker.[209] That case was challenged by William L. Banks who argued that disapproval of black reparation does not mean approval of racism. Slavery, with its cruelty, disregard for human dignity, rape and murder, remains a stain on the character of America. But no monetary compensation can nullify the fact, history, or banality of slavery. Banks argued from a strongly fundamentalist religious perspective that the God of the Bible is no respecter of persons, no receiver of faces or races.[210] In turn, Larry J. Perodin responded, making his acse for such reparations. Why, he asked, were reparations denied ex-slaves in 1865 by the government? Rather the day slavery ended segregation became the new norm for Blacks. Keep them separate, put them on an island. Through the years reparations have been vaguely talked about and skirted around as if

207Ruprecht Fadem, Maureen. *Objects and Intertexts in Toni Morrison's Beloved.* Routledge, 2021.

208Bader, Eleanor J., "Making the Case for Slavery Reparations," *MS Magazine*, 21 February 2021.

209Bittker, Boris. *The Case for Black Reparations*. Beacon Press, 2003.

210Banks, William L. The Case Against Black Reparation. Infinity Publishing, 2013.

not necessary. Are reparations needed? Today the conditions of Black communities makes plain something is needed. Black Man Island contends the violence, lack of education, poor medical care, lack of good paying jobs are symptoms of the dire need for reparations. He challenged America to answer the call to nullify the effects of slaver by awarding reparations.[211]

Black Congresswoman Sheila Jackson Lee, in 2021 authored the reparations bill known as H.R. 40, arguing that no level of opposition to it would discourage the quest. Lee's bill has support from many Democrats, including House of Representatives Speaker Pelosi Vice-president Harris, and President Joe Biden. As a first step to making the country pay for its racist past, many Democrats want to establish a Congressional commission to examine slavery and discrimination dating as far back as 1619. After thorough consideration, the commission is expected to recommend appropriate remedies, one of which will likely be monetary compensation.[212] There is stiff opposition from Republicans.

Robert Johnson, founder of Black Entertainment Television, is one of the most outspoken proponents of reparation payments. He has argued that America must atone for its slaver past and continued systemic racism by paying African-Americans reparations to make them economically equal to white Americans. Johnson, the first black billionaire in the United States, has put a price tag on the debt America owes to African-Americans at $14 trillion. "Nobody talks about cash, but black people understand cash," Johnson told Fox News. Under his proposal, an estimated 40 million African-Americans would each receive $350,000 in direct cash payments, payable over 30 years and costing the average taxpayer roughly $2,900 a year. The $350,000 would signify the wealth disparity between African-Americans and white Americans, according to Johnson. "Slavery, Jim Crow laws and racial discrimination were a wealth transfer from African Americans to white people. It's time to make amends and give it back."[213]

211Perodin, Larry J. *Black Man Island: The Case for Reparations*. London: Future Now, 2020.

212"Biden Supports Payment of Slavery Reparations for Blacks,"*The Herald*, 26 February 2021. The same story appeared in the *New York Times* and *Washington Post*, along with other major and minor newspapers.

213New York Times, 5 June 2020. See also Schultz, Marisa, "Robert Johnson's Big Idea: $14 trillion in slavery reparations to African-Americans," *Fox News The Big Idea*, 26 June 202o.

Reparations in Theory

As with all movements, there must have been some collaborating justification offered, usually by academic and intellectual critics. Such was the case for reparations for enslavement. Some of the more important supporters from the nation's higher educational system include the following individuals.

Charles James Ogletree Jr. (1952---) is an American attorney and law professor who is currently the Jesse Climenko Professor at Harvard Law School, the founder of the school's Charles Hamilton Houston Institute for Race and Justice, and the author of numerous books on legal topics. He is co-chairman of the Reparations Coordinating Committee (RCC). Founded in December 2000, the Reparations Coordinating Committee and originally called the Reparations Assessment Group, this organization has attempted to obtain reparations through litigation. The organization consists of prominent lawyers, academics and authors. Responding to RCC, in 2001 the Center for the Study of Popular Culture, through its president David Horowitz, attempted to purchase advertising in various student newspapers around the country. Entitled "10 Reasons Why Reparations for Slavery is a Bad Idea—and Racist, Too" most newspapers refused to print it. Of the 71 newspapers to which the advertoisement was submitted, only 28 printed it.

Ogletree, who writes extensively on the issue, is one of the key figures in helping to galvanize the modern movement for reparations. In 2004 Harvard disciplined Ogletree for the plagiarism of six paragraphs from Yale scholar Jack Balkin's book, *What Brown v. Board of Education Should Have Said* which he used in his own book, *All Deliberate Speed: Reflec*tions *on the First Half-Century of Brown v. Board of Education.*[214] He has appeared as a commentator on such programs as Nightline and Meet the Press. A prominent legal theorist, he has made a reputation in taking a hard look at complex constitutional issues of law and in criminal justice issues

Randall Robinson (1941---) is co-chairman of the Reparations Coordinating Committee (RCC) and former president of TransAfrica Forum, which lobbies on U.S. foreign policy issues affecting Africa and the Caribbean. He first came to national attention when he began organizing sit-ins at the South African embassy in Washington, D.C.,

---

214 "Charles Ogletree" in Wikipedia; Mineo, Liz. "Honoring Charles Ogletree". *The Harvard Gazette,* 3 October 2017.

protesting against the Afrikaner government's apartheid policy. He authored the 2000 bestseller *The Debt: What America Owes to Blacks*, which helped to further galvanize the movement. Robinson often casts Fidel Castro in a favorable light, and is a sharp critic of capitalism and the United States. In *The Debt,* Robinson wrote, "I will say what few of us will say aloud. . . . Many blacks—most, perhaps, though I can't be sure—don't like America."[215] *The Debt* was centered on an intricate outline of the substantial reparations which he had come ro assume that the United States owed to descendants of former slaves. Compensation should be offered to African-Americans as a means of redressing centuries of both *de jure* and *de facto* discrimination and oppression directed at the group. In the book Robinson argued in favor of the enactment of race-based reparation programs as restitution for the continued social and economic issues in the African-American community, such as a high proportion of incarcerated black citizens and the differential in cumulative wealth between white and black Americans.

In *The Debt*, Robinson wrote, "Lamentably, there will always be poverty. But African Americans are over-represented in that economic class for one reason and one reason only: African slavery and the vicious climate that followed it."[216] That gap "has been resolutely nurtured since in law and public behavior. It has now ossified. It is structural. Its framing beams are disguised only by the counterfeit manners of a hypocritical governing class."[217] In one of the opening observations that Robinson made he described a tour he took of the U.S. Capitol, in which a guide pointed out that the building was built largely with slave labor. He then launched a vicious attack on what the Capital stands for, essentially saying it is based on a lie. "I thought, then, what a fitting metaphor the Capitol Rotunda was for America's racial sorrows. In the magnificence of its boast, in the tragedy of its truth, in the effrontery of its deceit."

Robinson found support in *Black Wealth, White Wealth*. In that book, Shapiro and Oliver attempt to provide an economic explanation for the gap, saying that because blacks could not own property

---

215 "Randall S. Robinson, Dr.". *Who's Who Among African Americans.* Detroit: Gale. 2011. See also "Randall Robinson" in Wikipedia. Robinson, Randall. *The Debt: What America Owes to Blacks*, Plume, 2001. See also, Robinson, Randall. *The Reckoning: What Blacks Owe to Each Other*. Plume, 2002

216 Robinson, *The Debt*, p. 8

217 Ibid., p. 204.

under slavery, they could not accumulate assets to pass on from generation to generation.[218] Melvin L. Oliver was Vice-President of the Ford Foundation's Asset Building and Community Development Program and was on leave from UCLA where he is Professor of Sociology and Social Policy. Thomas M. Shapiro is Professor of Sociology and Anthropology at Northeastern University. He is the author of *Population Control Politics: Women, Sterilization, and Reproductive Choice*. Their *Black Wealth/ White Wealth* sought to demonstrate how an analysis of private wealth uncovers a revealing story about race in America. An examination of how assets are created, expanded and preserved reveals a deep economic divide between blacks and whites. Charting the changing structure of inequality over many generations, the authors examine how and why many blacks have had difficulty accumulating wealth and opportunities for a better life. In combining quantitative data from over 12,000 households and interviews with a range of black and white families, the racial face of wealth in America is measured and conceptualized.

In 2001, Professor Robinson resigned his position as head of TransAfrica, emigrating to St. Kitts, where his wife, a member of a prominent Kittitian family, was born. He discussed his decision in his book, *Quitting America: The Departure of a Black Man from his Native Land*. In it he argued that both the domestic and foreign policies exploited minorities and the poor.[219] In *The Debt*, Randall Robinson suggested that a thousand African Americans per day walk through the halls of Congress to make certain that its politicians "would never stop seeing our faces, never stop hearing our demands."[220] He has subsequently taught at the law school operated and controlled by the Pennsylvania State University.

Maureen E. Ruprecht Fadem, who teaches English at Kingsborough Community College, part of the City University of New York (CUNY), describes herself as a scholar-activist whose work centers around colonialism, empire, race, racism and the residual impact of slavery. She wrote her recent book[221] to provoke a reckoning

---

218 Shapiro, Thomas M. and Melvin L. Oliver. *Black Wealth, White Wealth*. Routledge, 1995.

219 Robinson, Randall. *Quitting America: The Departure of a Black Man From His Native Land.* Plume Books, 2004

220 Robinson, *The Debt*, p. 247.

221Ruprecht Fadem, Maureen. *Objects and Intertexts in Toni Morrison's Beloved.* Routledge, 2021.

with the ways enslavement has tainted race relations in the U.S. and calls for reparations to repair the emotional, social and political damage it has caused. Such reparations, Fadem argues, would be the logical culmination of Morrison's literary campaign. Fadem, following Morrison's lead, argues that reparations for slavery are an essential component of making the U.S. more equitable. It is also the only acceptable method of eradicating the brutal slave past. Her argument utilizes Toni Morrison's 1987 novel, *Beloved,* to highlight the necessity of grappling with the brutality of "that peculiar institution," as slavery was once known. Both support monetary reparations for those whose genealogies include enslaved fore-parents as a foundational first step, but also advocates the building of monuments to pay homage to those forced into servitude.[222]

What Morrison laid out in fiction had been outlined much more fully in a non-fictional work by Boris Bittker.[223] That case was challenged by William L. Banks who argued that disapproval of black reparation does not mean approval of racism. Slavery, with its cruelty, disregard for human dignity, rape and murder, remains a stain on the character of America. But no monetary compensation can nullify the fact, history, or banality of slavery. Banks argued from a strongly fundamentalist religious perspective that the God of the Bible is no respecter of persons, no receiver of faces or races.[224] In turn, Larry J. Perodin responded, making his case for such reparations. Why, he asked, were reparations denied ex-slaves in 1865 by the government? Rather the day slavery ended segregation became the new norm for Blacks. Keep them separate, put them on an island. Through the years reparations have been vaguely talked about and skirted around as if not necessary. Are reparations needed? Today the conditions of Black communities makes plain something is needed. Black Man Island contends the violence, lack of education, poor medical care, lack of good paying jobs are symptoms of the dire need for reparations. He challenged America to answer the call to nullify the effects of slaver by awarding reparations.[225]

222Bader, Eleanor J., "Making the Case for Slavery Reparations," *MS Magazine*, 21 February 2021.

223Bittker, Boris. *The Case for Black Reparations*. Beacon Press, 2003.

224Banks, William L. The Case Against Black Reparation. Infinity Publishing, 2013.

225Perodin, Larry J. *Black Man Island: The Case for Reparations*. London: Future Now, 2020.

Robert Johnson, founder of Black Entertainment Television, is one of the most outspoken proponents of reparation payments. He has argued that America must atone for its slaver past and continued systemic racism by paying African-Americans reparations to make them economically equal to white Americans. Johnson, the first black billionaire in the United States, has put a price tag on the debt America owes to African-Americans at $14 trillion. "Nobody talks about cash, but black people understand cash," Johnson told Fox News. Under his proposal, an estimated 40 million African-Americans would each receive $350,000 in direct cash payments, payable over 30 years and costing the average taxpayer roughly $2,900 a year. The $350,000 would signify the wealth disparity between African-Americans and white Americans, according to Johnson. "Slavery, Jim Crow laws and racial discrimination were a wealth transfer from African Americans to white people. It's time to make amends and give it back."[226]

Dorothy Tillman (1947---) is a Chicago city councilman and a leading reparations activist. Tillman was a field staff organizer for Reverend Martin Luther King's Southern Christian Leadership Conference. Elected to serve as an alderman in Chicago in 1985, she has earned a reputation as a major political figure in city politics. She frequently becomes involved in issues such as inner-city education, housing and homelessness. Always an outspoken and controversiial figure, during one session of the Chicago City Council, Tillman produced a pistol from her handbag and waved it around. Tillman was convicted for criminal trespassing at an Alabama hospital, an event which occurred in March 2008 during a dispute over medical records. She was fined and received a suspended sentence.[227]

Ms Tillman was a staunch advocate of payment of substantial compensation as reparations for slavery. She was most successful in having a number of resolutions passed in support of the concept. She authored a bill, passed unanimously in 2002, forcing companies who perform contracts with the council to declare any past ties with slavery. In early 2005, Tillman led a campaign against a $500 million re-

---

226New York Times, 5 June 2020. See also Schultz, Marisa, "Robert Johnson's Big Idea: $14 trillion in slavery reparations to African-Americans," *Fox News The Big Idea*, 26 June 202o.

227 "Dorothy Tillman," in Wikipedia. Olen, Helaine, "Gun-toting Aldermen have Law on their Side," *Chicago Tribune*, 19 November 1991. Since aldermen are legally conservators of the peace, they may carry concealed weapons which would otherwise be forbidden.

financing deal with the Bank of America because she alleged it had strong ties with slavery in its early history. In the case of the Bank of America, these links are allegedly through FleetBoston Financial, a company which Bank oif America acquired in 2004. Providene, a predecessor of Fleet Boston, was reportedly founded by a slave owner in 1791. Tillman sponsored Chicago's slave disclosure law in 2003 which has subsequently served as a model for other municipal disclosure ordinances.[228] Penalties for failing to fully reveal all information on past ties to slavery are substantial.[229]

Cornel Ronald West (1953---) is a professor of Religion and African American Studies at Princeton University, and a Reparations Coordinating Committee (RCC) member. West (1953---) is an American political activist and social critic. The grandson of a Baptist minister, West focuses on the role of race, gender, and class in American society and the means by which people act and react to their "radical conditionedness". His book *Prophesy Deliverance! An Afro-American Revolutionary Christianity* (1982) attempted to fuse Christianity and Marxism. Other books include *Beyond Eurocentrism and Multiculturalism* (1993) and *Race Matters* (1993). West has publicly disagreed with Louis Farrakhan's anti-Semitism

Ta-Nehisi Paul Coates (1975--) is an American author and journalist who was born in Baltimore, Maryland. His father, William Paul Coates, was a Vietnam War veteran, former Black Panther, publisher, and librarian. His mother, Cheryl Lynn (Waters), was a teacher. Coates' father founded and ran Black Classic Press, a publisher specializing in African-American titles. The Press grew out the George Jackson Prison Movement. Black Classic Press was established with a table-top printing press in the basement of the Coates family home.

Nehisi gained a wide following during his time as national correspondent at *The Atlantic* magazine, in which he wrote about cultural, social, and political issues regarding African Americans included a discussion of the grassroots organization, the Contract Buyers League. The focus of Coates' article was not so much on reparations for slavery, but was instead a focus on the institutional racism as prac-

228 Dorothy Tillman was interviewed by The History Makers on September 5, 2002. Tape four, "Dorothy Tillman talks about her political actions in favor of reparations."

229 Spielman, Fran, "Aldermen May Punish Firm for Concealing Slavery Ties," *Chicago Sun*, 5 June 2005

ticed in housing discrimination.[230]

His fame spread after the penned an article for *The Atlantic,* "The Case for Reparations." Coates claimed that he had worked on that story for almost two years, weighing various alternatives for compensation for blacks whose ancestors had been enslaved. Among other books, he had read and was greatly influenced by Rutgers University professor Beryl Satter's book, *Family Properties: Race, Real Estate, and the Exploitation of Black Urban America.* Professor Satter related a history of redlining that while denouncing presumed white supremacy. Coates has also written for *The Village Voice, Washington City Paper*, *Time* magazine,*The New York Times Magazine, The Washington Post, The Washington Monthly*, and *O*. Three of his nonfiction books: *The Beautiful Struggle, Between the World and Me*, and *We Were Eight Years in Power: An American Tragedy*.He has also written a Black Panther series and a Captain America series for Marvel Comics. His first novel, *The Water Dancer*, was published in 2019 and is a surrealist story set in the time of slavery, concerning a superhuman protagonist named Hiram Walker who possesses photographic memory, but who cannot remember his mother, but is able to transport people over far distances by using a power known as conduction.

Despite his personal nihilism, he is living proof that the American Dream is alive and well, and he is a living refutation of the apocalypticism, resignation, indignation and hopelessness regarding the American experience that informs his misanthropic imagination.

Coates has been a magnet for conservative black critics who have attacked Coates along several lines. The common criticism lies in the racial reductionism of Coates' vision and his hyperinflation of what he calls white supremacy as the single causal explanation for black oppression and suffering in the United States. He has called for blacks to disengage from civic life which his critics have hailed as morally irresponsible. He offered a very pessimistic analysis of the prejudicial nature of race relations without viable solutions. This, they claim, betrays the vision of a true moral intellectual, and also of an analytic journalist. He has refused to confront his youth when he was terrorized by the fears of his own suffering at the hands of violent blacks. That fear of his own race, his critics charge, he has transplant-

230Coates, Ta-Nehisi, "The Case for Reparations". *The Atlantic*, June 2014. See also Roig-Franzia, Manuel, "With Atlantic Article on Reparations, Ta-Nehisi Coates Sees Payoff for Years of Struggle," *Washington Post*, 18 June 2014.

ed to white society in general.

Reading Coates, they accuse, one gets the impression that the psychology of fear he attributes to black people is a projection of his own personal psychological make-up: he is deathly afraid of his own race, but, out of a sense of racial shame, finds it easier to blame white people for the endemic black-on-black violence to which he was systemically subjected to as a child, beginning with the beating inflicted on him by his own father. This is a rather unfair burden to download upon white people by a man who his personal demons. Some of the African-Americans who reject Coates see him as merely a loud-mouth spokesman of a neo-liberal emerging black elite. It is also true that the American political left, for a long time, had a very masochistic relationship with its left-leaning, anti-American black intellectuals such as Coates.[231]

Coates is deeply committed to a wholly amoral view of the world. More importantly, he denies that whites have the moral capacity or will necessary to foster strong positive moral sentiments about the lives of black people. Neither do Caucasians care about black suffering and misery. Even his most ardent liberal white supporters have expressed grave concern about his words. Many of them believe that Coates loathes them because they are white. He has clearly demonstrated how much he hates them as part of the ruling 'majoritarian pigs' he describes in *Between the World and Me*. He claims that these people who have created the policies and racial infrastructures majoritarian .rule have the doomed lives of black people. As an integral part of his wholesale indictment of white America as a country ruled by majoritarian pigs, he has refused to show sympathy for the heroic white or even black firefighters who died in the World Trade Center in the aftermath of 9/11 attack. He writes that they were not human to him; rather, they were menaces of nature; they were the force, the comet, the storm which could, with no justification, shatter his body. It is obvious that his thought cannot progress upward so long as he maintains his loathing of supposed white prejudice against blacks.[232]

Deadria Farmer-Paellmann is a lawyer-activist, who gained notoriety in 2002 after filing suit in a New York federal court demanding reparations payments from corporations such as Aetna Insur-

---

231Warren, Calvin L., "Black Nihilism and the Politics of Hope," *New Centennial Review* 15: 1 (2015), pp. 215-48.

232 Hill, Jason, "The Black Nihilism of Ta-Nehisi Coates," *Spiked*, 18 May 2018

ance, Fleet-Boston Financial, and CSX railroad. In 2000, Farmer-Paellmann, then a student at the New England School of Law, discovered that Aetna, Inc., based in Hartford, Connecticut., had a history of insuring the lives of slaves. The company issued an apology but the episode marked the beginning of the reparations crusade against alleged corporate slave profiteers. She alleged that these companies or their "predecessors in interest" profited from slavery. Farmer-Paellmann is credited for popularizing the slavery reparations movement through her groundbreaking research exposing corporate complicity in slavery. Born in 1966, Farmer-Paellmann spent her early years in East New York, in a single-parent household headed by her mother who depended on public assistance. When Farmer-Paellmann was about seven years old, the family moved to the largely white Brooklyn enclave of Bensonhurst, where they became the only African-American family in the immediate area. She is a freelance legal researcher and reparations activist, acting as executive director of the Restitution Study Group, Inc.

Edward Fagan (1952---) was the attorney who represented Richard Barber and Deadria Farmer Paellmann, who were plaintiffs in two separate lawsuits against several U.S. companies for their alleged role in slavery. Born to a conservative Jewish family, Fagan was prominent in the Holocaust-related lawsuits against European companies, using many of his previous arguments honed in Holocaust cases. Fagan, who is white, has vowed to file additional slave-reparations lawsuits throughout the country. In April 2002 Ed Fagan filed a class action lawsuit against eighteen companies, including FleetBoston, CSX Corporation, Aetna, Union Pacific Railroad, R. J. Reynolds Tobacco Company, and Lehman Brothers, accusing the companies of having "unjustly enriched (themselves) through profits earned either directly or indirectly from the Trans-Atlantic slave trade and slavery between 1619 and 1865, as well as post-Emancipation slavery through the 1960s". In January 2004 Judge Charles R Norgle dismissed the lawsuit because Fagan failed to establish a clear link between plaintiffs and the companies. He has since lost his law license as a former American reparations lawyer. He was disbarred for his conduct involving dishonesty, fraud, deceit, or misrepresentation. Fagan lost his license in both New York and New Jersey for failing to pay court fines and fees and for stealing client money and escrow trust funds from Holocaust survivors.[233]

Patrisse Cullors, born in 1983, is a black artist and activist and a co-founder of the Black Lives Matter movement. Cullors created the #BlackLivesMatter hashtag in 2013 and has written and spoken widely about the movement. Other topics on which Cullors advocates include abolition of the prison system, ending capital punishment, and LGBTQ rights. She co-founded the prison activist organization known as Dignity and Power Now, which advocated a civilian oversight board for California jails. Cullors has borrowed ideas from various critical and nihilistic theories from around the world,.

Ms Cullors has defines herself as one who is committed to abolishing prisons, the police and militarization, a position she says is inspired by "a legacy of black-led anti-colonial struggle in the United States and throughout the Americas." She also favors reparations for what she describes as "the historical pains and damage caused by European settler colonialism", in various forms, such "financial restitution, land redistribution, political self-determination, culturally relevant education programs, language recuperation, and the right to return or repatriation." As she wrote, "The United States, the world's largest jailer and is also the world's greatest perpetrator of war and the most extensive purveyor of human rights atrocities at home and abroad, laying claim to over 800 military bases around the world. Our task is not only to abolish prisons, policing, and militarization, which are wielded in the name of public safety and national security."[234]

She is the author of *When They Call You a Terrorist: A Black Lives Matter Memoir.* In her work and on her interviews she frequently cites various convicted criminals, revolutionaries, nihilists, and communists. She praised Weather Underground member Eric Mann as her intellectual mentor during her earliest years. She draws on various dissidents as her inspiration, such as black feminist Audre Lorde and her "Black, queer, feminist lens." .She drew upon Angela Davis for her "political theories and reflections on anti-capitalist movements around the world", her work towards "a broader anti-racist and anti-

---

233 "Edward Fagan," in Wikipedia. See also Covaleski, John , "Ethics Charges Leveled at Lawyer Who Fostered Holocaust Settlement." *New Jersey Law Journal,* 20 January 2005. See also Walder, Noeleen G. "Lawyer Disbarred for Failing to Pay Sanctions, Fees in Holocaust Case." N*ew York Law Journal,* 12 December 2008.

234Cullors, Patrisse, "Abolition And Reparations: Histories of Resistance, Transformative Justice, And Accountability," *Harvard Law Review,* 10 April 2019.

war movement", and her fight against white supremacy in the United States. Franz Fanon was another inspiration in his "work on colonial violence in Algeria and across the Third World [making] timely connections" for the understanding of the context in which black people live throughout the world. She also freely cited Karl Marx, Vladimir Lenin and Mao Zedong, who, she asserted, provided "a new understanding around what our economies could look like."[235]

Black Religious Leaders and Reparations

One of the earlier quasi-religious figures to support reparations for slavery was radio evangelist Reverend M. J. Divine, better known as Father Divine, and born George Baker (c. 1876—1965). He was an African-American spiritual leader from about 1907, until his death. His full self-given name was Reverend Major Jealous Divine, and he was also known as "the Messenger" early in his life, but later claimed to be God. He founded the International Peace Mission movement, formulated its doctrine, and oversaw its growth from a small and predominantly black congregation into a multiracial and international church. Due to his ideology, many consider him to be a cult leader, rather than a clerrgyman. He made numerous contributions toward his followers' economic independence and racial equality. He was one of the earliest leaders to argue clearly for "retroactive compensation", and the message was spread via International Peace Mission publications. Father Divine was particularly concerned with the downtrodden of society, including but not limited to Blacks. He was opposed to people accepting welfare. He believed in capitalism. In his opinion, capitalism was not at fault but that various individual were to blame for involuntary servitude. He taught that Americans could make it better if they had positive thoughts and channeled God's spirit.

On July 28, 1951, Father Divine issued a "peace stamp" bearing the text: "Peace! All nations and peoples who have suppressed and oppressed the under-privileged, they will be obliged to pay the African slaves and their descendants for all uncompensated servitude and for all unjust compensation, whereby they have been unjustly deprived of compensation on the account of previous condition of servi-

---

235Jenkins, Aric, "Black Lives Matter Co-Founder Patrisse Cullors on Her Book," *Time* magazine, 26 February 2018; Walcott, Rianna, "How the Founder of Black Lives Matter Started a Global Movement," *Dazed,* 5 April 2018.

tude and the present condition of servitude. This is to be accomplished in the defense of all other under-privileged subjects and must be paid retroactive up-to-date."[236]

Father Divine required that his followers think of themselves as simply Americans, believing that America was the birthplace of the "Kingdom of God", which would ultimately encompass truths of all religious principles, promoting equality and brotherhood. His Movement thought of the United States Declaration of Independence, the Constitution, and the Bill of Rights as inspired documents, believing that they outlined a more ideal life. The cult established an International Modesty Code which forbade smoking, drinking alcoholic beverages, and using profanity. The code also forbade soliciting or accepting tips or bribes, receiving presents, "undue mixing of the sexes," and women wearing slacks or short skirts and men wearing short-sleeve shirts.[237]

Louis Farrakhan was born Louis Eugene Walcott on 11 May 1933. He is an American religious leader, political activist, and anti-Semite who heads the Nation of Islam (NOI). Earlier in his career, he served as the minister of mosques in Boston and Harlem and was appointed National Representative of the Nation of Islam by former NOI leader Elijah Muhammad.

After Warith Deen Mohammed reorganized the original NOI into an orthodox Sunni Islamic group known as the American Society of Muslims, Farrakhan began to rebuild the NOI as "Final Call". In 1981, he officially adopted the name "Nation of Islam", reviving the group and establishing its headquarters at Mosque Maryam.[238]

The Southern Poverty Law Center (SPLC) describes the Nation of Islam as a black nationalist hate group. The SPLC has condemned Farrakhan's antisemitic statements as has the Anti-Defamation League (ADL) and similar self-appointed watch-dogs.

236Watts, Jill. *God, Harlem U.S.A.: The Father Divine Story.* University of California Press, 1992. See also Hoshor, John. *God in a Rolls Royce: The Rise of Father Divine, Madman, Menace, Or Messiah.* Hillman-Curl. 1936. See also John Gordon Melton, "Father Divine (American religious leader) in Britannica Online Encyclopedia". Britannica.com.

237 Logan, Rayford W. and Michael R. Winston, eds. "Father Divine". In *Dictionary of American Negro Biography*. Norton, 1982, p. 179.

238"Louis Farrakhan" in Wikipedia. See also Gardell, Mattias. *In the Name of Elijah Muhammad: Louis Farrakhan and The Nation of Islam*. Duke University Press, 1996.

According to the SPLC, the NOI promotes a "fundamentally anti-white theology" which is tantamount to an ideology which teaches "innate black superiority over whites". Some of his remarks have been heard as homophobic.[239] Farrakhan has repeatedly denied referring to Judaism as a "gutter religion" by explaining that he was instead referring to what he believed was the Israeli Government's use of Judaism as a political tool. Many, including Malcolm X's family, have accused Farrakhan of being involved in the plot which successfully assassinated Malcolm X. Naturally, Farrakhan has disputed such assertions on many occasions including the SPLC characterizations.

Desiring to establish a viable enterprise to help employ Islamic converts while acting as a source of income, Farrakhan sought to create some business. In 1985, Farrakhan obtained working capital in the amount of $5 million, in the form of an interest-free loan from Libya's Islamic Call Society, to be repaid within 18 months which was to be used to create a toiletries firm with black employees. Libyan President Muammar Gaddafi had also offered Farrahkan guns to secure his black nation. Farrakhan said that he told Gaddafi that he preferred an economic investment in black America. In January 1996, when Farrakhan visited Libya, Gaddafi pledged him a gift of $1 billion along with a personal stipend of $250,000. As economic activity between the two countries had been restricted by the US government since 1986 following allegations of Libya's connection to terrorism, the financial transfer was blocked. It was unclear if Gaddafi would have been in a position to finance the money transfer.[240]

In October 1995, he organized and led the Million Man March in Washington, D.C., which took place on 15 October. One of the event's official purposes was to demand "full and complete reparations for the descendants of slaves.". In 2015, he led the 20th Anniversary of the Million Man March which he titled Justice or Else. Again he called for reparations. His organization published *The Secret Relationship Between Blacks and Jews*, which claims that Jews were instrumental in the slave trade. Farrakhan has demanded land grants for blacks rather than money transfers.

Because of age and health issues, he has recently reduced his responsibilities with the NOI. Nonetheless, Farrakhan has continued

239 "Louis Farrakhan". Southern Poverty Law Center; "The Nation of Islam" and "Louis Farrakhan: America's Leading Anti-Semite"".Anti-Defamation League.

240 "Charm of a Snake," *Investor's Business Daily*, October 17, 2005

to deliver sermons and speak at NOI events He was banned from Facebook in 2019 along with other public figures considered to be extremists because of his bigoted views.

Jesse Louis Jackson (1941---) whose birth name was Burns is an American political activist, ordained Baptist minister, and politician. He was a candidate for the Democratic presidential nomination in both 1984 and 1988. He has served as shadow U.S. Senator for the District of Columbia from 1991 to 1997. Early in his career Jackson referred to Jews as "Hymies" and New York City as "Hymietown" in remarks to a black *Washington Post* reporter and the degree of his antisemitism has been a matter of question ever since. Jesse Jackson praised Venezuela and its communist leader in 2005, saying that there is no evidence that the country represents a threat to the region. He praised the Chavez government's most important issues.[241]

Jackson is the founder of the organizations that merged to form Rainbow/PUSH. Jackson hosted "Both Sides with Jesse Jackson" on CNN from 1992 to 2000. In recent years, he has become adept at accusing corporations and other entities of racism, prompting them to grant money and concessions to Jackson's organization and associates. It is a practice that lends itself well to the slave reparations issue. Jackson's methods are reflected in the large revenues of his Citizenship Education Fund (CEF). (In 2001, the National Legal and Policy Center filed a formal complaint that the CEF operates outside of its tax-exempt status.) Interestingly, Jackson advocates giving slave reparations payments not to slave descendants directly, but to nonprofit organizations (e.g., Rainbow/PUSH) that focus on the black community.[242]

Alfred Charles Sharpton (1954---) is an American political and racist activist, ordained Baptist minister, and politician. In 1969, Jesse Jackson appointed Sharpton to serve as youth director of the New York City branch of Operation Breadbasket, which focused on the promotion of new and better jobs for blacks. He burst onto the national scene in 1987 with the Tawana Brawley hoax, in which a black teenager falsely claimed she had been raped by a gang of whites In 1971 Sharpton founded the National Youth Movement, designed to

---

241 *Washington Post,* 28 August 2005.

242 "Jesse Jackson," History, Jesse Jackson – HISTORY. See also "Jesse Jackson," in Wikipedia. See also "Jesse Jackson," in Biography, 17 November 2017, updated 22 June 2020.

raise resources for impoverished youths. In 1991, Sharpton founded the National Action Network, an organization designed to increase voter education, to provide services to those in poverty, and to support small community businesses. In 2004, he was a candidate for the Democratic nomination for president. He hosts his own radio talk show, "Keepin' It Real," and in 2011 was named the host of MSNBC's "Politics Nation," a nightly talk show.. In 1991, after a Hasidic Jewish driver in Brooklyn accidentally killed a seven year-old black, Sharpton participated in anti-Semitic riots, and at the funeral denounced "diamond merchants" in a veiled reference to Jews. In 1995, after a dispute between a Jewish store owner and black tenant, Sharpton's National Action Network staged protests filled with anti-Semitism and violent language. A protester shot four store employees and set the store on fire, killing three more.

Democratic Party and Reparations

The Democratic Party, while not explicitly endorsing reparations, appears to be gradually accepting the idea. During the 2000 presidential race, the Democratic Party's Platform Statement officially adopted a plank supporting the establishment of a federal commission to examine the history of slavery and "to make appropriate recommendations on behalf of the American people." In addition, a growing number of books, lectures, websites, rallies and various grassroots groups press the reparations issue.[243]

During the 2000 presidential election campaign, Al Gore expressed his support for the notion of reparations. At a primary debate in Harlem early in 2000, both Gore and Bill Bradley refused to condemn reparations when the topic was brought up. And during a rally in Tulsa, OK Gore reportedly said reparations were "a definite possibility."11 As noted earlier, the 2000 Democratic Party Platform Statement endorsed the principle of reparations.

The idea spread throughout the Democratic Party. In April 2002, then-California Governor Gray Davis indicated his support for slave reparations, declaring, "Clearly, we want to right any wrongs and do justice to people who were taken advantage of, if that is the case. I believe that will be the case." He also signed a law forcing insurance companies to disclose information about any ties to slavery they had a century and a half ago. The governor of Michigan, Jennifer

243 www.democrats.org/about/ 2000platform.htm

Granholm, also supported reparations. She declared before the NAACP that "I support reparations as well, and supported John Conyers' bill."

The Green Party signed on. Presidential candidate Ralph Nader's 2000 platform explicitly endorsed reparations. The platform states that "people of color have legitimate claims in this country to reparations in the form of monetary compensation for these centuries of discrimination." Although Nader did not run as the Green Party candidate in 2004, the Green Party Platform included language supporting reparations.

Reparations in Congress

Such groups include the National Association for the Advancement of Colored People (NAACP), the Southern Christian Leadership Conference and the National Urban League. Congressmen regularly raise the issue, most notably Rep. John Conyers (D-MI). Since 1989, Conyers has been pushing a bill asking Congress to establish a commission to study reparations proposals for African Americans. Many Democratic members of Congress continue to throw their support for Rep. Conyers' reparations bill, "The Commission to Study Reparation Proposals for African Americans Act" (H.R. 40). It would "establish a commission to examine the institution of slavery, subsequently de jure and de facto racial and economic discrimination against African-Americans, and the impact of these forces on living African-Americans, to make recommendations to the Congress on appropriate remedies, and for other purposes." (Conyers chose the bill number "40" to reflect the "40 acres and a mule" the U.S. government allegedly promised freed slaves). Conyers first introduced the bill in 1989. [244]

Although Congress has never acted on it, he vows to keep reintroducing it until it's passed into law. Conyers argues that "just as we've discussed the Holocaust and Japanese internment camps, and to some extent the devastation that the colonists inflicted upon the Indians, we must talk about slavery and its continued effects." If Democrats regain control of the House of Representatives, Conyers, who would likely become the chairman of the House Judiciary Committee, has pledged to immediately take up the reparations issue.4 At

---

244 Decker, Bret M., "The Coming Reparations Boondoggle," *National Review Online,* 18 June 2000. See also www.house.gov/conyers/news_ reparations.htm

last count, 22 congressmen have co-sponsored the bill. Influential liberal interest groups are also lending support to a reparations commission. In February 2006, the House of Delegates of the American Bar Association formally urged Congress to establish a commission to study the effects of slavery and make recommendations to address those effects. To date, Congress has not acted on it.

At the first National Reparations Convention in Chicago in 2001, Howshua Amariel, a Chicago racial activist, proposed that the federal government would be required to make reparations to proven descendants of slaves. In addition, Amariel demanded "For those blacks who wish to remain in America, they should receive reparations in the form of free education, free medical, free legal and free financial aid for fifty years with no taxes levied," and "For those desiring to leave America, every black person would receive a million dollars or more, backed by gold, in reparation." At the convention Amariel's proposal received approval from the 100 or so participants. Nevertheless, the question of who would receive such payments, who should pay them and in what amount, has remained highly controversial, since the United States Census does not track descent from slaves or slave owners and relies on self-reported racial categories.[245]

On July 30, 2008, the United States House of Representatives passed a resolution apologizing for American slavery and subsequent discriminatory laws

Reparations have been a recurring idea in the politics of the United States, most recently in the 2020 Democratic Party presidential primaries.[246] The call for reparations has intensified in 2020, following various insurrections that charged police brutality and demanded defunding of the police. Calls for reparations for racism and discrimination in the U. S. are often made by black communities and authors alongside calls for reparations for slavery. The idea of reparations remains highly controversial, due to questions of how they would be given, how much would be given, and who would pay and

245 Shepard, Paul Shepard (February 11, 2001). "U.S. slavery reparations: Hope that a race will be compensated gains momentum," *Seattle Times*, 11 February 2001; Simons, Bright, "Ghanaian President Stirs Controversy Over Slave Trade Reparations," worldpress.org, 11 February 2001; and Chen, Michelle, "Bill to Study Slavery Reparations Still Facing Resistance," The NewStandard, 27 March 2007.

246 Hagen, Lisa,"2020 Democrats' Support for Reparations Lacks Details," *US News & World Report,* 27 February 2019.

who receive them.

U. S. Representative Sheila Jackson Lee, Democrat from Texas, introduced H.R. 40, calling for reparations for enslavement. She claimed that was it a needed step on the "path to restorative justice." The House Judiciary Committee voted on April 14, 2021, to recommend the creation of a commission to study the possibility of paying reparations to the descendants of enslaved people in the United States. The measure, H.R. 40, would establish a 15-person commission to offer a "national apology" for slavery, study its long-term effects and submit recommendations to Congress on how to compensate African Americans. Any federal reparations bill faces long odds of being enacted due to Republican opposition, but this is the furthest this effort has advanced since a similar bill was first introduced over 30 years ago. Lee's bill has support from many Democrats, including House of Representatives Speaker Pelosi Vice-president Harris, and President Joe Biden. As a first step to making the country pay for its racist past, many Democrats want to establish a Congressional commission to examine slavery and discrimination dating as far back as 1619. After thorough consideration, the commission is expected to recommend appropriate remedies, one of which will likely be monetary compensation.[247] There is stiff opposition from Republicans.

As the U.S debates reparations for descendants of U.S. slavery, looking to Africa might help clear a path forward, according to my research on African history and the African diaspora.

Reparations in the States

The Asheville, North Carolina, City Council voted unanimously in July for reparations that would take the form of helping businesses and providing housing and health care. The Asheville, city council approved reparations on a 7–0 vote on July 14, 2020. "[B]udgetary and programmatic priorities may include but not be limited to increasing minority home ownership and access to other affordable housing, increasing minority business ownership and career opportunities, strategies to grow equity and generational wealth, closing the gaps in health care, education, employment and pay, neighborhood safety and fairness within criminal justice," the resolution reads. The

247"Biden Supports Payment of Slavery Reparations for Blacks,"*The Herald*, 26 February 2021. The same story appeared in the *New York Times* and *Washington Post*, along with other major and minor newspapers.

resolution establishes the Community Reparations Commission which will make make concrete recommendations for programs and resources allocations to ultimately carry out the reparations. The Asheville City Council also voted unanimously on June 9, 2020 to remove two confederate monuments as a result of demands made by a group called "Black Asheville Demands" and the work of the Racial Justice Coalition with led the push for the effort. The City Council meeting had so much community engagement public comment was extended for an extra hour beyond the normal meeting time.[248]

Other local governments considering reparations in some form include Amherst, Massachusetts; Providence, Rhode Island; and Iowa City, Iowa.

In California, elected officials in Manhattan Beach in Los Angeles County announced a bill to restore property now known as Bruce's Beach to the Black family whose resort on that ocean-side property was wrongly seized by city officials in 1924.

In Washington, D. C., Georgetown University has announced a fundraising goal of $400,000 a year to benefit the descendants of the 272 slaves who were sold to help keep the college afloat almost 200 years ago. Now students who had voted to pay for it through additional fees will not have to do so. Georgetown University in 2016 agreed to give admissions preference to descendants of the 272 slaves, formally apologized for its role in slavery and renamed two buildings on its campus to acknowledge the lives of enslaved people. In April, 2019 students at Georgetown University voted to increase their tuition by $27.20 to benefit the descendants of the 272 slaves sold by the Jesuits who ran the school in 1838. The student led referendum was non-binding. Later that year, after further pressure and follow up from the Georgetown University Student Association the university eventually moved forward with a similar proposal without the students' covering the cost with a tuition increase.[249]

In March 2021 Evanston, Illinois, became what is believed to be the nation's first city to offer reparations to Black residents who

248Burgess, Joel, "In historic move, Asheville approves reparations for Black residents," *Citizen Times,* 14 July 2020; "City OKs monuments' removal, pending county approval," *Citizen Times,* 15 June 2020; and "In historic move, North Carolina city approves reparations for Black residents," *Citizen Times,* 15 July 2020.

249 "Georgetown University announces reparations fund to benefit descendants of slaves once sold by the school," *New York Times*, 30 October 2019.

have suffered housing discrimination. The modest but historic resolution directs initial funding of $400,000 from the city's Local Reparations Fund, funded mostly by a new tax on legal marijuana. The fund will award up to $25,000 to 16 eligible households to help with a home purchase, repairs or improvements. Applicants must have been Black residents between 1919 and 1969 or a direct descendant. They also may qualify if they experienced housing discrimination because of the city's policies or practices after 1969.[250]

The North Carolina legislature considered a state-wide disclosure law in 2005. Representatives Larry Womble and Earl Jones sponsored the proposal which would have required companies to "disclose any and all records of participation in or profits derived from slavery." The bill never made it to the floor for consideration.

In California, Governor Gavin Newsom appointed five individuals to serve on the newly formed Task Force to Study and Develop Reparation Proposals for African Americans. The formation of this task force was made possible by the Governor's signing of AB 3121, authored by then-Assembly member Shirley Weber (D-San Diego), which established a nine-member task force to inform Californians about slavery and explore ways the state might provide reparations. "California is leading the nation, in a bipartisan way, on the issue of reparations and racial justice, which is a discussion that is long overdue and deserves our utmost attention," said Governor Newsom. "Last year, I signed into law a number of key bills focused on leveling the playing field in our society and ensuring that everyone has a fair shot at achieving the California dream. The appointment of individuals with an expansive breadth of knowledge, experiences and understanding of issues impacting the African American community is the next step in our commitment as a state to build a California for all."

The five individuals selected by the Governor to serve on this task force represent diverse backgrounds and meet the statutes required by law, which include choosing one candidate from the field of academia with expertise in civil rights and an additional two appointees selected from major civil society and reparations organizations that have historically championed the cause of reparatory justice. Other key factors considered for committee candidates included a background in economics and community development, health and

---

250Page, Clarence, "U.S. still struggles with issue of reparations," *Philadelphia Tribune,* 9 May 2021.

psychology, law and criminal justice, faith-based and community activism, and an expertise in the historic achievement of reparatory justice. The Task Force to Study and Develop Reparation Proposals for African Americans (Reparations Task Force) will have a total of nine members, with two individuals appointed by the Senate and two members appointed by the Assembly.[251]

City councils in Los Angeles, Detroit, Cleveland, Chicago, Dallas and Atlanta have endorsed Conyers' H.R. 40 seeking reparations. In October 2002, two years after it voted to endorse H.R. 40, the Chicago city council, in a 44-0 vote, approved an ordinance requiring city contractors to inspect their records on whether they or their predecessor companies profited from slavery, and turn over all paperwork to the city if such evidence is found. In May 2003, the Los Angeles City Council approved legislation that requires businesses seeking city contracts to disclose any profits made from slavery. In June 2004, Detroit passed a similar measure. The Philadelphia City Council unanimously passed a disclosure law in March 2005. Modeled on the Chicago ordinance, Philadelphia's measure requires companies doing business with the city to search their records and disclose if they profited from slavery. In 2005 Milwaukee, Wisconsin, adopted a similar measure.

In June 2021 a Massachusetts town council approved a fund to pay reparations to Black residents to atone for slavery, discrimination and past wrongs, which several town officials suggested an initial seed investment of more than $200,000 from surplus budget funds. The Amherst Town Council voted 12-1 in favor of establishing the fund. A two-thirds vote of the council is required to authorize any spending from it. Michele Miller, co-founder of Reparations for Amherst, a local advocacy group that pushed for the fund, said her group hopes to establish a private fund to help the town's efforts. "We look forward to supporting the African Heritage Community to implement a robust and sustainable reparative plan," Miller said.[252]

Reparations Suits in Federal Courts

Building on Farmer-Paellmann's legal theory, reparations suits

---

251 California Governor Gavin Newsom Announces Appointments to First-in-the-Nation Task Force to Study Reparations for African Americans (goldrushcam.com) 8 May 2021.

252 Klapper, Rebecca, "Massachusetts Town Will Seed $220K to Begin Reparations for Black Residents," *Newsweek*, 24 June 2021.

against corporations proliferated. Richard E. Barber, a former deputy executive director of the NAACP, filed a lawsuit in Newark, New Jersey, targeting New York Life Insurance, the Wall Street investment firm Brown Brothers Harriman & Co., and the railway company Norfolk Southern. Enter Edward Fagan who predicted that "This is just another step in a series of upcoming political and legal moves that will address the issue of reparations for American slave descendants. Eventually, the six reparations lawsuits filed were consolidated into one federal suit seeking an unspecified amount of money from no less than nineteen corporations representing some of the nation's largest companies.

Reparations lawyers argued that the corporations' ancestors profited by insuring slave ships, insuring slaves for their owners, using slaves, or financing businesses built with slave labor. As it was, on 26 January 2004, Illinois U.S. District Judge Charles Norgle dismissed the suit on the grounds that it was not the courts role to render judgment on such claims, noting that it is "the president and Congress [which] have the constitutional authority to determine the nature and scope of relief . . . not the courts. Judge Norgle wrote, "Plaintiffs' attempt to bring these claims more than a century after the end of the Civil War and the formal abolition of slavery fails," U. S. District Judge Charles R. Norgle said. Further, the plaintiffs' claims "are beyond the constitutional authority of this court" and that the lawsuit claimed no specific connection between the plaintiffs and the companies named as defendants."[253]

Having dismissed the original suit without prejudice, Ms Farmer-Paellmann refiled a class action suit against many of the same companies under the legal theory of unjust enrichment. The amended complaint alleged violations of consumer protection and corporate fraud. The suit charges that corporations had business relationships, including through mortgage loans, connected to slavery but lied about those ties. On 6 July 2005 Judge Norgle made his second in a 104-page opinion. Judge Norgle ruled that the plaintiffs did not prove that they were personally injured by slavery, noting that a genealogical tie to slaves is not enough to prove injury. He made reference to the potential negative consequences of paying reparations. Specifically, he ruled that "present-day Americans are not morally or legally liable for

253 *In re African-Am. Slave Descendents Litig.*, 304 F. Supp. 2d 1027 (N.D. tll. 2004

historical injustices, that the debt to African Americans has already been paid, and that reparations talk is divisive, immersing African Americans in a culture of victimhood." Judged Norgle thought that it was legally and morally ridiculous to hold a company responsible for 150-year-old commercial transactions, such as loaning money with slaves as security or granting loans for the purchasing of slaves.[254]

Judge Norgle's opinions raised two arguments against the slavery class action suit. He ruled that the slavery class action should be dismissed because the plaintiffs have no standing to sue in federal court under Article III of the U. S. Constitution[255], and because the suit runs afoul of the U.S. Supreme Court's "political question" doctrine. Citing the Supreme Court's 1962 decision of *Baker v. Carr*[256], the federal courts should not attempt to adjudicate questions which are non-justiciable; that is, not susceptible to being resolved in court, because they are inherently political - and thus better suited to resolution by other branches of government.[257]

Reparations from Corporations

Beginning in January 2005, four of the nation's leading banks —JPMorgan Chase; Wachovia; Bank of America; and Lehman Brothers—have admitted some sort of financial dealings with slavery. Various state and local laws required the banks to disclose any and all such transactions. Each company has significant financial interests in the demanding cities and so to keep their activities legal all four banks complied with the prevailing legislation.

The first company to give in to the demands of black militants was JPMorgan Chase. In January 2005, the bank announced that it had conducted a thorough and complete review of its earliest business records and had discovered that two of its predecessor banks in Louisiana owned slaves who had been used as collateral for loans to Loui-

254 See Epstein, Richard A., "The Case against Black Reparations," *Boston University Law Review* 84 (2004), pp. 1177-92.

255 *In re African-Am. Slave Descendents Litig.*, 304 F. Supp. 2d at 1044-75

256 *In re African-Am. Slave Descendents Litig.*, 304 F. Supp. 2d at 1053-63, asserting that each Baker factor is grounds for dismissing the plaintiffs complaint.

257Rotenberk, Lori, "Slavery Reparations Lawsuit Dismissed," *The Boston Globe*, 27 January 2004; *Washington Times*, 27 January 2004. Judge Norgle's opinion was published as *In re African-American Slave Descendants Litig. See also* Sebok, Anthony J., "*The Lawsuit Brought by African-Americans Seeking Compensation from Corporations for The Wrongs of Slavery: Why the Opinion Dismissing the Suit Is Unpersuasive," Legal commentary on Findlaw, 8 August 2005.*

siana plantation owners. JPMorgan's connection to slavery was complex and convoluted. Between 1831 and 1865, Canal Bank and Citizens Bank accepted 13,000 slaves as collateral on loans and had found it necessary to repossess some 1,250 of those slaves after plantation owners defaulted on loans. The banks merged in 1924 to form Canal Commercial Trust & Savings Bank which failed in 1933 during the Great Depression. Its deposits were placed in The National Bank of Commerce of New Orleans, which later became the First National Bank of Commerce. Bank One acquired First National Bank of Commerce in 1998.[258]

Rather than confront the reparations activists, JPMorgan Chase chose to apologize for its tenuous tie to slavery. It created a $5 million college scholarship fund for black college students in Louisiana. Company executives erroneously thought that this apology and a multi-million dollar payoff would buy off the reparations lobby. It miscalculated and the bank has been plagued with its supposed past misdeeds ever since.[259]

Other banks fell in line quickly. Bank of America, as we saw in our entry on Tillman, owned up to having had ties to slavery.[260] Wachovia suddenly admitted to its sins of decades past.[261] The list continued to grow and branch out beyond financial institutions. Companies which provided various forms of energy have become possible targets for reparations suits and pressure campaigns because some of them reportedly used slaves to lay oil lines beneath cities. The Reparations Coordinating Committee announced that it plans to sue various colleges and universities which it alleges have profited from slavery. The Committee specifically cited Harvard, Yale, Princeton, Brown and the University of Virginia. Some of these universities, such as the University of Mississippi, the University of Virginia, and University of South Carolina, were built using slave labor. In other cases, some of the early benefactors were slave owners and thus must be punished for how they obtained wealth. Various mining companies

---

258 Spielman, Fran, "Reparations Leaders Rip Bank's Scholarship Offer," *Chicago Sun-Times*, 23 January 2005.

259 Spielman, Fran, "Reparations Leaders Rip Bank's Scholarship Offer," *Chicago Sun-Times, 23* January 2005

260 Wisniewski, Mary, "Bank of America Admits Ties to Slavery," *Chicago Sun-Times,* 25 August 2005

261 Smitherman, Laura, "Wachovia Apologizes for Slavery Ties of Predecessors," *Baltimore Sun*, 2 June 2005

also reportedly relied upon slaves to dig for coal and harvest salt. Even newspapers could become potential targets because many profited by printing runaway slave notices beginning in the eighteenth century.[262] In this way, by capitulating to absurd demands, banks made themselves conspicuous and long-lasting targets. By apologizing for alleged involvement in slavery and attempting to appease activists with multi-million dollar donations, the banks have created touch areas for continual demands for ever more reparations payments.

Fictitious Tax Refunds

One tactic used to obtain so-called reparations payments was to file income tax forms seeking substantial refunds and citing a bogus "Slave Reparations Act" or non-existent "black inheritance tax refund." In 2002 the Internal Revenue Service (IRS) warned against filing false tax claims tied to reparations. In March 2002, responding to a surge in frivolous claims for the non-existent slave reparations tax credit, the U.S. Department of Justice filed civil suits in Mississippi and Virginia to prohibit tax professionals from preparing returns that claimed such refunds based on this spurious tax credit. Prior to that, the IRS disclosed it had paid out as much as $30 million to persons (including at least four current or former IRS employees) who had claimed such a credit in 2000 and part of 2001. One woman reportedly received a half-million dollars using this scam.[263]

Reparations in England

England's High Court of Justice ordered the Metropolitan Police Service and the Lambeth London Borough Council to pay $130,000 in damages to Black activists from the Nation of Islam Monday, with the judge ruling that the agencies worked together to prevent insurrectionist Louis Farrakhan from giving a 2017 speech on slavery reparations. The High Court's Justice Neil Stephen Garnham ruled that Met Police and the Lambeth city breached the human rights of 34 Black representatives from the U.K. Nation of Islam ahead of an August 2017 event called the 4th Africa International Day of Action. Organizers had scheduled Farrakhan to deliver a remote speech about reparations to Kennington Park event attendees. His planned remarks

---

262 Flaherty, Peter and John Carlisle, "The Case Against Slave Reparations," National Legal and Policy Center, 2004.

263 Flaherty and Carlisle, *op. cit.*, p. 14.

cited hundreds of years of the trans-Atlantic slave trade as justification for seeking modern reparation benefits. Nation of Islam lawyers rejected police claims that Farrakhan's speech was blocked solely to avoid threats of "disorder."

Metropolitan Police, citing Farrakhan's long history of anti-Semitic remarks and "extreme views," were criticized by the High Court for having issued a narrowly tailored event permit that ultimately prevented Farrakhan from remotely calling in to give the speech at all. The High Court on Monday agreed with the Nation of Islam plaintiffs who brought a complaint that accused police and the city council of proactively stifling the discussion on reparations, thus "unlawfully infringing" upon the claimants' rights under the Human Rights Act of 1998.

“My clients just wanted to talk about reparations for the historical and continuing effects of slavery," plaintiff attorney Andre Clovis told the court on behalf of the 34 Black activists from the Detroit-based Nation of Islam. "The Lambeth City Council and the Metropolitan Police, by eliminating Plaintiffs' ability to speak their minds, sought to suppress their ability to think about matters of central importance to their own being." Garnham said authorities from both the local Lambeth city council and Metropolitan Police imposed an illegal ban on Farrakhan's scheduled broadcast about slavery reparations. They were ordered to collectively pay the $130,000 (£92,250) in damages in addition to $250,000 in legal fees. Clovis said Lambeth City Council and police have spent nearly $2 million fighting this case since 2017, and have continually denied any and all wrongdoing.
"[This has] served to compound the insult my clients felt and it was a serious abuse of public funds [which were] deployed not for the benefit of their local community, but to hide wrongdoing and to protect their own reputations."

The Lambeth City Council and officials with the Metropolitan Police expressed regret over how the incident was perceived, with spokesperson James Berry issuing a written statement that "the Metropolitan Police Service has no desire to stifle speech on reparations." Berry noted that it was Farrakhan's long history of expressing "extreme views" and potentially violence-inciting rhetoric which had law enforcement on edge prior to the 2017 event. Martin Forde, legal counsel for the claimants, dismissed authority concerns over Farrakhan's inflammatory past remarks about Jews, Adolf Hitler and "anti-termites." Speaking to the court Monday, Forde said the Nation of Islam leader has been "misrepresented in a very sensationalized way in the media" for decades.[264]

The Case against Reparations

There have been many objections launched against the payment of reparations for slavery.[265] It is, of course, legally and morally absurd to hold companies responsible for commercial what were then perfectly legal transactions made well over a century earlier.

As we saw in the case of Edward Fagan, one argument for reparations payments to descendants of slaves is based in reparations paid to victims of World War II. Those advocating slave reparations who make this argument have misapplied logic. This is clearly a case of false analogy. In the cases of Holocaust and Japanese internment reparations, the payments went to the actual victims of the wrongdoings or to the victims' immediate families, not to the descendants of victims. Recent, generally successful, lawsuits undertaken by Holocaust survivors seeking to extract payments from German companies that profited from slave labor during the Nazi era but again apply to survivors of this horror or their immediate successors.

Another alleged case of reparations payments involved payments made to several Native American tribal nations. In 1986 the Ottawa tribe living in Michigan received $32 million based on an 1836 treaty. These were not reparations payments at all, but rather were legal settlements involving land disputes between Native American tribes and the U.S. government, determined under legally binding treaties between sovereign nations. According to the Bureau of Indian Affairs, in the 1800s the U.S. government sometimes acquired land, mineral rights and other property from Indian tribes without adequate compensation. Many treaties, for example, contained provisions for the cessation of Indian lands to the U.S. government, yet the Amerindians had never been compensated for ceding those lands.[266] Actually, the Amerindian leaders would have preferred having the land rather than the money.

---

264 Fearnow, Benjamin, "Police Ordered to Pay Nation of Islam $130K for Blocking Louis Farrakhan Reparations Speech," *Newsweek*, 12 May 2021.

265 Flaherty, Peter and Carlisle, John, "The Case Against Slave Reparations" National Legal and Policy Center, October 2004.

266 Masci, David, "Reparations," Issues in Race, Ethnicity and Gender: Selections from the CQ Researcher, *Congressional Quarterly*, Washington, D.C., 2001

There is a legitimate question as to who should pay the demanded reparations. A very small percentage of Americans have ancestors who owned slaves. Approximately three-quarters of whites in the antebellum South did not own slaves. In the United States, blacks frequently owned other blacks as slaves. For example, about one-third of the 10,600 free blacks in New Orleans in 1860 were slave owners. Various Amerindians, notably the the Cherokees, enslaved blacks extensively. There are many black Americans, most of them recent immigrants, do not have ancestors who were U.S. slaves. Virtually all economic disparity between descendants of former slaves and the descendants of free blacks largely disappeared within just two generations following emancipation, which suggests that slavery had little effect on the economic condition of future generations. At the height of the slave trade, there were nearly as many slaves within Africa as there were in the Americas. Around 1800, roughly one-tenth of the resident population in Africa were slaves, about 2.5 million people. By 1850, there were more slaves in Africa, 10 million, than in the Americas. Of an estimated 9.6 million African slaves who arrived in the Americas from the sixteenth through the nineteenth centuries, less than 5 percent came to what is now the United States.

Defunding the Police

Defund the police is a slogan that supports divesting funds from police departments and reallocating them to non-policing forms of public safety and community support, such as social services, youth services, housing, education, healthcare and other community resources. Activists who use the phrase may do so with varying intentions; some seek modest reductions, while others argue for full divestment as a step toward the abolition of contemporary police services. Activists that support the defunding of police departments often argue that investing in community programs could provide a better crime deterrent for communities; funds would go toward addressing social issues, like poverty, homelessness, and mental disorders. Police abolitionists call for replacing existing police forces with other systems of public safety, like housing, employment, community health, education, and other programs.

One recent law student chose four different ways to conceptualize the act of defunding the police. To defund the police can refer to a long-term policy aim to abolish the police, to recalibrate what police do in society, to create accountability measures through conditional funding, or simply to save government resources. These four interpretations of defunding are not mutually exclusive. Each meaning tells us something about the movement."Defund" is a transitive verb that means "to withdraw funding from or "to withdraw financial support from. Colloquially, defunding refers to either a reduction in, or the elimination of, funding. Public debate turns on social interpretations of the word in the context of policing.[267] The "defund the police" slogan became closely associated with the George Floyd protests which erupted in May 2020. The slogan was popularized by the Black Visions Collective shortly after the death of George Floyd.

Critics of the police argue that the one consistent finding in the social science literature is that if we really want to reduce crime, education equity and the establishment of a work infrastructure is the best approach. A study using 60 years of data found that an increase in funding for police did not significantly relate to a decrease in crime. Throwing more police on the street to solve a structural problem is one of the reasons why people are protesting in the streets. Defunding

267 Eaglin, Jessica M., "To 'Defund' the Police," Stanford Law Review Online, 73: 120 (2021).

police—reallocating funding away from police departments to other sectors of government—may be more beneficial for reducing crime and police violence.[268]

Origins of the Movement

The Black Lives Matter, Movement for Black Lives, and other protesters, rioters, insurrectionists, and activists have used the phrase to call for police budget reductions and to delegate certain police responsibilities to other organizations. Many trace the advocacies of these organizations, and the assertion that black lives mattered as much as white lives, to W. E. B. DuBois.

William Edward Burghardt Du Bois (1868–1963) was an American sociologist, socialist, historian, Pan-Africanist, author, writer and editor. Born in Great Barrington, Massachusetts, Du Bois grew up in a relatively tolerant and racially integrated community. After completing graduate work at the University of Berlin and Harvard University, where he was the first African American to earn a doctorate, he became a professor of history, sociology and economics at Atlanta University. Du Bois was one of the founders of the National Association for the Advancement of Colored People (NAACP) in 1909.

In 1911, DuBois had joined the Socialist Party of America. However, he supported the Democrat Woodrow Wilson in the 1912 presidential campaign, and was forced to resign from the Socialist Party. In 1913, Wilson, a Virginia segregationist, placed all black employees, regardless of job or department, in the same building so Caucasian employees would not have to work in close proximinity with them. Still, DuBois remained remained convinced that socialism was an excellent way of life. Nine years after the 1917 Russian Revolution, DuBois visited the Soviet Union, where he was struck by the poverty and disorganization he encountered in the Soviet Union, yet was impressed by the intense labors of the officials and by the recognition given to workers. Although DuBois claimed that he was not familiar with the communist theories of Karl Marx and Vladimir Lenin, he concluded that socialism might provide the better path towards racial equality than capitalism. Although Du Bois generally endorsed socialist principles, his politics were essentially pragmatic. For example, in 1929, he endorsed Democrat Jimmy Walker for mayor of New

---

268 Ray, Rashawn, "What does 'defund the police' Mean and Does it Have Merit? Brookings Institute, Friday, June 19, 2020

York, rather than the socialist Norman Thomas, believing that Walker could do more immediate good for blacks, even though Thomas's platform was more consistent with Du Bois's views.

In *Black Reconstruction*, first published in 1935, W. E. B. DuBois wrote about "abolition-democracy", which advocated for the removal of institutions that were rooted in racist and repressive practices, including prisons, convict leasing, and white police forces. He described the difference between white and black laborers.

> It must be remembered that the white group of laborers, while they received a low wage, were compensated in part by a sort of public and psychological wage. They were given public deference and titles of courtesy because they were white. They were admitted freely with all classes of white people to public functions, public parks, and the best schools. The police were drawn from their ranks, and the courts, dependent upon their votes, treated them with such leniency as to encourage lawlessness. Their vote selected public officials, and while this had small effect upon the economic situation, it had great effect upon their personal treatment and the deference shown them. White schoolhouses were the best in the community, and conspicuously placed, and they cost anywhere from twice to ten times as much per capita as the colored schools. The newspapers specialized on news that flattered the poor whites and almost utterly ignored the Negro except in crime and ridicule.[269]

In the 1960s, insurrectionists such as Angela Davis advocated for the defunding or abolition of police departments.

The book *The End of Policing*, authored by Alex S. Vitale, and published in 2017, has been called the instructional manual for the movement to defund the police. Alex S. Vitale is a contemporary author who is professor of sociology at Brooklyn College. He has served at that institution as as the coordinator of the Policing and Social Justice Project. His writing has appeared in the *New York Times, The Nation, The Appeal, USA Today, Vice News,* and other left-of-center media outlets. In one recent book, Vitale focused on the drive to improve quality of life in New York City and other American cities. In particular, he asserted that, in the 1990s, New York City politicians focused on restoring the fundamental moral order, which included the "zero tolerance" campaign advocated by then Mayor Rudolph Giuliani. It brought about a major overhaul of laws dealing with prostitution, graffiti, panhandling, and homelessness in the city.

269Du Bois, W. E. B. *Black Reconstruction.* Harcourt, 1935, ch. XVI

This, he claimed, marked a shift toward prioritizing the needs of the middle and upper classes over and against the lower classes. The book examined how such changes impacted various New York neighborhoods, the New York Police Department, and city politics.[270]

When first published, *The End of Policing* was met with a mixed reception. Positive reviews praised his writing style and the fine detailing in his research. The negative reviews argued that Vitale's proposed solution of abolition of the police was too extreme. However, there was a small number of reviews that claimed that his solution was not extreme enough.

Following the George Floyd protests, Vitale's work received wider public interest. He became a darling of the leftist media, interviewed constantly on his ideas on alternatives to the police. Media outlets such as National Public Radio, the Intercept, Jacobin, The Nation, band The Independent, Democracy Now,and The Daily Show, hung on his every word. Be became the mentor to the various movements that sought to defund or abolish the police.

The idea of defunding the police, presumably in each and every American community, can be traced to the Black Lives Movement and Alicia Garza. Alicia was born out of wedlock to a single mother in Oakland, California, in 1981. During her first four years she lived with her black mother and uncle. After her mother married , she lived with her Jewish stepfather. During her teens, she engaged in agitated on behalf of various causes, including birth control. She graduated from the University of California, San Diego, in 2002, having majored in anthropology and sociology. In 2003 she met Malachi Garza, 24, a transgender person. In 2004, Alicia came out as homosexual. In 2008, she married Malachi and took the name Garza, settling in Oakland.

Opal Tometi, born in 1984, is the daughter of Nigerian immigrants, the oldest of three children, who grew up in Phoenix, Arizona, but now lives in Brooklyn, New York. She received a Bachelor of Arts degree in History from the University of Arizona; a Masters in Communication and Advocacy from Arizona State University; and an honorary doctor of science degree from Clarkson University. She was formerly a case manager for survivors of domestic violence. Ms Tometi was a co-founder of Black Lives Matter. Tometi has been

---

270Vitale, A. S. *City of Disorder: How the Quality of Life Campaign Transformed New York Politics*. NYU Press, 2009.

credited with setting up the social media portions of the movement. She is the former Executive Director of the United States' first national immigrant rights organization for people of African descent, the Black Alliance for Just Immigration.[271] As a co-founder of the Black Lives Matter, she recently called for a boycott of the British royal family following Meghan Markle's claims of royal racism in her interview with Oprah Winfrey.

Garza is credited with creating the slogan, "Bl;ack Lives Matter," after the July 2013 acquittal of George Zimmerman in the death of Trayvon Martin. Specifically, she lamented, "I continue to be surprised at how little Black lives matter." Garza's post became popularized after protests emerged in Ferguson, Missouri, following the death of Michael Brown. Garza led the agitation in Ferguson, and helped organize Black Lives Matter chapters across the United States. Garza has been credited with popularizing the use of social media for mass mobilization in the United States; a practice called "mediated mobilization.

Garza's first book, *The Purpose of Power: How We Come Together When We Fall Apart,* was published in October 2020 by Penguin Random House. It has been advertised as "an essential guide", the book tells Garza's story as an activist and shares lessons for future activists. Various publications, especially of the political Left, such as *The Guardian, The Nation, The Feminist Wire, Rolling Stone, HuffPost* and *Truthout*, have published her opinions.. She also worked with Special Projects at the National Domestic Workers Alliance and People Organized to Win Employment Rights (POWER) in the San Francisco Bay Area.

In 2018 Garza launched Black Futures Lab, whose announced goal was to engage with advocate organizations to advance policies that make black communities stronger, starting with the Black Census Project, which was a survey included questions on subjects such as political attitudes, organization affiliation, experiences with racism and police violence, and the perceptions of various social movements. It plans to use the results of the Black Census Project to agitate for various perceived important legislative and policy issues. The Project has also focused on the black LGBTQ community.

271Dalton, Deron, "The Three Women Behind the Black Lives Matter Movement," *Madame Noire*, 4 May 2015. See also "Black Lives Matter Founders Chosen As Glamour's "Women Of The Year," *Essence*, 2 November 2016.

According to Garza, white supremacists, right-wing militias, back by racist police, were responsible for most violence on the West Coast in 2020. "And who gets blamed for that," she charged, "is people who are protesting to raise the issues of justice, to raise the issues of dignity and to fight back against police violence in our communities."

Garza and her organization has traced a line from chattel slavery to Jim Crow to the creation of the first police departments in the United States, seeing all as part of a gigantic conspiracy against blacks, most notably against the many black women who have been assaulted and killed by law enforcement. In 2018, Garza announced that the language that white Americans use is, "Well, if they hadn't been committing a crime, then there would not have been a problem." She asserted that the prevailing Caucasian mentality sheds light on the violence, particularly at the hands of law enforcement, because the police have "always been directed against Black and indigenous Americans." Garza has repeatedly called for the defunding of police departments, reminding Americans that the struggle toward liberation must include drastically shifting the power given to American law enforcement. Her constant claim is that police departments are step-children of chattel slavery in the United States. It is her opinion that "Policing as a system is incredibly corrupt, period. There are people inside of these departments who want to reinstate a level of integrity into these departments and they should be commended. But they cannot do that on their own . . Policing as a whole in this country is deeply, deeply corrupt and cannot be reformed." [272]

In a recent interview, Garza made her views on police clear. She said:

> What we are dealing with right now is a disease that has plagued America since its inception. Convicting a few cops isn't going to deal with that disease. We've been trying hard this year to be clear that state violence is bigger than police terrorism. Although police terrorism plays a specific role on behalf of the state, it is not the totality of what state violence looks like or feels like in our communities. We've been shifting the narrative to talk about state violence being structural racism. Given that,

272Quoted in Segura, Olga M., "The History of Policing in the United States Is About Controlling Black Lives," Teen Vogue on Microsoft News, 15 March 2021. See also Goodman, Amy, "Alicia Garza on Being Targeted in Armed White Supremacist Plot as Trump Stokes Fires of Racism," Democracy Now! 27 October 2020.

> what we are lifting up here is that we need a bigger vision than just Band-Aid reforms—we need to move towards a transformative vision that touches on what's at the root of the problems we are facing.[273]

Most recently, the Black Lives Matter movement has been buckling under its own success, with tensions rising between local chapters and national leaders over the group's goals, direction and distribution of the vast amount of money it has collected. From the beginning, Black Lives Matter was a grassroots effort, born in the streets with no central hierarchy. The idea: to keep power concentrated in the hands of its members, the people. The master controller is known as the Black Lives Matter Global Network (BLMGN). By the end of June 2020, the Black Lives Matter Global Network had raised more than $13 million in donations, with much more to come, and it had cemented its role as a political power and organizing force.[274]

Ms Tometi, long with self described "queer" co-founders Alicia Garza and Patrisse Cullors, has had BLM call for the extermination of the white race, not just what it styles white privilege. BLM defines white supremacy as white males who identify as heterosexual. Only white males with a gender identity among the fifty-eight or so Facebook-recognized gender identities other than heterosexual or "straight", are not considered subhuman. The vast majority of BLM activists, supporters, and financial backers are white so-called progressives.[275]

Patrisse Cullors, born in 1983, is a black artist and activist and a co-founder of the Black Lives Matter movement. Cullors created the #BlackLivesMatter hashtag in 2013 and has written and spoken widely about the movement. Other topics on which Cullors advocates include abolition of the prison system, ending capital punishment, and LGBTQ rights. She co-founded the prison activist organization known as Dignity and Power Now, which advocated a civilian oversight board for California jails. Cullors has borrowed ideas from various critical and nihilistic theories from around the world,.

273Smith, Mychal Denzel, "A Q&A With Alicia Garza, Co-Founder of #BlackLivesMatter: The force behind the burgeoning movement talks about the resurgent fight for black liberation," *The Nation*, 24 March 2015.

274King, Maya, "Black Lives Matter Power Grab Sets Off Internal Revolt," *Politico,* 10 December 2020.

275See Fernando, Ivan. "Progressive professor urges white male students to commit suicide during class," 18 November 2013 on Diversity Chronicle website. See also "Opal Tometi" on Conservapedia

In a newly surfaced video from 2015 Ms Cullors declared that she and her fellow organizers are "trained Marxists" – making clear their movement's ideological foundation, according to a report. "The first thing, I think, is that we actually do have an ideological frame. Myself and Alicia in particular are trained organizers," she said, referring to BLM co-founder Alicia Garza. "We are trained Marxists. We are super-versed on, sort of, ideological theories. And I think that what we really tried to do is build a movement that could be utilized by many, many black folk," Cullors added in the interview with Jared Ball of The Real News Network.

While promoting her book *When They Call You a Terrorist: A Black Lives Matter Memoir* in 2018, Cullors described her introduction to and support for Marxist ideology. She fully accepted the Marxist line regarding the creation of wealth: "This country was created from stolen land and stolen labor. And from a moral perspective, but also from a practical one, everybody knows that when you steal, you're always looking over your shoulder because you know that somebody may steal it back."[276]

Ms Cullors has defines herself as one who is committed to abolishing prisons, the police and militarization, a position she says is inspired by "a legacy of black-led anti-colonial struggle in the United States and throughout the Americas." She also favors reparations for what she describes as "the historical pains and damage caused by European settler colonialism", in various forms, such "financial restitution, land redistribution, political self-determination, culturally relevant education programs, language recuperation, and the right to return or repatriation." As she wrote, "The United States, the world's largest jailer and is also the world's greatest perpetrator of war and the most extensive purveyor of human rights atrocities at home and abroad, laying claim to over 800 military bases around the world. Our task is not only to abolish prisons, policing, and militarization, which are wielded in the name of public safety and national security."[277]

She is the author of *When They Call You a Terrorist: A Black Lives Matter Memoir.* In her work and on her interviews she frequently cites various convicted criminals, revolutionaries, nihilists, and

276Steinbuch, Yaron, "Black Lives Matter Co-founder Describes Herself as a Trained Marxist," New York Post, 25 June 2020.

277Cullors, Patrisse, "Abolition And Reparations: Histories of Resistance, Transformative Justice, And Accountability," *Harvard Law Review,* 10 April 2019.

communists. She praised Weather Underground member Eric Mann as her intellectual mentor during her earliest years. She draws on various dissidents as her inspiration, such as black feminist Audre Lorde and her "Black, queer, feminist lens." .She drew upon Angela Davis for her "political theories and reflections on anti-capitalist movements around the world", her work towards "a broader anti-racist and antiwar movement", and her fight against white supremacy in the United States. Franz Fanon was another inspiration in his "work on colonial violence in Algeria and across the Third World [making] timely connections" for the understanding of the context in which black people live throughout the world. She also freely cited Karl Marx, Vladimir Lenin and Mao Zedong, who, she asserted, provided "a new understanding around what our economies could look like."[278]

By 2021 two of the three co-founders of BLM, Alicia Garza and Opal Tometi, had left the BLMGN, although they have continued to speak on its behalf. Patrisse Cullors, its remaining co-founder, assumed the role of executive director of the group and made many decisions without the input of local chapters. The ten complaining local chapters signed have signed a letter which laid out a half-dozen points of contention and long-standing grievances. Cullors has been the cause of most complaints, they said, arguing she made a power grab when she appointed herself executive director of the Black Lives Matter Global Network. These chapters also said that there has been a lack of transparency over money the movement has raised and how chapters can access it. Since Black Lives Matter formed in 2013, the chapters complained they've received scant financial support, despite repeated promises.

Campaign Zero was founded as an organization which focused on containing perceived police violence. However, BLMGN criticized it for advocating for solutions they argued were far too modest and did not go nearly far enough in defunding and hemming in the police. Its #8CantWait campaign called for an eight-step approach to ending police violence, but BLMGN rejected that program, saying it was filled with half-way measures which had already been tried and failed. Moreover, BLMGN argued, that #8 relied on shoddy data that was

278Jenkins, Aric, "Black Lives Matter Co-Founder Patrisse Cullors on Her Book," *Time* magazine, 26 February 2018; Walcott, Rianna, "How the Founder of Black Lives Matter Started a Global Movement," *Dazed,* 5 April 2018.

unsustainable. Campaign Zero was originally led by Johnetta Elzie, DeRay McKesson, Brittany Packnett Cunningham and Samuel Sinyangwe. Seeing the apparent futility of opposing BLMGN, it issued a public apology for rushing out the campaign so quickly. Cunningham later resigned from Campaign Zero. It was obvious that no modest program of police reform would satisfy BLMGN.

Partial Defunding

When abolitionists talk about responding to police violence, they often refer to the Illinois Reparations for Police Torture Victims Act drafted in response to the heinous acts of torture by the Chicago Police Department under the leadership of the late Jon Burge. This legislation provides non-financial reparations for survivors and their families, including an official apology, free psychological counseling, free education at the City Colleges, and job training; it mandates that public schools teach about the torture in eighth- and tenth-grade curricula. The City of Chicago set aside $5.5 million to financially compensate living survivors of the torture. In Chicago, money in the police budget is set aside in the police budget to fund civil lawsuits that the City anticipates will result from police misconduct each year.[279]

Advocates of defunding claim that it is a common misconception that "defunding the police" mandates completely stripping law enforcement of all of their funding. While while some organizations are indeed calling for the abolition and dismantling of police altogether, ro some "defunding the police" means only partially dismantling the traditional units and reducing police department budgets and redistributing those funds towards essential social services that are often underfunded, such as housing, education, employment, mental health care, and youth services.

One of those agitating for partial defunding is Christy E. Lopez, a professor at Georgetown Law School and a co-director of the school's Innovative Policing Program. Professor Lopez recently wrote in an op-ed piece published in *The Washington Post,* entitled "Defunding the Police." In making it all sound so good and wholesome, she asserted that the movement seeks only "the shrinking the scope of police responsibilities and shifting most of what government does to keep us safe to entities that are better equipped to meet that need," she explained. "It means investing more in mental-health care

279 "Chicago t o Pay $5.5 million," *Chicago Sun,* 26 June 2015.

and housing, and expanding the use of community mediation and violence interruption programs."

In a fundamental error of logic, those advocating defunding assume to be factual that the police are generally ill-equipped to address various societal problems, and to deal with suspects who are mentally ill, retarded, disoriented, or deranged. Since police department budgets commonly consume a large portion of many cities' overall budgets, often significantly exceed funds for other areas such as education, employment, and other critical social services, it is police budgets that must suffer substantial decreases. It has been estimated that cities expend over $100 billion annually on policing nationwide. In a recent year, New York City allocated $6 billion to the funding of its police department, a budget that exceeded more than those of the health department, homeless services, youth and community development, and workforce development combined.

Governments have assigned police with the tasks of responding to a vast variety of social issues and crises, from homelessness to mental illness although they are rarely trained to handle such tasks. Proponents of defunding the police argue that investing in public health and social services, rather than in police, would constitute a more appropriate and effective means to meet the public safety needs of a community. Specifically, they argue, these social services would be trained so that they would be adequately prepared to address societal issues such as poverty, homelessness, and mental health more directly. Since the properly trained public servants would respond to social crises more appropriately than police, they would act as better deterrent to crime than law enforcement. Crime would therefore diminish, requiring fewer police.

Besides, activists point out, playing the inevitable race card, the police have historically been a harmful institution that perpetuates systemic racism. By redistributing these funds to essential social services and community programs, the idea is that the needs of a community can be more directly addressed without the harmful effects of prevalent police policies. Those endemic policies have been especially harmful for Black, Indigenous, and People of Color (BIPOC) who have disproportionately suffered from police brutality and violence.

"Defund the police" implies reallocating or redirecting funding away from the police department to other government agencies funded by the local municipality. Defund does not necessarily mean abolish the police. And, even some who say abolish, do not necessarily mean to do away with law enforcement altogether. Rather, they offer this metaphor: they want to see the rotten trees within police departments cut down and fresh roots replanted. Critics of police offer Camden, New Jersey, as a good example of what they seek. Nearly a decade ago, Camden disbanded its police force and dissolved the local police union. This approach seems to be what the anti-police elements in Minneapolis want do in some form, although even tiny nuances are important.

Different from abolishing and starting anew, defunding police highlights fiscal responsibility, advocates for a market-driven approach to taxpayer money, and has some potential benefits that will reduce police violence and crime.

The Movement for Black Lives boasts that the movement's core idea — that black lives are valuable — and need to be protected from racist police-- has benefited from its embrace in popular culture, particularly the "unapologetically black" aesthetic, which merged black history and civil rights causes with fashion and art, with much favorable publicity garnered after it seeped into recent Hollywood productions. Anti-police activity is meaningless and harmful, according to leading black spokespersons, when people join marches and post "Black Lives Matter" but do not advocate for substantive changes in police policy.

In 2021, politicians in some large municipalities with an alleged history of police brutality have reallocated funds in line with the defund police movement. Los Angeles alter its police appropriations by at least $100 million, reassigning those funds to programs within the minority communities. San Francisco Mayor London Breed said that she will work with community groups to reprioritize its public safety funding. Baltimore City Council voted to reallocate $22 million, taking it away from the police department whose annual budget for 2021 was to have been over $500 million. The city council plans to redirect the funding to recreational centers, trauma centers, and forgivable loans for black-owned businesses. Authorities in Prince George's County, Maryland, decided to reallocate $20 million, taking it away from a new training facility which it had planned to build for its police department, although that money would not come out of the police department's budget. The same decision-makers also chose to remove student resource officers from the public schools. Other areas, such as Minneapolis, have advocated removing police officers from schools as well.

Police Recalibration

To defund the police can also mean supporting the idea that we need to reprioritize existing public resources to create healthier communities. Significant amounts of public resources go toward police, yet more policing does not always make a community safer, particularly when considering economically disadvantaged black and brown communities. Other forms of public spending could increase safety more effectively while also creating a more equitable society. While abolitionists seek to transform society by ending policing, recalibrationists seek to transform it by altering police responsibilities. Those changes can occur through reductions in funding to police. This reform would explicitly defund the police. The funding for this mental health services system would be appropriated from the police budget. Policymakers urging recalibration-oriented defunding reforms are deeply concerned with structural marginalization. To those advocating recalibration, the reduction in police funding does not equate with the long-term elimination of all police; rather, it is the transformation of their function in society.

As many as 90% of all calls made to the 911 system which have been referred to police are non-violent instances. Advocates for the defund movement like Phillip McHarris and Thenjiwe McHarris argue that shifting funding to social services that can improve things such as mental health, addiction, and homelessness is a better use of taxpayer money. This approach further enhances the push to decriminalize and destigmatize people with mental health conditions and addiction problems. They claim that there has been serious overcriminalization focused on people who are addicted to crack cocaine. They claim that that this shift in emphasis is long overdue.

Thenjiwe Harris has spent her political career calling for an end to presumed policies and practices which she alleges have led to acts of torture being frequently committed by law enforcement personnel. She went on to help organize efforts that addressed the alleged human rights violations which she asserts occurred during and after Hurricanes Katrina and Rita. She has actively opposed the imposition of solitary confinement and capital punishment. She has claimed that American law enforcement is committed to the use of excessive force. Mosy recently, Thenjiwe has been working with a team called Blackbird, which has focused on movement building. Blackbird provides communications, and organizing as well as policy and advocacy support to various organization which claim that they are committed to ending racism in the United States. Thenjiwe McHarris, was an important strategist in the Movement for Black Lives, the coalition formed by the three women who coined the phrase "Black lives matter." She said much of the movement's work has happened away from well-covered protests and speeches.

Anti-police activists across the country have developed relationships with state and local leaders while lobbying for governments to spend less on policing and more on housing, mental health and social work. These efforts have resulted in drug intervention programs in the District of Columbia. Among its claimed victories is the dispatching of social workers to 911 calls in Dallas, Texas.

One of the charges that BLM have made as justification for defunding the police is related to weaponry. Over the last several decades, the police, which had been created as localized public safety units, have instead embraced key advanced and highly lethal weaponry of the military. Police see these as weapons as vital parts of their mission to serve and protect. BLM has charged that law enforcement, at times, has deployed these weapons with disastrous results, largely because their training is insufficient. Some police departments have ignored the most important and crucial aspect of military dogma: avoid using your weapon if at all possible and then to use supreme discipline when deploying it.

In a 2016 survey taken by Pew, only about a third of black adults said that police in their community did an "excellent" or "good" job in using the right amount of force (33%, compared with 75% of whites), treating racial and ethnic groups equally (35% vs. 75%), and holding officers accountable for misconduct (31% vs. 70%).[280]

Who Supports Defunding?

The idea to cut, or even totally eliminate, funding to police departments strikes some observers as extreme. But activists say the rallying cry is the only sensible course of action after decades of piecemeal reform efforts that did little to change police culture. There is a

---

280 DeSilver, Drew; Michael Lipka; and Dalia Fahmy, "10 things We Know about Race and Policing in the U.S.," Pew Research, 3 June 2020.

group in the United States Congress that has advocated defunding the police. Its members include Representatives Alexandria Ocasio-Cortez (D-NY), Ilhan Omar (D-MN), Rashida Tlaib (D-MI), Ayanna Pressley (D-MA),and Mondaire Jones (D-NY). The so-called Squad works well with the American Civil Liberties Union (ACLU) since have called for a decrease in or cessation of law enforcement funding after the death of George Floyd in Minneapolis.

Ocasio-Cortez has been a vocal proponent of defunding the police, constantly defending her position on the issue. In 2019, Ocasio-Cortez joined Senator Bernie Sanders (I-VT) in demanding that the U.S. to follow New Zealand's total ban on semi-automatic weapons Jones has also called for a "partial defunding" of police forces. Omar called the Minneapolis police "rotten to the root" and demanded their dismantling last June. Tlaib recently called the American police "inherently [and] intentionally racist."

The ACLU released an opinion piece in the summer of 2020, claiming that defunding the police across the country would make America "safer." It noted a racist origin to police in the United States. "The first U.S. city police department was a slave patrol, and modern police forces have directed oppression and violence at Black people to enforce Jim Crow, wage the War on Drugs, and crack down on protests," the ACLU wrote. "When people ask for police reform, many are actually asking for this oppressive system to be dismantled and to invest in institutions, resources, and services that help communities grow and thrive." The ACLU stepped up its attack on police. "That's why many protesters and activists, following in the footsteps of Black-led grassroots groups, are demanding immediate defunding of police departments," the opinion piece continued. This civil liberties group claimed that the "basic premise" of defunding the police is to "cut the astronomical amount of money" that governments spend on law enforcement and give that money to "more helpful services like job training, counseling, and violence-prevention programs." Among other steps the ACLU demanded was that the Department of Homeland Security be disbanded after "years of chaos and impunity."[281]

One of those most adamant about defunding the police is Con-

281 Keene, Howard, "'Defund the Police' advocates lack effective alternatives for combating violent crime," Fox News, 20 April 2021. 'Defund the Police' advocates lack effective alternatives for combating violent crime (msn.com)

gresswoman Maxine Waters (D-CA). As reported exclusively by Fox News, a complaint filed with the House Committee on Ethics claimed outspoken police critic Congresswoman Maxine Waters, who was already accompanied by two armed officers with the Capitol Police and two U.S. Secret Service agents, requested two air marshals and two more marshals on touchdown to escort her in the airport. "Congresswoman Maxine Waters utilized numerous government resources inappropriately," the complaint reportedly said. "Federal Air Marshals were removed from a "High Risk" flight to cover Ms. Waters flight to Minnesota. The High Risk flight took off with no armed law enforcement on board leaving a gap in National Security." Sonya Hightower LoBasco, executive director of the Air Marshal National Council, told the outlet U.S. air marshals were removed from missions deemed "high risk" and reassigned to Waters's flight. "We still don't have any justification as to why government resources were utilized to fly Miss Waters out to Minnesota," Hightower LoBasco added. Congresswoman Waters is b best remembered for her controversial statements and actions during ex-policeman Derek Chauvin's trial. Not trusting that the jury would render a judgment that suited her, before a verdict was returned, the California Democrat demanded Chauvin be found "guilty, guilty, guilty" in the killing of Floyd following an arrest in Minneapolis last May.[282]

Attorney Ben Crump has represented the families of several black Americans who were killed in the line of duty by police officers. On CBS News' Sunday Morning interview, conducted on 16 May 2021, Crump described his daily legal fight against what he describes as the "legalized genocide of colored people" across America. CBS Reporter Ted Koppel pursued Crump regarding his use of the word "genocide," which the attorney defended his use of the word as the most descriptive he could think of to describe the police treatment of blacks. "Genocide is a very particular legal term with a very particular legal definition. You're a lawyer; you understand the power of words, Ben," Koppel asked Crump. "And when you accuse the United States in the twenty-first century of genocide, that has a lot of weight." "Exactly," Crump retorted. "When you think about what Black people have been suffering for 400 years in America, since

282 Roman, Carly, "Maxine Waters slams 'deceitful, lying' Fox News report that she requested air force protection on flight," **Washington Examiner**, 15 May 2021.

1619, when the first enslaved Africans were brought to America, I would argue that legalized genocide – when you think about how the very laws that are supposed to protect us are being used to kill us. When you think about what happens in every city, in every state, in every courtroom in America, every day, they're killing African Americans, they're killing marginalized people of color, using the law, whether it's killing them physically, or it's killing them legally with these trumped-up felony convictions."[283]

Partial defunding will never satisfy many of the protesters who march through American cities carrying signs displaying their various slogans. Reforms that merely remold are not enough, such activists say. Because, in their view, the system of law enforcement is totally broken and thus needs to be shattered entirely. "There is finally a growing awareness that the problems that are caused by police in this country are structural problems," said Alec Karakatsanis, executive director of Civil Rights Corps, a litigation nonprofit based in Washington, D.C. "You can't reform the core function of the police, you have to dramatically reduce the size of its oversight and transfer their resources into Black communities." Civil Rights Corps (CRC) is self-described as a non-profit organization dedicated to challenging systemic injustice in the United States' legal system that is built on white supremacy and economic inequality . It works to shift power to community-led movements, particularly those led by Black and Brown people who are most affected by this legal system, so they can build sufficient power to create structural change.[284]

The current annual police budget in Boston in $414 million, which is approximately fifteen percent of the city's total budget. What defunding advocates are calling for, in part, is a 10 percent reduction, with that $40 million going to public health and community programs that could reduce inequities. This is typical of demands made by one portion of the defunding advocates.

Alternatives to Police

The ACLU suggested in June 2020, that the nation should "embrace alternatives" to traditional law enforcement "like civil-

---

283 Fearnow, Benjamin, "Ben Crump Says He Wants to End 'Legalized Genocide': 'They're Killing African Americans'," Newsweek on line, 16 May 2021.

284 Civil Rights Corps.org 601 Connecticut Avenue NW, Suite 800, Washington, D.C. 20009

ian-led crisis intervention teams composed of highly trained professionals, including nurses, doctors, psychiatrists, and social workers, to respond to incidents with people who are in mental health crises." The great question is how American public safety would be preserved if the police were defunded.

Camden, New Jersey, is the only American city in recent history which purposefully dismantled and rebuilt its police force. That Camden is one of the country's poorest urban areas and was once considered its most dangerous. Scott Thomson, Camden's chief of police led the city's high-profile pivot to community policing beginning in 2013. He oversaw a steep decline in crime. For example, homicides in Camden reached 67 in 2012; the figure for 2019 was 25. Over the past seven years, the department has undertaken some of the most far-reaching police reforms in the country. In 2013, the mayor and city council dissolved the local police department. They signed an agreement with the surrounding county to provide shared services. The new county force is double the size of the old one. Increasing the head count was a trust-building tactic, says Thomson, who served as chief throughout the transition: Daily, non-crisis interactions between residents and increased. Police received de-escalation training and body cameras. The city installed more cameras and devices to detect gunfire. Camden's police department adopted an 18-page use-of-force policy in 2019 which was developed with the assistance of New York University's Policing Project. The rules emphasize that de-escalation has to come first. Deadly force, such as a chokehold or firing a gun or even a Taser, can only be used in certain situations, once every other tactic has been exhausted.[285]

Minneapolis has signaled it will try to reconstruct its police department, following the George Floyd incident, possibly along the lines employed by Camden. More typical than total dismemberment and rebuilding a new is the adoption of piecemeal reforms which leave the police departments essentially intact.

Defunding advocates point to Eugene, Oregon, as the poster child for success following major reconstruction. That police department pioneered a program beginning in 1989 called Crisis Assistance Helping Out On The Streets program (CAHOOTS) that dispatches trained social workers with specialization in crisis management rather

---

285 Holder, Sarah, "The City That Remade Its Police Department," *Bloomberg Businessweek,* 4 June 2020.

than police officers to most 911 calls that have a strong behavioral health component. The program tackles approximately twenty percent of all calls. The crisis workers do not carry handcuffs or any sort of weapon. In 2019, out of a total of about 24,000 calls, they called for police backup just 150 times. The funding for CAHOOTS is diverted from the Eugene Police Department. In Fiscal Year 2018 (July 2017 to June 2018) the contract budget for the CAHOOTS program was approximately $798,000 which funded 31 hours of service per day (this includes overlapping coverage), seven days a week.[286]

The New Orleans police department, once viewed as inherently corrupt, embraced a whole new commitment to transparency in recent years. Criminologists point to the changes implemented in the New Orleans Police Department as a model to be emulated elsewhere. For decades, a culture of racial discrimination and minority abuse within the department contributed to making Louisiana's incarceration rate the highest in the country, but without decreasing crime rates. The department's dysfunction was laid bare in 2005 after Hurricane Katrina. The Justice Department issued a consent decree to reform the police force, which remains in effect in 2021.[287]

The Minneapolis suburb of Brooklyn Center, scene of an incident in which police killed a black person under questionable conditions, has undertaken a major revision of police duties and functions along lines that are acceptable to some, but not all, defund the police activists. New divisions of unarmed civilian employees to handle non-moving traffic violations and respond to mental health crises. It also limits situations in which officers can make arrests and requires more de-escalation efforts by police before using deadly force. Its initiatives emanate from the resource banks of various movements and organizations which seek to defund the police.

The defunding police arguments regarding traffic services insist that this is an area where armed, uniformed police are unnecessary. Where police are engaging in traffic services, their intervention could result in more harm to other vehicles using the road. When a UPS truck was stolen in Florida during the course of a robbery in which no one was harmed, the police prioritized the recovery of the

---

286 CAHOOTS | Eugene, OR Website (eugene-or.gov)

287 "Improving Recruitment and Retention in the New Orleans Poliec Department" www.rand.org. New Orleans Police Department Operations Manual, 6 December 2015, https://www.nola.gov/getattachment/NOPD/NOPD-Consent-Decree

(likely insured) jewelry and capture of the robber over the safety of everyone else using the road. Several police cars engaged in a high speed chase, crashing into other vehicles on the road. Eventually, police exited their vehicles and began an outrageous shooting spree. Multiple innocent bystanders were killed in the process. Beyond situations like the horrific example above, police are more likely to stop Black people for supposed traffic "infractions," when no one's safety is at risk. What are the purpose of these stops? Oftentimes, a mere request to justify a traffic stop from a Black driver can result in the type of escalation that culminates in death, like Sandra Bland. Increasingly, police officers are using tactics like stealth cars that are difficult to identify as police vehicles in order to "catch" drivers by surprise. What is the purpose of this type of strategy? Why is a service that is meant to provide safety and security engaging in "gotcha" surprise tactics and targeting black people.[288]

A new Department of Community Safety and Violence Prevention would be formed to oversee efforts on community health and public safety, led by a director with public health expertise. Police are more likely to use lethal force when attending to an emergency call when a person is experiencing psychiatric distress. When an individual calls 911 when experiencing mental distress, what they need is expertise in de-escalation, social and health supports & services. Instead, they are met with multiple armed and uniformed police officers. The police have become the first point of access to mental health support for many under-funded communities. The defund police groups allege that police service is a dangerous option for people experiencing a mental health crisis—but for many, it's the only option. By defunding the police, significant resources can be reallocated to create a new community emergency services to support the mental health needs of our vulnerable community members. Teams trained in de-escalation and who root their work in community-informed practices could provide crisis support and care.

Brooklyn Center City council approved these changes less than a month after then-Brooklyn Center Officer Kim Potter, who is white, fatally shot Daunte Wright, a 20-year-old black motorist. The American Civil Liberties Union of Minnesota called the proposal "an important first move" in changing policing. But several police groups

288 Summary of argument from Alternatives To Police Services - Defund The Police

have raised concerns, saying parts of the resolution conflict with state law and will put public safety at risk.[289]

Those advocating the defunding of police argue that, because police are too heavily involved in minor matters, they are unable to respond correctly to investigation of major crimes. They argue as follows: Police are meant to provide investigation services for us in the event that we experience a theft or burglary or a similar crime. In the United States the clearance rates 2018 for motor-vehicle theft and burglary were less than 15 percent. For theft and property crime, the clearance rates were less than 20 percent. For robbery, the clearance rate was just over 30 percent and for arson, the clearance rate was less than 25 percent. Clearance rate does not mean solved cases. Clearance refers to cases in which a charge has been laid and police departments have been criticized for laying charges simply to get clearance rates up, even when an investigation does not lead to the charge that they ultimately lay. What this tells us, they say, is that police departments are not very good at investigation services. The problem gets worse when the police are investigating victims that are undervalued in our society.

The defunding advocates see an epidemic of missing and murdered black and indigenous women and girls and trans-people across North America which is, in part, due to the lack of seriousness with which police services attend to these disappearances.
If authorities were to defund the police, they could create new investigative services where diverse teams of researchers and investigators, with a mix of scientific, public health and sociological expertise are able to attend to all important investigative needs.

Additionally, government could put money into programs attending to the food security and housing security needs of people living under substantially reduced circumstances, thereby reducing the likelihood that desperate people unable to have their basic needs met would resort to the extraordinary step of attempting to meet their needs through theft.[290]

Decriminalization of many petty crimes has attracted the attention of many defunding organizations. They argue that most laws

---

289 "Minneapolis suburb OKs sweeping changes in policing policies," Associated Press, 16 May 2021.

290 Summary of argument from Alternatives To Police Services - Defund The Police

dealing with petty matters, as well as the fines associated with them, serve only to criminalize poverty, while not ensuring public safety. By dismantling and overturning such ordinances that criminalize people in public space, and especially those that criminalize poverty -- loitering, fare evasion, sleeping in public, public urination, public intoxication, solicitation, pan-handling-- police can concentrate on important investigations. Mental health and social welfare professionals would, under the defunding banner, deal correctly with such minor matters, and to the degree that is absolutely necessary. Decriminalization would ensure that individuals who use, possess, or sell drugs are not subject to arrest, detention or conviction. This removes the need for a police apparatus for enforcement of ineffective drug laws.

Funding would be rerouted to provide safe warm places to sleep, that is, meaningfully addressing the housing shortage and homelessness crisis in our cities. They assert that substantial social welfare programming offers far more safety than police harassment, ticketing, and criminalization. Governments would assure neighborhood safety by providing clean and accessible public toilets, free transit, harm reduction and safe injection sites, shelters for people who are inebriated, and investing in housing people rather than criminalizing their presence in public space. In nearly all municipal budgets in North America, the police are funded more than all of these quality of life supports combined: we can choose differently.[291]

---

291 Decriminalization - Defund The Police

Results of Defunding

Reasonable and responsible politicians and others advocate and support sensible police reforms that would increase transparency and make forces more professional and more accountable for their use of force, but "defunding" is the opposite of such reforms. To virtually all Americans, save only those most dedicated to defunding, the result is inevitable: greater crime, slow police response time, low police morale, mass resignations, and great reluctance to enter predominately black areas. Defunding police just might be one of the worst possible measures for curtailing police abuses.

Many police officers would now prefer to withdraw from highly charged scenes rather than risk becoming involved in incidents that turn into riots and civil insurrections. Why, indeed, should they risk harm when they see cowardly administrators allowing rioters to wreak havoc and burn and destroy? What we are seeing is the result of indecision. Military leaders are hampered by instructions to limit their effectiveness and withhold weapons systems, obviating the age-old military assumption that the only objective is total victory. Police are to try to restrain insurrectionists, but not harm them, allowing them to burn and destroy at will, until they finally tire of that game. In short, politicians jumped on a bandwagon in order to placate the woke mob. Murder rates were up 36% across the board in 2020, including in prominent jurisdictions that did not defund their police. But murders increased by 41% in Atlanta, 53% in Denver, and 78% in Minneapolis.

Democratic politicians at virtually every level, from President-elect Joe Biden down to local city councilmen, had reacted to recent incidents of real and alleged police misconduct by encouraging the "defund the police" movement. Realizing that they had made a grave mistake, Democrats tried to redefine the idea of "defunding" the police, relying heavily on cover from the liberal news media. "Defund," they began to assert, did not actually mean "defund" at all. Surely no one was going to victimize the men and women whose age-old assignment has always been restraining criminals, no matter how dangerous, who would destroy lives and property. To be certain, "defund" would now mean simply "reallocation." It might even mean that cities and states would spend more, not less, money on law enforcement. There would be a greater focus on alternative methods of conflict resolution through expanded social programs, along with expenditures of bribe money in high-crime areas. [292]

Police officers in smaller jurisdictions, or those primarily populated by people of color, are frequently paid less than those in metropolitan areas. For example, in Hillsdale, a suburb of St. Louis, Missouri, new officers earn $13.50 an hour after a probationary period, less than hourly workers at Target. Low wages force many officers to take extra jobs, leaving them tired and unprepared to deal with a high-stress police situation. One cannot automatically assume that the most poorly-paid make the worst police, but low pay increases the chances that a community will not attract the best officers. In Memphis, Tennessee, use-of-force complaints almost doubled as officers in an understaffed department were required to work overtime.[293]

Illinois State Police reported an increase in fatal car accidents due to a decrease in motorcycle traffic officers after 2010 budget cuts. In order to raise funds for the department, the state implemented a policy wherein for each citation, such as a speeding ticket, $15 is dedicated to support the state police. Used in several states and many communities, and called "citation taxation," departments taking a cut of each citation written is a common fund-raising strategy. Such tickets often cost residents more than expected. The worst is California where a $100 traffic ticket while bearing the nominal fee of $100 in state assessment fees, bears such additional assessments as $70 in county assessment fees, $50 in court construction fees, $20 for emergency medical fees, among other fees resulting in an almost $500 ticket for rolling through a red light. While no one wants to pay a $500 traffic violation ticket, the poor are especially ill-equipped to pay such tickets.[294]

In the thirty largest U. S. cities, police shootings have dropped about 30 percent, and some cities have seen larger drops. In some of these cities, additional education and training have accomplished

292 Kokai, Mitch, "Results of defunding the police," *The Locker Room*, 6 January 2021. "They really are 'defunding' the police, and it's not going well," Editorial in *Washington Examiner*, 5 January 2021.

293 Weichselbaum, Simon and Nicole Lewis, "Support for Defunding the Police Department Is Growing. Here's Why It's Not a Silver Bullet.," themarshallproject.org, 9 June 2020.

294 Police Executive Research Forum, "Is the Economic Downturn Fundamentally Changing How We Police?," policeforum.org, December 2010; Dieterle, C. J."Citation Nation," city-journal.org, 4 April 2017.

much for de-escalation of tense events, stricter use-of-force policies, and greater officer accountability, all of which costs money. Contrary to the woke-asserted war against black people by white police officers, few are actually killed by white officers each year. An analysis of the Philadelphia, Pennsylvania, police department found white officers were least likely to shoot an unarmed black person, with a threat perception failure (TPF) rate of 5.2% with black suspects. Black officers had an 11.4% rate, and Hispanic officers a 16.7% rate.[295]

Portland's Experience

On 10 August 2020 Portland, Oregon, was experiencing its seventy-fifth day of protests against racial injustice and police brutality. Portland saw 100 consecutive days of often violent protests last year sparked by the May 25, 2020, death of George Floyd. Police in Portland, Oregon, declared a riot on after officers observed protesters damaging multiple businesses. Beginning with about 150 people, rioters gathered and began marching from Irving Park in north Portland and headed south on N.E. Martin Luther King Jr. Blvd around 7:15 p.m. The insurrectionists threw objects at police and pepper sprayed members of the community. Police say they also shattered windows at several businesses, including two phone stores, a coffee shop, a computer store, a community bank, a hotel, a restaurant, a financial office and two realty offices.

Rioters defied orders to disperse and threw rocks, along with frozen or hard-boiled eggs at police. Vandals threw commercial-grade fireworks at police officers, injuring two, police said. The face of one police victim was "partially melted" from the firework. Some other officers were treated at the scene. Some demonstrators filled pool noodles with nails and placed them in the road, causing extensive damage to a patrol vehicles. Portland, Oregon, has set a good example of how quickly the breakdown of the rule of law can lead to anarchy and violence.[296]

The city of Portland responded by reducing its police spending by $16 million in August. The move dissolved the area's Gun Violence Reduction Team, School Resource Officers and Transit Divi-

295 Emily Bazelon, Emily, "A Discussion about How to reform Policing," New York Times, 13 June 2020; Fachner, George and Steven Carter, "Collaborative Reform Initiative: An Assessment of Deadly Force in the Philadelphia Police Department," phillypolice.com, 2015

296 "Riots Declared in Portland," *The Oregonian,* 31 October 2020.

sion Program and redirected the funding to social services programs.

By March 2021, Mayor Ted Wheeler was calling for nearly $2 million in additional funding for the police force and other agencies, citing a rise in homicides and other violent crime in 2021. At the time of his request, there had been 20 homicides in Portland and more than 200 shootings. Wheeler's proposal would use the additional funding to bring back a uniformed team of officers to seize guns and work to prevent shootings. The team would also respond to and investigate shootings.

The police team was reestablished, but no new funding was given to the Portland Police Bureau. Instead, the mayor and city council approved roughly $6 million for community organizations to do anti-violence work and authorized the addition of two dozen unarmed rangers to patrol parks and neighborhoods.

By May 2021 a new poll found that, despite a summer of protest against the police last year, a vast majority of residents in Portland, Oregon did not want to see a decrease in law enforcement presence. According to a survey commissioned by *The Oregonian*/ OregonLive, seventy-five percent of Portland-area residents said they do not want policing in the city to dip below its current levels. Half said they want more cops on the streets, while twenty-four percent said they want policing levels to remain the same. Less than a quarter of Portland-area residents believe there should be fewer police officers on the streets. Just fifteen percent of respondents living in the city proper said they wish to see a decrease in police presence. The findings came after just a year of local protests during which "defund the police" became a major rallying cry.

The new poll also found that forty-two percent of Portland's residents think downtown Portland is "much less safe" today than it was one year ago; twenty-one percent of respondents said the area was "somewhat less safe" while twenty-seven percent said it was "about the same." Only two percent of respondents described downtown Portland as "much safer" and four percent thought it was "somewhat safer." More than half of respondents, fifty-three percent, described feeling "very unsafe" in downtown Portland at night.[297]

Democratic Portland Mayor Ted Wheeler chose to make a

---

297 Hutzler, Alexandra, "75% of Portland Residents Don't Want Decrease in Law Enforcement Presence Despite Calls to Defund the Police, Newsweek, 18 May 2021.

moral appeal to the protesters and appease their demands rather than confront the insurrectionists who burn and looted his city. Subsequently, he pushed for Portland to adopt a grab bag of left-wing ideas. One of the most prominent demands being defunding the police, which at that point had become a national initiative for activists around the country. Wheeler had rebuked then President Donald Trump, rejecting his offer to send the National Guard to restore order in the city. The response of the Portland City Council to the destructive riot was to reduce the police budget by nearly $16 million. As a consequence, wanton vandalism on one federal building or another has essentially become a norm in Oregon.[298]

`

Defunding the Police in Minneapolis

A coalition of defund activists have pushed for an amendment to the city charter that would allow them to replace the Minneapolis Police Department after a coalition of activists submitted their petition containing the 20,000 signatures to amend the Minneapolis charter. The coalition's proposed amendment would replace the police department with a new Department of Public Safety and shift authority over the police from the mayor to the City Council. The petition comes as the city of Minneapolis remains under pressure to overhaul policing after George Floyd's fatal encounter. A Justice Department probe into the department's policing practices has compounded that pressure.

A majority of council members committed to replacing the police force with a more holistic agency in the days after Floyd's death last summer, but that effort stalled. A current proposal by three council members mirrors of the protesters' coalition to establish a public safety department, and would include police officers and other divisions for a comprehensive approach to public safety beyond law enforcement. The city council, not the mayor, would have direct oversight over the police. In response to the defund movement, city council cut nearly $8 million from Mayor Jacob Frey's $179 million policing budget for 2021 and redirects it to mental health teams, violence prevention programs and other initiatives.[299]

The defund coalition is comprised of at least twenty organiza-

---

298 Stepman, Jarrett, "Portland Proves that Defunding the Police Is a Giant Mistake," *The National Interest*, 20 March 2021.

299 "Minneapolis to shift $8 million from police budget amid defund the police movement," *Minneapolis Star Tribune,* 10 December 2020.

tion, including the ACLU, Twin Cities Coalition for Justice, and Reclaim the Block. Antonio Williams, an activist with the People's Canvass boasted that the 20,000 signatures was a broad community-wide "screaming indictment" of the police.[300] The coalition has a half0million dollar backing from the Open Society Policy Center which is tied to billionaire George Soros.[301]

By late winter 2020-21 Minneapolis had backtracked on its original push to defund the city's police department in the wake of George Floyd's death. Angry and frightened residents begged the city to hire more officers, citing longer response times and increased violent crime. The city faced a different kind of lawsuit, this one at the hands of mainstream community members, including African-Americans, who are trying to force officials to add more officers to the force because of increased violence, especially gun-related incidents. Since the City Council voted to divert $9 million from the $178 million police budget, crime has noticeably spiked.[302]

By February 2021 the department had only has 638 officers available to work, approximately 200 fewer than usual. An unprecedented number of officers quit or went on extended medical leave after Floyd's death and the unrest that followed. The City Council then voted unanimously to approve $6.4 million in additional funding that police had requested. The city updated its application process for police recruits to include questions about whether they have lived in Minneapolis, have degrees in criminology, social work, psychology or counseling, and whether they volunteer or participate in programs such as the Police Activities League.[303]

Some 200 former Minneapolis police officers and firemen have left city employment amid the civil unrest that happened in the wake of the Floyd's death. Many were claiming to have suffered physical injuries or post-traumatic stress in the fallout that occurred on consecutive nights of civil unrest that included the burning of the headquarters of the third precinct. An attorney representing the former law enforcement officers, is working to settle the workers' compensa-

---

300"Activists Continue Push to Ax Minneapolis Police," Associated Press, 4 May 2021.

301 *Minneapolis Star Tribune*, 10 February 2021.

302 Defunding Minneapolis police, a spike in crime, and a lawsuit by residents | Sharyl Attkisson

303 "Minneapolis push to defund police backfires after residents complain of slow response times, increase in crime," Fox News 14 February 2021.

tions packages with City Hall, and settlements require approval by City Council. One package is for $250,000, though more realistic estimates settlements average about $175,000 each, bringing a total price tag of around $35 million.[304]

Rioters gathered in Minneapolis' Uptown area protesting the killing of a black man authorities say had fired a gun. Demonstrators, protesting the shooting death of Winston Boogie Smith Jr., on 3 June 2021. Members of a U.S. Marshals task force stated that Smith had fired a gun at police who responded in kind. Smith was wanted on a weapons violation and fired a gun before two deputies shot him while he was inside a parked vehicle. Members of the U.S. Marshals Fugitive Task Force were trying to arrest him on a warrant for allegedly being a felon in possession of a gun. The rioters, accepting the word of Smith's family and friends who described Smith as a devoted father of three who was often harassed by police, ignored the facts of the situation. The insurrectionists blocked intersections and ignited fires nearby. Minneapolis police made 27 arrests in connection with the disruption of traffic and the arson. Police arrested 26 for rioting and one was facing a weapons charge.[305] Two facts are important. The suspect had a handgun at the time of the shooting, and, as a felon, was not permitted under prevailing law to possess a handgun. The Minnesota Bureau of Criminal Apprehension will spearhead an independent investigation of the incident.[306]

Defunding Elsewhere

Los Angeles has cut its police budget by $150 million. Seattle has cut $69 million. San Francisco has cut $60 million over the next two years. Denver has cut $50 million. All the cuts are between 10 and 20% of the cities' police budgets." Moreover, cities such as Houston, Oakland, and Portland, Maine, have barred their police from serving in certain roles (on school grounds, for example), and Atlanta's mayor has even been talking about about closing the city jail.

304" Minneapolis Police Department suffered mass exodus, as some 200 officers left the force," Fox News, 4 May 2021.

305 "Fire Extinguished in Minneapolis Amid Protests Over Fatal Police Shooting," Yahoo News, 5 June 2021; Byrne, Kerry J., "Minneapolis unrest continues as Winston Smith Jr.'s family demands police shooting video," *New York Post*, 5 June 2021.

306 Kelley, Alexandra, "A team of U.S. Marshals was reportedly pursuing a suspect with a state arrest warrant," *The Hill*, 4 June 2021.

New York City, where the police commissioner recently eliminated the New York Police Department's plainclothes anti-crime unit, with those 600 officers being reassigned to "other positions." Commissioner Dermot Shea's recent decision was praised by New York City Mayor Bill De Blasio, who called the announcement of the change "very powerful." In the first week following the NYPD elimination of the special unit, shootings have more than doubled over the same week last year. There were 28 shooting incidents with 38 victims reported, compared to a total of 12 shootings for the entire week at the same time last year. "This is a permanent change," de Blasio said. "The personnel will be using new and different ways to fight crime more effectively and in a way that creates a better relationship with the community, and that's the way forward for this city and for the NYPD." [307]

Budget cuts for the New York City Police Department (NYPD) illustrate the cost-reductionist interpretation of defunding the police. In the face of severe financial deficits brought on by the COVID-19 pandemic and its effect on the economy, Mayor Bill de Blasio set out to reduce police funding as early as April 2020. In response to the protests following the death of George Floyd, in May, New York City Council members pledged to cut New York City's police spending by $1 billion. As the Council explained, these cuts would "limit the scope of the NYPD" and "show our commitment towards moving away from the failed policing policies of the past." Parts of the specific loss are the removal of $350 million in over time pay, reallocation of $400 million in the police budget, and 1160 unfilled positions in the department.[308]

Some individuals and organizations pushing for police reform continue to demand that fewer resources be provided to the police and more money earmarked for the community. They point to such expenditures as mediation programs, increased education funding and other preventive measures that do not include abolishing police —at least not yet at least. Several cities that elected to reduce funding for their police departments are now seeing two things happening: First, there has been a surge in crime rate, just as critics of defunding pre-

307 Chesnut, Mark, "Defunding Police Already Showing Results," *New York Post,* 24 June 2020.

308 Rubenstein, Dana and Je ffrey C. Mays, "Nearly $1 billion is shifted from police budget," *New York T imes*, 10 August 202.

dicted. Second, mayors and city councils have not only rescinded their defunding decisions, but have increased police funding to address these surges. Los Angeles was one of the first to announce the increase, which happened about three weeks later. New York also announced last week that it would also be re-funding its police force.

San Francisco police academy sergeant Rich Cibotti told "America's Newsroom" on Wednesday that it's "no surprise" the defund the police movement caused officers to "move on." Cibotti, who is a member of The San Francisco Police Officers Association, pointed out that his department is "losing a lot of people" and is "understaffed." He explained why he believes "a lot" of officers have been deciding to leave the profession. Cibotti warned that "unless we stop that from happening we're really going to have a problem." He referred to "an understaffed police department" noting there would be attacks on officers patrolling alone as was the case with a female officer who was attacked by a homeless person. The mayor introduced a budget proposal for the next two years that budgets $1 billion to address homelessness in San Francisco, in the midst of calls to defund police.[309]

St. Louis, Missouri, boasts the worst murder rate in the United States. Homicides are at a 50-year high, the police department has nearly 100 unfilled jobs, and the mayor's answer is to defund the police department and shut down a city jail. Tishaura Jones became the city's first black female mayor in April 2021. Ms Jones had campaigned on a promise to enact progressive criminal justice reforms. The size of the problem is overwhelming. St. Louis had 87 homicides per 100,000 residents in 2020, the worst rate in the country, even as the population has dwindled in that same time period. The mayor and some other city officials blamed the spike in violence on the corona virus pandemic. The problem with that explanation is that St. Louis also led the country before COVID-19 in homicides in 2019 with 65 per 100,000 population.[310]

Mayor Jones' Director of Public Safety Daniel Isom explained the mayor's plan this way: "Funding a comprehensive approach to violent crime is the best approach to reducing murders. This requires both police and partnering agencies adequately funded to support vic-

309 Kaplan, Talia, " 'No surprise' defund police movement causing officers to leave profession: California sergeant," Fox News, 2 June 2021

310 *St. Louis Post-Dispatch,* 21 May 2021

tims and hold offenders accountable. It also requires target arrest and prosecutions to get murderers and shooters off the streets and not filling jails with nonviolent offenders." And Mayor Jones argued that "more police doesn't prevent crime." In Mayor Jones' proposed city budget for 2022, she would cut $4 million from the police department and reallocate the funds to an affordable housing fund, victim support services, the city's Department of Health and Human Services and Civil Rights Enforcement Agency, which investigates housing, equal employment and public accommodation complaints. She also plans for the city to eliminate nearly 100 vacant police positions. The budget proposal also contains no future funding for the city's medium-security jail. Mayor Jones and her supporters see a need to move people through the system, and to find alternatives to jails for some of the offenses.[311]

A review of government homicide data reveals that the city of St. Louis has a higher murder rate than Honduras, El Salvador, South Africa, Venezuela, and Mexico. In fact, homicides in the city of St. Louis are 17 times greater per capita than those of the United States as a whole. The vast majority, more than 90%, of those who were murdered were black. Seventeen children under the age of 17 were killed. This move was celebrated by Missouri Democratic Representative Cori Bush, who said, "Today's decision to defund the St. Louis Police Department is historic. It marks a new future for our city." In Kansas City, where there were a record number of murders in 2020, the mayor and County Council last week approved taking over $40 million directly out of the Police Department and putting it toward social workers and community outreach.[312]

Chicago, under the woke spell, has been active in the defund movement. Among those murdered in the Windy City during Mayor Lori Lightfoot's recent 2021 watch, the Chicago *Sun-Times* listed of homicide victims lists 185 black victims, along with 23 Hispanics. The *Chicago Tribune* tracker states that 596 black people have been killed in Chicago in the last 365 days, along with 66 Hispanic victims.[313] The result of reducing police funding in Chicago was that during the first five months of 2021 there have been 225 homicides in

311 Fox News, 22 May 2021.

312 Schmitt, Eric, "Defunding the police is a dangerous reality in Missouri," *Washington Examiner,* 2 June 2021

313 Faria, Zachary, "'Progressive' racism is still racism, and it should not be tolerated or shrugged off," *Washington Examiner,* 18 May 2021.

Chicago, according to the *Chicago Sun-Times*. In just the first 139 days of 2021, 225 people have been killed during Mayor Lori Lightfoot's defunding campaign. It would seem unlikely that her support of defunding would reduce that number. The *Chicago Tribune* puts that number at 227 while noting that Chicago is 36 homicides ahead of its 2020 pace. It has done the mayor no good to place the blame on firearms or racist police.[314]

Bevelyn Beatty, who became a national figure when she defaced a Black Lives Matter mural in July 2020 was arrested in Chicago in August 2020 after she and other protesters failed to disperse while demonstrating outside of Chicago Mayor Lightfoot's home. They were protesting the mayor for "pushing to defund the police."[315]

Antonio Brown, an Atlanta city councilman and prominent advocate of the 'defund the police' movement had his car stolen in the middle of the afternoon by a group of school-aged children. The incident took place as Brown, who just joined the mayoral race in Atlanta less than two weeks before, was meeting with community leaders at a ribbon-cutting ceremony around noontime. Brown noted that one of the children "acted as though he had a gun." According to police the car, a Mercedes, was stolen by "several males." Brown claimed that "he held onto the car and was dragged about a block down the road before letting go." In 2020 Brown had voted in favor of cutting the budget of the Atlanta Police Department by $73 million. Regarding the thieves, Brown said, "The reality is this: We need programmatic initiatives in place to help support these kids to be able to give them another pathway instead of them of them committing crimes."The perpetrators dragged Brown alongside the vehicle for about a block before he released his grip.The Atlanta councilman is presently running for mayor on a platform of defunding the police, and has served as a member of Atlanta's city council since 2019. He was indicted in 2020 on charges that he lied about his income in order to obtain new credit cards and loans, which he allegedly used, in part, to purchase a Mercedes C300. He complained vigorously about the slow response time by police.[316]

---

314 Faria, Zachary, "'Progressive' racism is still racism, and it should not be tolerated or shrugged off," *Washington Examiner,* 18 May 2021.

315 *Chicago Tribune*, 6 August 2020.

316 *Atlanta Constitution,* 27 May 2021.See also Takala, Rudy, "Atlanta City Councilman Running on Defunding Police Dragged Behind Car by Robbers," Microsoft News, 27 May 2021.

The police budget in Boston stands at $414 million a year, or about 15 percent of the city budget. Leading the campaign to defund police is Monica Cannon-Grant who founded Violence in Boston, Inc. Ms Cannon-Grant was also one of the organizers of the Fight Supremacy Counter Protest and Rally that attracted 45,000 people in August 2020. She has explained her thoughts: "Instead of saying defund the police, you could say shift funds to invest in Black communities. The reality is we can scream defund, but this is a commonwealth, and it ain't gonna happen entirely," she said. "But those who say they just want to reform the police are just saying the rhetoric they think people want to hear to move on from this moment." She recognizes the unlikelihood of the city fully defunding the police, but what she will settle for is is a 10 percent reduction in the police budget, with that $40 million going to public health and community programs that could reduce inequities.[317]

Baltimore, Maryland, had the second-worst homicide rate and also its highest on record for that city in 2019 with 57 per 100,000. After choosing to defund the city's police department by $22 million for fiscal 2021, Baltimore is now increasing its police funding by $28 million after a large surge in crime. Baltimore's spending board approves a $28 million increase in police funding following a large surge in crime Baltimore's City Council defunded the police department by $22 million in June 2020.[318]

In 2017 Baltimore police were held responsible in part for the death of a black criminal taken in custody. Litigation brought federal court oversight of the police department, costing the city $1.5 million per year. Police have said they need more resources: more officers, more training, more technology. The federal consent decree now all but requires it. One political response was to defund the police. The federal courts have put a stop to that scheme, requiring instead additional police training and instruction, especially regarding sexual assault. From 2019 to 2020, the department said their hiring of city residents increased by 88%, they also hired more female officers and increased use of body cameras.[319]

---

317 Krueger, Hanna, "Amid cries to defund the police, what are the alternatives?", Microsoft News, 11 June 2020.`

318 *Baltimore Sun,* 19 April 2021, See also Lamb, Clint, "Baltimore Refunding Police by $28 Million after Crime Surge," 14 May 2021.

319 Kushner, Kelksey, "Federal Judge Overseeing Baltimore Police Cautions Against Defunding Department For Now," WJZ Baltimore Channel 13 CBS, 30

Asheville Police Department (APD) of North Carolina has ordered its officers not to respond to certain types of crimes so that the agency can adequately respond to calls for help amid a "staffing crisis." APD will no longer respond to 911 calls involving certain incidents where suspect information is not available; harassing phone calls that don't include threats to life, unless they are related to stalking or domestic violence; identity theft and other scams, and trespassing reports that don't involve pressing charges, among other incidents, the department said in a Wednesday announcement. In the wake of racial problems and disorder, APD staffing numbers have decreased by 84 officers since the start of 2020. According to the Police Executive Research Forum, APD boasted 238 sworn officers as of 2019.[320]

Legal Reaction

In 2021 Florida Governor Ron DeSantis announced the terms of the state's new Law Enforcement Protection Act.[321] Long subject of criticism for applying capital punishment, Florida reacted to Antifa/ BLM violence. Violent assembly and blocking a roadway are felonies. Those coming from out of state to participate in a riot may be subject to enhanced sentences. The law provides mandatory minimum jail sentence of six months imprisonment for striking a law enforcement officer, including with a projectile, during a violent or disorderly assembly. It also provides additional penalties for assault and battery of a law enforcement officer during a violent or disorderly assembly. There are added penalties for participation in a violent or disorderly assembly by an individual from another state.

The law provides new and enhanced penalties for criminal offenses to aid in combating rioting, looting and related violence. It is a third degree felony when seven or more persons are involved in an assembly and cause damage to property or injury to other persons. It is also a third degree felony to obstruct traffic during an unpermitted protest, demonstration or violent or disorderly assembly. A driver of an automobile is not liable for injury or death caused if fleeing for safety from a mob. It is now a first degree misdemeanor for a participant in a violent or disorderly assembly to harass or intimidate a per-

April 2021.

320 Pagones, Stephanie, "North Carolina police department stops responding to certain 911 calls amid 'staffing crisis'," Fox News, 4 June 2021

321 The Combating Violence, Disorder and Looting and Law Enforcement Protection Act , 21 September 2020.

son at a public accommodation, such as a restaurant. RICO liability attaches to anyone who organizes or funds a violent or disorderly assembly.

Local governments in Florida which refuse to protect their citizens from organized violence lose their protection under sovereign immunity and citizens whose lives and property are disrupted may sue those governments for failure to protect and maintain order. Florida communities and municipalities that defund police will lose future financial aid and grants. The law terminates state benefits and makes anyone ineligible for employment by state/local government if convicted of participating in a violent or disorderly assembly. No bond or bail until first appearance in court if charged with a crime related to participating in a violent or disorderly assembly; rebuttable presumption against bond or bail after first appearance.

In his press release promoting the legislation, Governor DeSantis said, "Our right to peacefully assemble is one of our most cherished as Americans, but throughout the country we've seen that right being taken advantage of by professional agitators, bent on sowing disorder and causing mayhem in our cities," Further, remarked, "I will not allow this kind of violence to occur here in Florida. The legislation announced today will not only combat rioting and looting, but also protect the men and women in law enforcement that wake up every day to keep us safe."Peaceful protesting is a constitutional right, but looting and disorderly rioting are not."

Almost immediately a self-styled social justice group the Legacy Entertainment & Arts Foundation, filed a lawsuit in federal court in Orland against Florida Governor DeSantis, claiming that the new law violates First Amendment protections of free speech and association. This suit was filed just two days after he signed a bill to create tougher penalties for people who participate in violent protests. The lawsuit also alleges the law was passed in racist response to protests "against the murders of minorities by the hands of police officers," citing the deaths of Breonna Taylor, George Floyd and Elijah McClain. It alleges statutes in the law "are written with the intent of defining any such protest as a 'riot' or participation in such protest as 'inciting a riot,'" and the statutes "retaliate against those subjected to these laws with excessive bail, fines or cruel and unusual punishment as a means of hindering the speech of dissenting opinions." The complaint also says the new law "unconstitutionally threatens to impose liability" on people "expressing their rights to free speech regardless of their intent to incite violence, the likelihood that their speech will result in violence, or the imminence of the intended violence." Finally, it also alleges the law's terms are "overbroad," "reaching" and vague, common themes in such lawsuits.[322]

Reaction against Defunding

Some sociologists, criminologists, and journalists have criticized aspects of the police defunding movement. In the United States, politicians from both the Democratic and Republican parties have spoken against defunding, although Republicans have sought to link Democrats to the movement in congressional races. This became a heated issue in the 2020 presidential race because incumbent President Donald Trump virtually accused his opponent Joe Biden of advocating defunding and that, if elected, Biden would move in that direction. Among the general public in the United States, the concept of defunding is unpopular.

How do Americans generally view the issue of defunding? Americans are divided along partisan and racial lines in their evaluations of police. Across four measures of police performance, white adults are consistently more positive about the performance of police around the country than Black adults, and Republicans are much more positive than Democrats. In a survey of American attitudes toward law enforcement, two-thirds of respondents said that individual officers should be held legally accountable for using excessive force, but few of those polled said they would support cutting police budgets. The results of the survey conducted by the Pew Research Center were significantly skewed by the race and political persuasion of those answering the questions. The poll, conducted from June 16-22, 2020, was taken during the nationwide protests and riots over alleged police brutality. The survey asked questions of 4,708 adults.

One demand advanced by many of the protesters, that of significantly reducing funding for the police, brought objections from 75% of those surveyed. Seventy-three percent said they thought funding for the police should either stay about the same (42%), be in-

---

322 Farrow, Claire, "Gov. DeSantis sued in federal court over Florida's new 'anti-riot' law," WTSP News, 22 April 2021. WTSP.com. See also"Florida's New Anti-Riot Law Has a Nasty Surprise for Rioters Who Surround Cars," *Western Journal*, 17 April 2021.

creased a little (20%) or a lot (11%). Less than 25% supported the decrease in public funding of police. Fewer than half of black adults (42%) say spending on policing in their areas should be reduced, although that is double the share of white adults who favor cutting funding for their local police (21%).

Pew's findings showed that, overall, opinions of the police have become less favorable today than in a similar poll conducted by Pew four years ago. Two-thirds (66%) of those surveyed rejected the notion of "qualified immunity," that is, that individual officers should be shielded from lawsuits unless they commit clear violations of the law. That majority agreed that "civilians need to have the power to sue police officers in order to hold them accountable for excessive use of force or misconduct." As viewed by race, 86% of Black respondents agreed with the statement, while 60% of whites and 75% of Hispanics did. There was a similar gulf along party lines, with 84% of those who consider themselves Democrats or lean that way agreeing with the statement. By contrast, a majority (53% to 45%) of those who identify as Republican or lean Republican disagreed with ending qualified immunity.[323]

How far are Americans willing to go in restraining police action? The Pew survey found the following: More than 60% of individuals in Pew's poll believe civilians should be able to sue police officers for excessive use of force. The legal doctrine of "qualified immunity" generally protects officers from being held personally liable in lawsuits unless they commit clear violations of law. A proposal to limit qualified immunity has emerged as a major stumbling block in the congressional debate over policing policies and procedures. However, only 32% of those surveyed say that, in order for police officers to do their jobs effectively, they need to be shielded from such lawsuits. More than eight-in-ten black adults (86%) favor permitting citizens to sue police officers to hold them accountable for misconduct, as do 75% of Hispanic adults and 60% of white adults.[324]

A clear majority (58%) of Americans say police around the

323Neuman, Scott, "Police Viewed Less Favorably, But Few Want To 'Defund' Them, Survey Finds," in America Reckons with Racial Injustice on National Public Radio, 9 July 2020. See also Neuman, Scott, "Police Viewed Less Favorably, But Few Want To 'Defund' Them, Survey Finds," National Public Radio, 9 July 2020.

324Pew Research, "Majority of Public Favors Giving Civilians the Power to Sue Police Officers for Misconduct," 9 July 2020.

country do an excellent or good job of protecting people from crime, which has gone down a bit from the share who agreed with this four years ago (62%). A favorable view of police is held by 78% of Republicans and those independents who lean toward Republicans, but 43% of Democrats and independents who support Democrats. Two-thirds of white adults (67%) say the police are doing a good or excellent job of protecting people, while just 28% of Black adults say the same. Half of Hispanic adults say police do an excellent or good job of protecting people. However, there have been double-digit declines in the shares who say police forces do an excellent or good job of using the right amount of force for each situation (from 45% in 2016 to 35% today), treating racial and ethnic groups equally (47% to 34%) and holding officers accountable when misconduct occurs (44% to 31%). Republicans say that police are doing an excellent or good job of using the right amount of force for each situation (61%) and treating racial and ethnic groups equally (64%). About half of Republicans (51%) say that police around the country are doing an excellent or good job of holding officers accountable when misconduct occurs. Fewer than two-in-ten Democrats rate police positively in these areas.

The decline in all three measures have been comparable among black and white adults. Democrats are far less positive about police performance than they were in 2016, while the change among Republicans has been less pronounced. Only 10% of Democrats say police around the country do an excellent or good job in treating racial and ethnic groups equally, down from 27% in 2016. Nearly two-thirds of Republicans (64%) have a positive view of how police around the country do in treating racial and ethnic groups equally, which is a modest decline from four years ago (71%).[325]

Seventy-five percent would support civilian oversight boards to investigate officers accused of misconduct, including the use of excessive force. Seventy-four percent would like to see officers required to live in the area they work in. Ninety percent or more support creating a federal database to track misconduct by police officers and more training on non violent police tactics. Only one-eighth of those surveyed, just 12%, support significant defunding and the reallocation of much of traditional police budgets to social activities and agencies.[326]

325Ibid.

326Zea, Lindsey, "What the Public Really thinks about Defunding the Police," What the public really thinks about defunding the police (better-cities.org)

An anti-police communications professor at Cypress College who talked down to a student over his presentation and condemned his presentation by belittling his presentation was dismissed from her position. An outspoken advocate of the "cancel culture" she claimed, before a virtual class of sophomore students, that calling 911 during an armed home invasion would actually further put her life in danger. The faculty union came to her rescue immediately by accusing Cypress College of "failure to be anti-racist" and creating a "chilling effect" on workplace safety after it fired, It stated that the "United Faculty stands in solidarity with all our faculty in protecting their academic freedom and the right to a safe work environment, free of hostility and threats to their physical safety and emotional well-being." The same Union said nothing of the rights of students to hold opinions, even if they are traditional and conservative, and to be free of ridicule from faculty mentors who disagree.[327]

Antiracists are racist on their own terms to the extent their favored policies contribute to inequity. In fact, many such policies seemingly will, and historically have. Consider policing, for example. Antiracists see the criminal justice system as systemically racist, in large part because minorities are incarcerated at disproportionate rates —rejecting or ignoring that those rates might reflect disproportionate underlying criminal activity. Therefore, antiracists argue that equity demands a raft of policies aimed at weakening the power of police forces, up to and sometimes including abolishing them outright. But it is only logical that if the authorities are to back off, if not disband altogether, then crime-ridden areas will get significantly worse. Over the last year, 2020, as antiracism rampaged through American society in an anti-cultural revolution, violent crime—and, in particular, homicide rates—rose at historic rates. While the American sociopolitical atmosphere remains charged with antiracism, the Biden administration is signaling a return to consent decrees that may well have the effect of hamstringing police departments. Police have recently been demonized by large swaths of the political class, and there is anecdotal evidence suggesting many may have been tactically backing off, given the hostile climate. Similarly, the New York Police Department is seeing an unprecedented mass of retirements.

Fortunately, the dramatic rise in violent crime we are witnessing comes from a historically low base. Violent crime has, overall, de-

---

327 *Washington Examiner,* 7 May 2021.

clined significantly over the last several decades. While there are many contributors, it stands to reason that among the most influential were policies diametrically opposed to the current antiracist agenda, including the embrace of "broken-windows policing," increases in the size of police forces and keeping criminals off the streets and behind bars. It stands to reason that a reversal of these policies may well disproportionately punish those in high-crime areas, often with large minority populations, thus generating greater inequity.

Regarding the police, antiracists see the criminal justice system as systemically racist, in large part because minorities are incarcerated at disproportionate rates. It becomes wholly immaterial that those rates might reflect disproportionate underlying criminal activity. By rejecting or ignoring the factual situation, they argue that the higher rates are caused by greater police efforts against minorities or even by police setting up and falsely arresting minorities. The antiracists argue that equity demands a raft of policies aimed at weakening the power of police forces, up to and sometimes including abolishing the police outright.

Destroy All Monuments

To many radical protesters, it is high time to remove from buildings, to parks, to museums, monuments, statues, and memorials in public spaces monuments which force people to interchangeably honor, celebrate, commemorate, and/or remember incidents and people who were at one point in time deemed important in the history of that place and space. But history marches on, people change, and so does the culture. As one protester posted on social media, "We have an obligation to destroy all monuments that glorify: hate, murder, violence, torture slaves, slaughter of animals by the tens of thousand, humiliate women, practice religious intolerance and being mean to migrants."[328] Misusing Alexis deTocqueville's term, some of the more philosophical vandals who wish to destroy all monuments refer to their presence as examples of soft despotism.

These self-appointed censors claim that there is no universal law that suggests that public statutes and memorials must remain in perpetuity where they were erected, or even exist at all. Objects placed in our public spaces can change with time, citizen preferences, economic conditions, and cultural shifts. In fact, most cities in post industrialized democracies recognize this situation. That is why there is usually a branch of government, such as a department of public works, that overseas public monuments, and sometimes there is a committee that represents different constituencies that reviews these sorts of things. The process, however, gets into trouble when it is out of sync with contemporary culture and current history.

At the center of the current controversy are statutes of racists, colonizers, individuals who led campaigns of genocide, and all symbols of racist activity such as confederate flags. The protests of the summer of 2020 against the killing of George Floyd by a police officer in Minneapolis highlighted what many so-called anti-racists see as the pervasive racial injustice that has persisted throughout the two hundred year history of the United States.

These objections have been accompanied with a significant upsurge of desecrating these monuments with graffiti, and, in some cases the total destruction of statues they deemed controversial. These acts of vandalism have naturally drawn some news and social media attention, with some reports siding with the vandals. Because these

328 Blogspot, 20 August 2017.

acts are criminal in nature, city, state, and federal governments spend much paying law enforcement salaries to protect the memorials. In some other jurisdictions municipal governments have sought to placate the vandals by allowing them to place what is sometimes called street art in other public places.

The present reality is that the United States has come to a vital crossroad. It must decide if the anger of the opposition which is demanding social condemnation of these displays justifies destruction of monuments and memorials erected decades ago. Charging that allowing such memorials to remain seems to laud various individuals and chapters in our collective history which are odious to some is a violation of their rights, protesters have demanded that governments act or the protesters will take matters into their own hands. The protesters assert that it is unacceptable to wait for action by committees that review requests for erecting and mothballing statutes. It is time for them to act, and to act fast before protesters turn to self-help and destroy what they do not like. To many, that sounds a great d eal like outright blackmail.[329]

The protesters, supposedly seeking social justice, seek to purge the United States of all monuments relating in any way to the Confederacy have been rapidly expanding their enemy list to include virtually all white people who have been memorialized throughout American history. The Founding Fathers who owned slaves are on the list which will undoubtedly expand as other deviations from current sensibilities are elaborated.

There is an unfortunate assumption that monuments outlive their usefulness, that some memorials represent an end to an historic epic, No longer serving a purpose among the living, outmoded memorials must be destroyed, or at least substantially altered. One of the best known critics of monument building, Lewis Mumford (1895-1990), said that by allowing to remain all architecture which no longer resonates for the living, we are turning our cities into tombstones. The truly alive and conscious intellects, Mumford asserted, know when it it is a time to destroy just as some know when it is a time to build,[330] or, as the Bible say, "“To every thing there is a sea-

329 Ross, Jeffrey Ian, "Time to remove offensive memorials, monuments, and statues," 2 July 2020. Time to remove offensive memorials, monuments, and statues – Jeffrey Ian Ross

330 Lewis Mumford was an American historian, sociologist, philosopher of technology, and literary critic. Particularly noted for his study of cities and urban ar-

son, and a time to every purpose under the heaven."[331]

The protesters have have an inclination to revere the very few monuments seen as good, but rejecting, and thus wanting to destroy, those seen as evil. But when a society begins to pick and choose it runs the extreme risk of coming into a conflict with those who hold contradictory views. While there may be a general consensus as to which one is good and which one is bad, there is the legitimate question if that disapproval truly warrants that the bad monument should be destroyed. In a pluralist society people we must allow competing views as well or else we are guilty of hypocrisy and censorship.

Put another way, evil has no life of its own, but rather attaches to existing being which is good. It is right to condemn the evil, but wrong to condemn the being. Presumably, someone may find an exception among the thousands of public and private memorials, but in general it is reasonable to assume that they were constructed because of the good found in that person, and not the evil. In some cases, that is self-evident, requiring no proof. The monuments raised to George Washington were tributes to his inspiring leadership in our darkest hours, and not to his role as a slave owner. Hate the slave owner, but respect the greatness of the man. One attack on Washington and wife Martha starts with their ownership of three hundred enslaved people who toiled on their Virginia plantation. Further, he ripped nine of them away from their families to join him when he set up the government in New York, where slavery was not outlawed until 1807. snatched African enslaved people's teeth and showcased them as his own. Antoine Fuqua is set to direct and serve as executive producer for a pilot about the contradictions surrounding George Washington's first term in office. The series, t1o be entitled *The President*, was created by Brian Burns and William N. Collage will expose such evil things about the Father of his Country.[332]

Origins of Memorials

If not the first act of destruction of monuments, one of the ear-

---

chitecture, he had a broad career as a writer. Mumford made signal contributions to social philosophy, American literary and cultural history and the history of technology

331 Ecclesiastes, 3: 1.

332 Stidhum, Tonja Renée, "Antoine Fuqua to Direct Series Highlighting Hypocrisy of Enslaved People Owner George Washington," Microsoft News, 3 June 2021

liest acts occurred on 7 June 415 BC, in Athens, Greece. Some unknown persons desecrated various statues of the god Hermes in Athens. This senseless act occurred during the disastrous Peloponnesian War (431-404 BC), just as the Athenians were preparing for the expedition to. Priests warned that the desecration had angered the gods, and the Athenians suffered a crippling defeat from which the polis never quite re covered.

The first monument to be destroyed was an equestrian statue of British King George III, originally executed by the British sculptor Joseph Wilton. It had been commissioned in 1764 and cast in lead covered with gold leaf, and depicted showed George dressed in a Roman toga astride a horse. It was a shameless copy of a statue of Roman Emperor and philosopher Marcus Aurelius. George and his horse were set up on a tall pedestal in Bowling Green Park, New York City. On 9 July 1776, when the Declaration of Independence was read for the first time in New York City, to celebrate it a group of patriots pulled down George's statue, and melted it down to make bullets with which to fight the British. When British troops arrived in November of that year they retaliated by destroying a statue of William Pitt which grateful colonists had erected in appreciation of his work to repeal the hated Stamp Act.

Opposition to these statues and memorials is not wholly a new phenomenon. To a small degree, some of this process has been being going on since the erection of the monuments. Opposition ebbs and flows, due to a myriad of factors including burn out by different political actors The main argument against Confederate memorials is that the vast majority of monuments to Confederate leaders were erected to honor their service to the Confederacy, whose main reason for existing was to protect and extend slavery. We may trace the origins of the movement to remove Confederate memorials to the 1870s, when black anti-slavery orator Frederick Douglass (1817-1895) condemned early efforts to honor Confederates on par with those who fought for the Union. Douglass denounced what he called the "nauseating flatteries" bestowed on Confederate General Robert E. Lee, from which "it would seem . . . that the soldier who kills the most men in battle, even in a bad cause, is the greatest Christian, and entitled to the highest place in heaven."

Ignoring him, the South created many memorials, not the least of which was at Stone Mountain, Georgia. An enormous rock relief on its north face, the largest bas-relief artwork in the world, which depicts three Confederate leaders, Jefferson Davis, Robert E. Lee, and Thomas "Stonewall" Jackson. In 1926 both the Congress and President Calvin Coolidge approved issuance of a Commemorative silver U.S. half dollar, bearing the words "Stone Mountain", as a fundraiser for the monument.

The federal government established the Gettysburg National Military Park Commission in 1893 following sponsorship of necessary legislation by Congressman Daniel Sickles, a veteran of that battle. In 1933, administration of the GNMP was transferred to the National Park Service (NPS). During the Great Depression the federal government undertook various projects using the Civil Works Administration and the Civilian Conservation Corps. Various states constructed monuments extolling the virtue, courage, and fortitude of their troops. The battlefield boasts the largest number of Confederate memorials anywhere. There are, of course, similar monuments in other Civil War battlefields, especially throughout the South, some of which were federally constructed, some established by state s, and a few created by private organizations.

To the protesters, the argument was simply: most of these Confederate monuments were built not immediately after the Civil War but in the South following enactment of so-called Jim Crown laws. of The white Southerners had developed a cult of the Glorious [but lost] Cause. In this retelling of history, Confederate soldiers were not landed gentry fighting to maintain their right to own other human beings, but were outnumbered but noble rebels, fighting against a tyrannical government for a right to maintain their way of life and that "peculiar institution" of slavery. The protesters argued that the statues, plaques, and obelisks that appeared in cities all over the South in memory of this myth were designed as points of nostalgic pride for white Southerners and ominous reminders of systemic racial terror for black Southerners.[333]

Buttressing the Confederate post-war pride were a host of publications, such as the *Confederate Veteran*, and host of rendezvous encampments and reunions. Hollywood blasted these remembrances in a movie entitled *They Won't Forget* (1937) in which the main event occurs on Confederate Memorial Day. The Yankee who is accused of

333 Squires, Camille, "All the Monuments to Racism That Have Been Torched, Occupied, or Removed," *Mother Jones*, 12 June 2020.

murder is chosen because he neglected to honor that day.

One group of nihilists asked, "How do you remove a racist monument? This week, the world is witnessing all the satisfyingly destructive ways." It bragged that they had discovered a "bronze disease" which, when it infected a statue, created an irreversible corrosion. The article boasted that protesters in Richmond, Virginia, had toppled a statue of Confederate President Jefferson Davis. More would surely follow. As justification they cited a 2016 report by the Southern Poverty Law Center, dated 2016 which claimed that such works of art had been part of a larger campaign of terror. While some cities are starting to remove Confederate statues, a 2019 update to the report found that 1,747 Confederate symbols still stand. The removals of these emblems have become a proxy for the larger fight against racism.[334]

The protesters view the recent removal, destruction, and/or defacement of statues of Confederates, slave traders, colonizers, and other known bigots, and the images circulating of these fallen monuments, as an accelerated example of *cultural* work which enlightened activists have been engaged in for decades, although with less publicity and public attention. When they been met by hesitation and red tape from bureaucracy, they have chosen to take direct action. While some have chosen to meet opposition with counterarguments, they insist that what is called historic preservation is really rhetoric emanating from people who want to uphold white supremacy.

A little known figure today, Confederate General Williams Carter Wickham (1820-1888) was a Virginia lawyer, plantation owner and politician. At the Virginia Secession Convention of 1861, Wickham voted against secession, but after fellow delegates and voters approved secession, he remained loyal to his state and became an important Confederate cavalry general. After the American Civil War, Wickham became a Republican in a heavily Democratic state, and served in the Virginia Senate. Seeking to help the South rebuild, and dedicated to bringing the sections of the nation together, he became an important leader of industry, serving as president of the Chesapeake and Ohio Railway Company. The statue, which demonstrators toppled at night, and was taken after to an unknown destination after it was pulled down. One person alleged that the statue was taken away by the National Guard. "That is a testament and a symbol to show

---

334

how fast these statues can be removed," one protester said. "These statues are hate that everyone knows about."[335]

Rename that School

Part of the movement to assault monuments encompasses the removal of names the protesters deem offensive from various public buildings, especially schools where delicate minds may be encouraged to honor slaveholders and other undesirables. Charleston, West Virginia, removed the name of its native son, Thomas "Stonewall" Jackson fr om its high school. California has a long list of undesirable names along with a recommended list of those now in good grace. Caltech removed the name of its founding president and first Nobel laureate, Robert A. Millikan, from campus buildings because he supported eugenics. USC stripped the name of former university President Rufus B. von KleinSmid from a prominent campus building. David Starr Jordan was a Indiana University professor of zoology from 1875 to 1885 and then served as IU's seventh President from 1885 to 1891. He then left to be founding president of Stanford University. Jordan Hall, Jordan River, Jordan Avenue and the Jordan Parking Garage were all named in his honor. Buildings were renamed because some people disagree with certain statements and views that Jordan held. Stanford University removed the name of its founding president, David Starr Jordan, from campus buildings and streets, while the Los Angeles Board of Education changed the name of its school to simply Jordan High.

Occasionally, little damage is done. In 1944, Liberty Hyde Bailey named an area of the Cornell University campus the "Cornell Plantations" to serve as a botanic teaching area. That department earned an international reputation. In response to the demands of black students who claimed the word "plantations" reminded them of slavery, it was renamed the "Cornell Bonatic Gardens."

For decades, Princeton University had honored Woodrow Wilson, who served as both President of Princeton and of the United States, by naming its public policy school after him. In 2020, Princeton removed his name from the school, citing Wilson's well-known racist views. The State University of New York at New Paltz renamed six buildings that were named after former slaveholders. One of the

---

335 Gorman, Sean and Moreno, Sabrina, "Confederate statue removed from Monroe Park," *Richmond Times-Dispatch,* 7 June 2020.

twelve residential colleges at Yale University had been named in honor of U.S. Vice President and Senator John C. Calhoun, a proponent of slavery and states rights, but that was changed in 2017.

A Florida school board voted to change the names of several schools in its district that honored leaders in the Confederacy. Duval County School Board in Jacksonville, Florida, voted on Tuesday to change the names of six schools, with each receiving a 5-2 vote in favor of the change. The board also voted to keep the names of three others, including one named after President Andrew Jackson. "At this point in time, it's important to start thinking about who we want to be," board Chairwoman Elizabeth Andersen told First Coast News. "As a board, we were listening to our community members and wanting to move forward so that every student that walks in our building understands that they are respected, that they are capable of achieving their highest potential, and that all of their lives matter." Joseph Finegan Elementary will become Anchor Academy, Stonewall Jackson Elementary will become Hidden Oaks Elementary School, Jefferson Davis Middle will become Charger Academy, Kirby-Smith Middle will become Springfield Middle School, J.E.B. Stuart Middle will become Westside Middle School, and Robert E. Lee High will become Riverside High School, according to the Associated Press. A total of 12 schools bear the names of Confederate figures in Florida, Anderson said. Tuesday's decision changes half of them.[336]

Results of Monument Destruction

When protesters pull down, deface, or otherwise destroy what they have judged to be racist monuments, whether erected by governments and by some other institution, they are forcing a reckoning. These protesters apparently actually believe that they are creating something new by adding to a space that was once dominated by only a single narrative. They are claiming an epiphany which not only rivals, but wholly surpasses, the accomplishments of the subject of a hated monument.

One of the early objects of hatred was Christopher Columbus. Accused of multiple crimes, not the least of which was enslavement of natives in the Caribbean, he was seen as the first enemy in the Western Hemisphere. Protesters claimed that Columbus was a psy-

---

336 Smith, Haley Victory, "Florida school board votes to change Confederate-honoring school names," *Washington Examiner*, 2 June 2021.

chopath who killed, enslaved and raped countless innocent people. He does not deserve to be remembered as anything other than the vile and disgusting creature he really was. In Baltimore, the world's oldest memorial to Christopher Columbus was vandalized by at least three hundred militants who the n threw the statue in the harbor.[337]

New York City through its mayor, Bill de Blasio, ordered an inquiry into whether Columbus Circle in Manhattan and its eponymous statue should remain in place or be renamed and the statue removed. Boastful demonstrators dragged a statue of Christopher Columbus into a pond. New York renamed the holiday Indigenous People Day. The public first heard of the alteration of the holiday only when the city Department of Education put out the new school calendar, referring to October 11, formerly Columbus Day, now called by its new name. Angelo Vivolo, president of the Columbus Heritage Coalition, protested: "At this time when we strive for unity and respect for the civil rights of all, Mayor De Blasio and his education department violated the civil rights of tens of thousands of Italian American students in New York City," [338]

Los Angeles has renamed Columbus Day, now calling it Indigenous Peoples Day. A statue of Christopher Columbus in San Francisco was vandalized the day before the federal holiday commemorating his arrival in the Americas in 1492. City workers cleaned up the statue at the foot of Coit Tower on Telegraph Hill that had been covered in red paint, along with graffiti on the base that read "Destroy all monuments of genocide" and "Kill all colonizers."[339]

In Boston, a statue of Columbus was beheaded. The headless statue on Atlantic Avenue, with the explorer's head lying on the ground in front of it, had been the target of unknown vandals. City officials said it's not the first time the monument has been defaced. "This particular statue has been subject of repeated vandalism here in Boston," Mayor Marty Walsh..[340] In Salt Lake City, vandals splashed

---

337 Maxouris, Christina, "Baltimore protesters toppled a Christopher Columbus statue and threw it in a harbor," CNN, 5 July 2020.

338 Slattery, Denis and Gartland, Michael, "De Blasio claims he wasn't looped into Columbus Day name change," *New York Daily News,* 5 May 2021. See also Roberts, Georgett Roberts and Carl Campanile, "Italian-Americans rip de Blasio over cancel of Columbus Day in schools," *New York Post,* 12 May 2021.

339Graff, Amy, "'Destroy all monuments of genocide': Christopher Columbus statue in San Francisco vandalized," *SFGATE,* 14 October 2019

340 Fitz-Gibbon, Jorge, "Christopher Columbus statue beheaded in Boston," *New*

red paint all over a bronze sculpture of open hands. While paint can be washed away, corrosion is irreversible. A leftist Egyptologist, whose life work presumably lay in discovering and preserving monuments, shared step-by-step instructions on how one might pull down an obelisk with ropes using brute force, and otherwise effectively destroy historic monuments. Professor Sarah Parcak, of the University of Alabama at Birmingham, shared detailed instructions on how to remove obelisks and even included a diagram on how people can "safely" destroy monuments. She posted her instructions on social media for who might be interested in how to pull down an obelisk safely from an Egyptologist who "never ever in a million years thought this advice might come in handy," she tweeted..[341]

In Philadelphia, the statue of Francis Lazzaro Rizzo (1920-1991), the divisive former Democratic mayor of Philadelphia and police commissioner who was known for violent and racist law enforcement in the city and for telling people to "vote white" and who vigorously opposed desegregation, has been vandalized several times. Over the years, the statue has drawn attention from activists, who have often vandalized or reframed it. In 2012, it was yarn-bombed with a pink bikini. A few years ago, Monument Lab commissioned an Afro-pick sculpture from Hank Willis Thomas and placed it near the statue as a form of dialogue. During the first night of protests in Philadelphia in 2020, red paint was thrown over the bronze Rizzo. The next morning city employees were busy removing the paint.

In San Francisco, protesters defaced and toppled a statue of Ulysses S. Grant, who led the Union Army during the U. S. Civil War. Vandals in San Francisco, California, toppled a statue of Ulysses S. Grant, the 18th president of the U.S. who led the Union Army during the Civil War, among other monuments at Golden Gate Park on Friday. This act occurred on Juneteenth, a black holiday which celebrates the emancipation of slaves in the United States. Nearly 400 protesters were reported at the scene, according to police, who did not engage with the demonstrators. Despite significant damage perpetrated upon public property, no arrests were made, NBC Bay Area reported. The statue of Francis Scott Key, the author of the lyrics to "The

York Post, 10 June 2020.

341 Jones, Kipp, "Professor Gives Detailed Instructions to Rioters on How To Successfully Destroy Monuments," *Western Journal,* 1 June 2020. See also Jones, Jonathan, ""'Anarchist Professor Gives Detailed Plan on How To Safely Tear Down and Destroy National Monuments," *Western Journal,* 2 June 2020.

Star-Spangled Banner," were also torn down. The insurrectionists alleged that Grant owned one slave before the start of the Civil War. It was far less clear why Key was an object of scorn.[342]

Protesters tied ropes around, and tried to topple, a statue of former president Andrew Jackson in Lafayette Square Park, in the nation's capital, but were stopped by law enforcement officials. In Portland, Oregon, a mob scribbled graffiti on a statue of George Washington, pulled it down, and burned an American flag over his head. Another statue of George Washington was defaced in Baltimore, and a statue of Thomas Jefferson was ripped down in Portland, while still other statues and memorials were targeted.

The statue of President Theodore Roosevelt outside the American Museum of Natural History in New York City will officially be removed due to complaints of it being a symbol of racism and colonialism. The New York City Public Design Commission voted unanimously on Monday to relocate the statue that has stood at the museum steps since 1940 and depicts the twenty-sixth President flanked by a native aborigine and African man.[343] Perhaps the vandals should dynamite the heads of the presidents from Mt. Rushmore.

BLM Murals

Black Lives Matter murals that now appear on streets in more than seventy U.S. cities have emerged as a form of anti-white protest. Bewildered and indecisive local governments, not certain how to react to these painted protest signs, have generally done nothing to prevent their appearance. Many fear having to defend in lawsuits should they prevent the painting on city streets. In Washington, D.C., the first rendition of the famous yellow letters was painted by the District of Columbia Department of Public Works, under the direction of Mayor Muriel Bowser. The mural design quickly spread to cities in deep--blue states, like Sacramento, California, and deep-red ones, like Birmingham, Alabama, where local officials blessed the projects. Most cities with BLM protest murals have also allowed police to protect them and arrest any who dare to desecrate them.

The reaction of public authorities to desecration of black mili-

342 Kim, Soo, "San Francisco Protesters Tear Down Union General Ulysses S. Grant's Statue," *Newsweek,* 20 June 2020.

343 Price, Greag, "Teddy Roosevelt Statue To Be Removed From Outside American Museum Of Natural History Over Complaints Of 'Racism,' 'Colonialism'," Microsoft News, 24 June 2021.

tant art work was quite different from acts of vandalism against art associated with famous Caucasians. Springfield, Massachusetts, Mayor Domenic Sarno, who participated in painting the mural on Saturday, Sept. 12, said he is "disheartened" by the desecration of the mural on Court Street. The mural, which had tall yellow letters that spell out BLACK LIVES MATTER, was defaced by apparent "burn out" from tires, Sarno said. He ordered police to find and charge the vandals.[344]

Two people were charged with a hate crime after they partially defaced a "Black Lives Matter" mural in Martinez, California. Various militants, some local and some from other states, members painted a "Black Lives Matter" mural as a protest against alleged police brutality. The city of Martinez had issued them a permit from the city, and their design featured yellow block letters spelling out the words "Black Lives Matter" on the road in front of the county courthouse in the East Bay city. Shortly after the mural was completed, two white people arrived with buckets of black paint and paint rollers. When witnesses tried to stop them, they began scoffing at the Black Lives Matter movement. They told protesters to go back to New York, saying the movement is not welcome in her town. One counter-protester asserted that "There is no oppression, there is no racism. It's a leftist lie," and blamed police-related deaths on people resisting arrest. The police arrested the counter-protesters charging them with three misdemeanors, including a hate crime.[345]

Vandals in Oak Park, Illinois,a village in Cook County, Illinois adjacent to Chicago, painted over a Black Lives Matter street mural on Scoville Avenue. They painted over certain letters to make the mural read, "ALL LIVES MATTER." Those espousing BLM assert that the phrase "all lives matter" is commonly used as a refutation and criticism of the Black Lives Matter movement. The militants claim the phrase dismisses racial inequity and systemic racism in American society. Volunteers painted the brightly colored "BLACK LIVES MATTER" message, which was completed and unveiled at the end of last month. The Oak Park Area Arts Council funded the project.[346]

---

344 Palpini, Kristin, "Two Days After Painting, Black Lives Matter Mural Vandalized In Western Mass, " *Hampden Daily Voice,* 15 September 2020.

345 Sharkey, Bridget, "2 People Who Vandalized A Black Lives Matter Mural Charged With A Hate Crime City police chief calls damage 'divisive and hurtful.'" *Simplemost*, 13 July 2020.

346 Sheridan, Sherry, "Black Lives Matter mural vandalized," *Journal of Oak Park and River Forest*, 8 July 2020; also updated on 23 February 2021.

England Reviews its Monuments

The Church of England has planned to review thousands of monuments in churches and cathedrals across the country that contain historical references to slavery and colonialism. There is considerable expectation that many offensive monuments will be removed. The Church supervises some 12,500 parishes and 42 cathedrals which must be thoroughly inspected for evidence of some offensive and contested heritage. Having identified offensive memorials, the Church will consult local communities on what action to take since decisions will be made at a local level. However, the the rules of Church guidance stress that ignoring contested heritage is not an option.

Among actions that local parishes may take are the removal, relocation or alteration of plaques and monuments, and the addition of contextual information. It is possible, but not likely, that in some cases, there may be no change.

The Archbishop of Canterbury Justin Welby, a political appointee who must be approved by the reigning monarch, called for a review of the Church's heritage following the English version of Black Lives Matter (BLM) protests last summer.

The BLM protests culminated in the toppling of a statue of slave trader named Edward Colston (1636-1721) in Bristol. The statue was a creation in bronze, which was intended to commemorate Colston's philanthropy, was originally erected in The Centre in Bristol, England. It was created in 1895 by the Irish sculptor John Cassidy and erected on a plinth of Portland stone. On 7 June 2020, the statue was toppled, defaced, and pushed into Bristol Harbour, but was recovered and put into safe storage by Bristol City Council. As the good Archbishop observed, some statues and monuments will have to come down.[347]

An American quasi-journalist reported her thoughts about the act of vandalism in the United Kingdom: "There is something cathartic — cleansing — about watching a statue of a British slaver who trafficked an estimated 84,000 people from Africa to the Americas get pulled down, rolled along the pavement, and dumped into a harbor. When I saw the statue of Edward Colston roll into the waters of Bristol Harbor in the United Kingdom, I squealed with delight. Never

347 Walker, Peter, "Pulling down Edward Colston statue was wrong". *The Guardian*, 8 June 2020.

mind that I was half a world away in the United States, watching on my laptop as these anti-racist protesters hauled Colston down. It was all the more gratifying because I was a world away. . . ."[348]

The Tower Hamlets Council removed the statue of the slave trader Robert Milligan who made his fortune in Jamaica. Milligan's statue had stood since 1813 in West India Quay. Removal was accomplished because of a petition signed by 4,500 town folk accompanied by a threat by Labour councillor Ehtasham Haque to organize a daily protest. One curious object of British protesters' hatred is Charles Grey, the politician who served as prime minister when slavery was abolished throughout the British Empire in 1833. He is faulted, not because of abolition of slavery, but because he saw to it that financial reparations were paid not to the ex-slaves but rather to the whites who had formerly owned the slaves.[349]

Other protesters in London defaced of the statue of Winston Churchill, the Tory prime minister who rallied Britain to defeat the Nazi Germany. Reportedly, Churchill thought that black people to be less capable than white people. White Anglo-Saxons were clearly the superior race. He judged Indians to be "a beastly people with a beastly religion." Still, a recent public poll showed about two-thirds of respondents thought it unfair to judge Churchill by modern standards and nearly all said his statue should remain.[350]

Joining the Archbishop of Canterbury was England's second ranking prelate, the Archbishop of York, and the two placed their stamp of approval on an anti-racism task force. The two Church dignitaries urged the Church of England to take decisive steps to address the legacy of its involvement in the slave trade, among other historical aberrations. Thus, the Church announced, "We do not want to unconditionally celebrate or commemorate people who contributed to or benefited from the tragedy that was the slave trade." Responding to the demands of BLM, Bristol Cathedral removed a window dedication to Colston.

The search for ancient expressions that are now unacceptable goes on. St Margaret's church in Rottingdean, Sussex, removed two

---

348 Johnson, Jane'a, "Confederate Monuments Getting Removed By Protesters Is a Statement of People Power," *TeenVogue,* 26 June 202.

349 Wootton, Dan, "We don't want historic statues to tear apart our future," *The Sun*, 10 June 2020.

350 Langfitt, Frank, "Desecration Of Statues With Racist Connections Triggers White Protests in the U.K.," National Public Radio, 17 June 2020.

headstones in its graveyard which contained racial slurs; and St Peter's in Dorchester has covered up a plaque commemorating a plantation owner's role in suppressing a slave rebellion.

The Church of England's director of churches and cathedrals, whose task it was to produce the guide, told the *Observer:* "Our church buildings and cathedrals are the most visible part of the Church of England, a Christian presence in every community. The responsibility to ensure they include, welcome and provide safe spaces for all is a vitally important part of addressing the way historic racism and slavery still impacts people today."[351]

In Ghent, Belgium, protesters put a bag over a bust of King Leopold II (1835-1909), doused it in red paint, and scrawled "I Can't Breathe" across it. This monarch had presided over a colonial regime in the Congo which was responsible for as many as ten million deaths as he sought to increase his personal fortune by extracting ivory and rubber using slave labor.

Future of Monuments

Global anti-racist protests have targeted monuments to racists, colonizers, and slavers. They have tagged them, torched them, even occasionally lobbed off a statue's head. Reactions to these efforts have been varied. On the one hand, some government officials have condemned the protesters, characterizing them as lawless mobs an d vandals, even threatened them with prison time. On the other hand, some local governments and universities have decided to capitulate, apologize profusely, and removal any and all statues deemed offensive, requiring no explanations as to why a subject had been selected for removal.

In June 2019 President Trump signed an executive order to protect American monuments, memorials and statues and threatened those who try to pull them down with prison sentences. President Donald Trump had put in place regarding existing monuments. Relying upon existing law, the President Trump issued an executive order calling for a 10-year prison sentence for those defacing or destroying federal monuments. Unsurprisingly, that vandalism stopped. During his speech at Mount Rushmore celebrating Independence Day last summer, President Trump said, "I am pleased to report that yesterday,

351 Sherwood, Harriet, "Church to consider removing or altering slavery monuments," *The Observer*, 9 May 2021.

federal agents arrested the suspected ringleader of the attack on the statue of the great Andrew Jackson in Washington, D.C." He made it clear that he would act decisively against acts of vandalism committed against similar public property by those who themselves have contributed little or nothing to society."I just had the privilege of signing a very strong Executive Order protecting American Monuments, Memorials, and Statues - and combating recent Criminal Violence," Trump tweeted. "Long prison terms for these lawless acts against our Great Country!" The new order was designed to fully implement existing laws which prohibit the desecration of public monuments and the vandalism of government property. The president's order withholds federal support tied to public spaces from state and local governments that have failed to protect public monuments, and withdraws federal grants for jurisdictions and law enforcement agencies that fail to stop their desecration.[352] By executive order, President Joe Biden revoked all protections for monuments and memorials.

President Trump then announced the creation of a new monument to the giants of our past. I am signing an executive order to establish the National Garden of American Heroes, a vast outdoor park that will feature the statues of the greatest Americans to ever live." Presumably fearing reaction by BLM and other protesters against some potential choices, President Biden countermanded plans to create a sculpture garden dedicated to various American heroes.[353]

The Andrew W. Mellon Foundation announced that it is spending $250 million over five years to build new monuments or memorials, add context to already existing ones and relocate others.[354] That offer of money comes at a time when the U.S. has been grappling with the question of what to do with the vast array of Confederate memorials located mostly in the South which the protesters have found offensive.

The head of the Mellon Foundation, said its present position is actually the culmination of years of study, inquiry, and work. Ms Elizabeth Alexander has headed the Mellen Foundation for the last two years came to the position with a background in African Ameri-

---

352 Phillips, Morgan, "Trump signs executive order to protect American monuments, memorials and statues," Fox News, 26 June 2019.

353 DeSoto, Randy, "Biden Cancels Trump's 'Garden of American Heroes' and Ends Exec Order Protecting Monuments," *Western Journal*, 14 May 2021

354 Santana, Rebecca, "Mellon launches $250 Million project to remake American monuments," Associated Press, 5 October 2020.

can studies and poetry. She previously held position at the Ford Foundation and was a featured figure at the Barack Obama inauguration.

Ms Alexander said the primary focus of the project is not the relocating of monuments but instead on helping ensure greater representation of historically forgotten or underrepresented communities. For example, she said less than 2% of the historic sites on the National Historic Register are about African Americans and the numbers are even fewer for Latinx, Asian American or Native American people. The money will build on grants the organization has already approved in recent years since Alexander's arrival at Mellon such as a $5 million donation in 2018 to the National Memorial for Peace and Justice in Montgomery that memorializes enslaved people and the history of lynching in America.

It would seem unlikely that storing monuments to disgraced figures would make sense. Presumably, once dethroned, these figures would be unlikely candidates for revived interest and rehabilitation. If only in the long run, protesters would be unlikely to settle for simple relocation. However, relocation of gravesites would seem to be the only alternative since even the most radical protesters would be disinclined to burn and scatter the mortal remains.

As law professor Ilya Somin has pointed out, even when vandals target monuments whose removal is justified, conducting the removal in this way is likely to be counterproductive. The point of removing Confederate monuments is not just to to get rid of the statues themselves, but to develop a strong social consensus that recognizes the wrongness of the Confederacy's cause. Removal through persuasion can help achieve that goal. Indeed, it has already taken major steps in that direction. The image of the Confederacy in popular culture today is vastly different from what it was several decades ago, even if there are still significant pockets of pro-Confederate sentiment out there. Removal through rioting and vandalism does no such thing. In the eyes of anyone who doesn't already support removal, it just makes critics of honoring the Confederacy look like a bunch of hooligans and thugs. Wanton destruction is unlikely to persuade; if anything, it is more likely to discredit the cause and spark a backlash.[355]

Over the last several years, approximately 130 Confederate monuments were removed, some even through peaceful means. Addi-

---

355 Somin, Ilya, "The Rights and Wrongs of Taking Down Monuments," *Reason,* 20 June 2020.

tionally, the last resting places of several prominent Confederates, including the President of the Confederate States Jefferson Davis, have been disturbed and the remains disinterred.

Where Will it End?

There are also the statues of others who have fallen into disfavor for one or another reason. For example, some have denounced explorer Christopher Columbus for his alleged atrocities against indigenous people. The effort to remove offensive monuments has gained new strength this year amid widespread protests which have focused on memorials as the most public displays of racial or other injustices.

The rioters and vandals generally have no sense of history or knowledge of its heroes as opposed to its alleged villains. Bent on total destruction of all important figures of the past, they have not limited their destructive activities to memorials whose removal may be justified. Among others, they have damaged or torn down such monuments as a statue of Ulysses S. Grant, the general who defeated the Confederacy, and who later sought to protect black rights during his term as president. They vandalized the Boston Common memorial to the 54th Massachusetts, which is the the African-American Civil War regiment made famous by the 1989 film *Glory*.[356]

Taking a new area of attack, vandalism has expanded to acts perpetrated against organized religion, damning it as idol worship and paganism. In Brooklyn, a statue of the Virgin Mary at Cathedral Prep School and Seminary in Queens also suffered an attack when an individual smeared it with the word "IDOL." Father James Kuroly, rector and president of Cathedral Prep, told the Catholic News Agency that the desecration of the 100-year-old statue was an "act of vandalism and hatred." In Boston at St. Peter's Parish Church, parts of a statue of the Blessed Virgin Mary were scorched after being lit aflame. According to some at the Boston Fire Department Fire Investigation Unit, "an unknown suspect had set fire to plastic flowers, which were in the hands of the statue, causing the face and upper body of the statue to be burned." In Ocala, Florida, a man lit the Queen of Peace Catholic Church on fire and crashed into the church with his minivan. The protester "poured gasoline in the church's foyer and ignited it, after crashing his minivan through the parish's front door" while parish-

---

356 Jacoby, Jeff, "Statue Toppling," *Boston Globe*, 12 June 2020.

ioners gathered inside for mass.[357]

In 2020 Florida passed new legislation that is clearly designed to contain lawless behavior within that state. One portion of that omnibus bill, entitled Prohibition on Destroying or Toppling Monuments, made it a second degree felony to destroy public property during a violent or disorderly assembly. Specific reference was to public monuments and memorials.[358] Rearing down monuments, including Confederate ones, is now a second-degree felony offense, meaning anyone who is charged with doing so would face a maximum of 15 years in prison.

Police reaction in Tulsa, Oklahoma, was quite different from the way police protected BLM signs in some other cities. When protesters showed up and began painting the familiar BLM sign on the city street, police ordered them to stop, calling it an act of vandalism. The officers formed a phalanx in a crosswalk, blocking off the street. Behind them, a group of about ten white men armed with rifles and bulletproof vests appeared, apparently a militia or police auxiliary. The protesters ignored police and chanted "Whose streets?" "Our streets!" successfully drowning out the officers' commands. The protesters continued their work and completed a mural that spelled out "BLM" in bright-yellow letters. Three people were arrested on the scene, and officers quickly began searching for more suspects. Mayor G. T. Bynum quickly issued a statement: "Vandalism of public property is not a peaceful protest. It is a criminal act." The city dispatched a clean-up crew which quickly removed the letters.[359]

The next obvious step which will go beyond removal and storage is total destruction. That had already begun with the attack on the monument in Asheville, North Carolina, dedicated to the former Confederate officer, governor, and United States senator Zebulun Vance. Erected in 1897, the statue is being removed, as are many such monuments across the country. But this removal is different for under the city's mandate, the monument must be destroyed rather than moved. This is clearly an advancement from plans for other Confederate monuments across the state that are being stored or moved rather than de-

---

357 Davidson, Jordan, "Catholic Churches And Statues Burned, Vandalized In String Of Targeted Attacks," *The Federalist,* 14 July 2020.

358 "Combating Violence, Disorder and Looting and Law Enforcement Protection Act", 21 September 2020. law passed Associated Press, 19 April 2021.

359 Luckerson, Victor, "The Defacement and Destruction of Black Lives Matter Murals," *New Yorker,* 19 November 2020.

molished. The destruction was expected to require two weeks. The Vance Monument is the third Confederate Monument to be removed in the past year from downtown Asheville's Pack Square.[360]

To some, the destruction of monuments will not end untiul even those depicting Jesus Christ are destroyed. Far-left activist Shaun King on Monday said all images depicting Jesus as a "white European" should be torn down because they are a form of "white supremacy." King made his remarks over a series of Twitter posts as historic monuments and statues have become the targets of anger and vandalism during Black Lives Matter protests. King was once a leading voice in the Black Lives Matter movement but fell from grace when his race was questioned and he was accused of being a Caucasian falsely portraying himself as black. "Yes I think the statues of the white European they claim is Jesus should also come down. They are a form of white supremacy. Always have been," King tweeted. "In the Bible, when the family of Jesus wanted to hide, and blend in, guess where they went? Egypt! Not Denmark. Tear them down."[361] King was also a surrogate for Senator Bernie Sanders (I-VT), in Brooklyn last year for his failed 2020 presidential bid.

---

360 *Charlotte Observer,* 17 May 2021. See also Randle, Brooke, "Vance Monument removal begins," *Asheville Mountain Xpress*, 26 May 2021.

361 Betz, Bradford, "Shaun King: Statues of Jesus Christ are 'form of white supremacy,' should be torn down," Fox News, 22 June 2020.

Made in the USA
Monee, IL
03 July 2021

72207708R00128